no-dig, no-weed GARDENING

Raymond P. Poincelot

Rodale Press, Emmaus, Pennsylvania

Printed in the United States of America on acid-free paper

Book design by Linda Jacopetti

Library of Congress Cataloging in Publication Data

Poincelot, Raymond P., 1944-
    No-dig, no-weed gardening.

    Includes index.
    1. Gardening. I. Title.
SB453.P578   1986   635   85-30012
ISBN 0-87857-611-8   hardcover
ISBN 0-87857-612-6   paperback

    4   6   8   10   9   7   5   hardcover
    4   6   8   10   9   7   5   paperback

Contents

Acknowledgments   v

Introduction   vii

Chapter 1 The No-Dig No-Weed Method   1
　　Why Do We Dig Gardens?   3
　　The Case against Digging   5
　　Tools for No-Dig Gardening   9
　　Tools for No-Weed Gardening   15
　　Helpful Accessories   16
　　Tool Simplicity   18

Chapter 2 Better Transplants—The Key to Success   19
　　Why Use Transplants?   19
　　Transplant Containers   21
　　Growing Media   27
　　Growing Areas   31
　　How to Grow Your Own Transplants, Step by Step   33
　　Caring for Growing Seedlings   41
　　Moving Outdoors   46
　　Growing Your Own Transplants Outdoors   49

Chapter 3 Planting the No-Dig Garden   51
　　Testing the Soil   51
　　Preparing the Garden for Planting   53
　　Planting the Garden   61
　　How to Use a Furrower   71
　　Raised Beds, Hills, and the No-Dig Method   75

Chapter 4 Feeding the No-Dig Garden   77
　　Water-Soluble Organic Fertilizers   79
　　Solid Fertilizers and Soil Amendments   86
　　Special Helpers   92
　　Step-by-Step Soil Improvement   93
　　No-Dig Soil Maintenance   99

Chapter 5 Mulching to Save Weeding and Watering **106**
  The Advantages and Disadvantages of Mulch 106
  How to Lay Down Organic Mulches 110
  The No-Weed Mulching System 112
  No-Weed Gardening without Mulch 120
  Solarization 123
  Watering Systems 124

Chapter 6 Beating Bugs and Diseases **133**
  Polyester Pest Protection 134
  Homemade Insect Traps 142
  Acceptable Sprays for Pest Protection 144
  More Ways to Outwit Pests 147
  Fighting Diseases 149
  Fences to Keep Out Big Pests 151

Chapter 7 Faster, Longer, Bigger Harvests **155**
  Cloches for Early Gardening 155
  Cloches for Late Gardening 161
  Efficient Gardening Techniques 162

Chapter 8 The No-Dig Vegetable Patch **174**
  Alphabetical information on growing vegetables 174

Chapter 9 The No-Dig Flower Garden **221**
  Alphabetical information on growing flowers 224

Appendix **251**

Index **257**

Acknowledgments

To my wife, Marian, and our three children, Raymond, Daniel, and Wendy, thanks for their love, patience, and support during my gardening and writing times. A special thanks to William Loefstedt, a friend and partner in horticulture. Without his ideas, support, and inspiration, this book could not exist. I also thank Anne Halpin for her editorial assistance and patience.

Introduction

I have loved gardening for as long as I can remember. From early childhood on, I had a garden. Oh, there were some interruptions here and there. When I went to college and lived in my first few apartments, I had no land. Then house plants were the closest thing I had to a garden. But I always came back eagerly to gardening when the possibility returned. To me gardening is a special part of life; it gives me a chance for personal satisfaction, a closeness with earth, and a feeling of naturalness.

I can't say that I have the same warm feelings about some of the work that goes with a garden. New gardeners sometimes drop by the wayside because of the labor involved. Old gardeners often are forced off the road when the burden becomes intolerable. A few years ago I found myself somewhere in the middle of the gardening road, having survived the start and wondering about the finish.

The work had not become intolerable yet, but it sure consumed a lot of my time. As such the garden was competing with my family time and other interests. If only gardening were easier, I wished.

My view was shared by a gardening friend, William Loefstedt. He is always questioning the basics, or what we take for granted in horticulture. Bill is an octogenarian who still gardens. He, too, wished gardening could be easier.

Sometimes wishes become reality with enough thought, work, and luck. That's what happened with Bill and me. We set out to create a form of gardening that was less work but still retained all the good results. We put considerable time and effort into the project, testing new ideas in our backyard gardens. Friends of ours also tried out some of the ideas. Other ideas were tested through my research at Fairfield University, where I also teach horticulture. Some ideas worked, others didn't. Our test gardens got better and the work became less.

We did succeed. This book presents a personalized approach to gardening. The approach is called, appropriately enough, no-dig no-weed gardening. Why not take a load off your gardening back and give it a try? If you do, I think you will go a lot further along the garden road.

Chapter 1
The No-Dig No-Weed Method

Each spring, for more years than I care to think about, I literally busted my garden's soil clumps. One could add that in the process, I "busted my own hump" to prepare the garden for planting. But like most dedicated gardeners, I wasted little thought on the hard work I did and the subsequent blisters and aches I suffered. I thought it was just part of what gardening was all about.

At first digging the garden was a challenge, a macho activity that proclaimed that spring was here to me, my family, and anyone else who looked. Then a sense of personal accomplishment took over, the blissful satisfaction of looking at a finely manicured seedbed. In the newly dug garden, the soil surface was smooth and free of lumps and clumps, and looking at it gave me the same feeling of calmness and cleanness that I get when I look at an expanse of freshly fallen snow, unmarked by footprints. In fact, I would get mad if a stray footprint from a neighborhood dog or cat marred the illusion. Heaven help anyone who walked on my garden after it was ready! I even regretted the fact that I made footprints when I planted the seeds. Sometimes I felt compelled to grab a rake and wipe out the offending footprints.

About four years ago, I began to question the hard labor involved in gardening. Whether my doubts arose as a consequence of age or wisdom, I don't know. But something inside me said gardens were for enjoyment and

1

for provision of food for the soul and body. I didn't enjoy the enforced spring ritual of digging the soil, even though I had gone from a shovel to a rotary tiller a few years before, and I didn't like weeding the garden, either. I thought of my options: Give up the garden or develop a better method of gardening. I loved gardening, so I couldn't give it up. My choice was simple: Look for the better method.

At that point either divine providence or lady luck entered my life. A phone call started me on the road to a better way.

In a previous job I knew an older man, William Loefstedt, an active octogenarian with a love for gardening and a mind that questioned all aspects of horticulture. Whenever our paths crossed, we would stop and chat about gardens. He had the unsettling habit of raising questions about gardening, the kinds of questions that seemed to have obvious answers, yet somehow didn't. When we parted he would say, "Think about it. Maybe next time you'll have the answer for me. Of course, I'll have some new questions for you." Some of the questions got answered, and others didn't.

Although I had changed jobs, I still got an occasional phone call from Bill. One day the phone rang and Bill asked, "Why do we dig?" I replied, "Funny you should ask. I was just wondering about that subject." We agreed to get together over lunch to discuss the topic. Bill said, "I also want to show you something then. Can you use a few pepper plants?" "Sure," I answered.

The day arrived and so did Bill. The back of his station wagon was incredibly loaded with garden paraphernalia: plants in various containers, empty trays and Styrofoam cups, buckets of sand, assorted garden tools, and many gardening magazines. There was hardly any room for Bill.

He stepped out with a smile and said, "Show me where you need a few pepper plants. I'll put them into the garden without digging." He handed me the pepper plants—they were growing in Styrofoam cups that had several slits in them—and he picked up a bulb planter with a short handle.

We walked into the yard and entered my garden. I pointed out a small, empty area. In one swift motion Bill bent over and with a thrust, twist, and pull, removed a soil plug from the garden. Next he deftly slid the root ball of the pepper plant from the cup. As he did, I noticed the healthy white feeder roots that covered the ball. He inserted the root ball into the hole left by the planter. It was a good fit.

"How's that for a no-dig transplant?" asked Bill with a smile. "Great," I answered, "but how would you plant seeds or onion sets?" Bill looked at me and said, "Those are questions for you to work on. We're just starting on the idea of no-dig gardening. Let's go to lunch. We have a lot to talk about." A thousand questions began to roll through my mind.

Over lunch we discussed the idea of a collaborative project on no-dig gardening. Bill wanted to find a way to garden without digging because digging was no longer an easy chore for him. The idea appealed to me because, while I am much younger than Bill, I realized that I no longer enjoyed digging my garden and felt that my time could be put to better use. We agreed to develop the concept of no-dig gardening.

Over a period of four years, Bill and I developed various procedures for a no-dig method of gardening. We had many lunch discussions together and tried out dozens of ideas in our test gardens. Some of the methods failed, some succeeded, and others changed as we experimented with them. In time we realized our concept had evolved into a no-dig no-weed form of gardening; hence, the title of this book was born.

We've been able to develop a system that works in any size garden, and that produces good yields of vegetables and beautiful flowers, too. Our system will let you have a terrific garden for a fraction of the work involved in conventional methods. And in this book I'm going to share our method with you, and show you step-by-step how to turn your garden into a no-dig no-weed success.

Let's dig into the subject by first asking the most basic question: Why dig?

Why Do We Dig Gardens?

Why indeed? To answer that question we must go back in our history to the days of the original thirteen colonies. For the colonists, the primary concern was farming. Gardens came second and were dependent upon adaptations of prevailing farm practices.

The prevailing practice was tillage, that is, plowing, sowing, and cultivating. The colonists plowed with a moldboard plow, which cut deeply into the soil and inverted a substantial layer, crumbling the soil as it turned it upside down. Next the farmers harrowed the soil to break up the lumps prior to sowing the seeds. As the plants grew they cultivated to destroy weeds.

This approach to farming was popularized in a book published in 1733. The author was Jethro Tull, and his book was titled, *The Horse-Hoeing Husbandry: Or an Essay on the Principles of Tillage and Vegetation.* Of course the machine drill, which Tull invented in 1701 for sowing seeds, was featured in his book.

Essentially, Tull invented the concept of row planting and advocated vigorous tillage (such as with the moldboard plow), preparation of seed-beds by harrowing, mechanical planting of rows, and weed control through repeated cultivations. His farming methods played a significant role in the emergence of the United States as an agricultural power second to none.

But what did this tillage system have to do with digging gardens? As I mentioned before, farming came first, and the luxury of home gardening followed. Farming methods served as the model for technology transfer into the garden. Vigorous tillage with a moldboard plow in turn inspired the spring digging of gardens. However, garden sizes usually did not justify the need or provide sufficient room for plowing equipment.

What simple hand tool gave the same soil-turning action as a mold-board plow? The standard garden spade. And the hand tools needed for harrowing and cultivating were the rake and hoe. The habit of digging the home garden became an ingrained custom that almost everyone accepted.

The Seeds of Dissent

Although today most of us still dig up our gardens, farming circles have for some time been questioning the wisdom of vigorous tillage. The seeds of agricultural tillage dissent were perhaps first sown over 30 years ago, by a Japanese farmer named Masanobu Fukuoka. He abandoned the traditional agricultural concept of tillage on his farm in Japan. Instead of plowing his fields, Fukuoka planted vegetables directly into fields of white clover.

Today we see variations of this method undergoing extensive investigation in certain segments of the agricultural community. These variations include the interplanting of legumes with corn, soybeans, or vegetable crops and the use of living mulch systems. The latter involves the growing of vegetables in grass and clover sod. Researchers are examining these no-tillage planting systems at the Rodale Research Center in Pennsylvania. Growers in Lackawanna County, Pennsylvania, are actually using the living mulch system.

Other farmers, especially organic farmers, have adopted conservation tillage. This practice is essentially that of reduced tillage. The farmer does not use a moldboard plow. Instead he uses some other plowing implement, such as a chisel plow, which tills the soil far less vigorously. Disk plowing is also popular. The main point is that the farmer keeps soil disturbance to a minimum, but is vigorous enough to insure weed control.

An extreme variation of the Fukuoka method is the no-till system. This way of farming allows no disturbance whatever of crop residues or mulches. The farmer plants the seeds by slicing or slotting directly through the surface residues. Herbicides rather than soil cultivation control the weeds. Although both traditional and organic farmers are increasingly practicing conservation tillage, the organic farmers are not employing the no-till methods because using herbicides goes against their beliefs.

So, why do we gardeners continue digging our gardens while the agricultural community is questioning and even eliminating the practice? Most likely we do it out of habit. One gardener who broke the digging habit was the late Ruth Stout, the author of numerous articles and books on gardening without digging. Her method depended on a year-round mulch. My method differs somewhat from Ruth Stout's approach. I have replaced her digging trowel with no-dig tools. You can still try her year-round organic mulch, but you can also use a mulch about which Ruth Stout had few kind words—black plastic. Stout's method requires a mulch, but my no-dig method works just as well without a mulch. A no-weed garden is also possible without a mulch, it just takes longer.

But like Ruth Stout, I broke the habit, and I'd like to convince you to stop digging your garden.

The Case against Digging

I don't think anyone will disagree with me when I say that digging a garden is hard work and consumes a lot of time. Bill and I agreed on this point, although his emphasis was a bit more on the hard work and mine on the time involved.

Is the work necessary? When I first thought about it, my answer was no. Let me explain why. First, think about the amount of dug and raked soil in your garden that is really used. Much of the prepared soil becomes either paths or the space between rows or beds. The actual soil you plant to seeds or transplants is only a fraction of the total area. My guess is that you use only 25 percent or less of the total soil surface area in terms of seed contact or root ball contact with transplants.

Some gardeners might argue this point, claiming that perhaps prepared soil throughout the garden makes for better root growth from the seedling or transplant. I would counter this objection with the following observation.

Perennial beds surround my sideyard walk and greenhouse perimeter. These beds contain, among other plants, assorted spring bulbs, summer lilies and phlox, and fall chrysanthemums. A gap occurs after the bulbs blossom and before the summer perennials flower. The bulb foliage, which must remain undisturbed even when it yellows and dries, makes the gap between blooming times even worse. I keep the bed looking nice by filling the gap with colorful annuals. Because I don't want to disturb the perennials, I don't do any digging when I plant the annuals. Instead I scratch in some seeds or put in transplants with a trowel.

These seeds and transplants go into soil that has little or no digging. As the plants grow, their roots eventually reach out into surrounding soil that has had absolutely no digging preparation. Yet these plants grow and thrive. In fact, they look every bit as good as those flowers I plant among the vegetables in the fully dug and raked soil of the main garden.

I can hear the skeptics saying, "Yes, but we know good reasons for digging garden soil. It controls weeds and improves the aeration and drainage of the seedbeds." Of course, you can rattle their complacency a bit when you mention the Ruth Stout method. The skeptics have a tough time explaining how she managed to grow such healthy, abundant crops without ever digging her garden. Perhaps they slough off Ruth's garden as an isolated case, or claim they don't want to bother with an all-year-round mulch. After all, they may say, no-dig gardening only works with a permanent mulch. Perhaps they feel they can't use a permanent mulch because their soil is too wet, or their garden has slugs or mice or some other recurring problem. To these skeptics I can reply that the no-dig method Bill and I have developed does not require a year-round mulch. It won't encourage slugs or mice to hide out in your garden.

To further convince you that you can have a great garden without going through the usual spring ritual of digging, I'm going to examine the supposed benefits of digging. Are they really so beneficial and necessary after all? Let's examine them one by one.

Weed Control

First, let's talk about weed control. It is true that turning the soil by digging buries any newly emerging weeds or ungerminated weed seeds lying near the soil surface. But I found over the years that my freshly turned garden quickly developed a luxuriant weed crop every spring, even though I cultivated it the preceding year. But I had a sparse weed crop in my perennial bed where I didn't dig or cultivate for weeds each year. Why did this happen? The answer lay in the soil.

Below the surface of any garden's soil lies a ticking time bomb: ungerminated weed seeds. Weeds produce prolific numbers of seeds. For example, the worst weed in my garden, purslane, can produce 190,000 seeds *per plant* in a single growing season. A lamb's-quarters plant can produce 72,500 seeds; plantain, 36,000; and chickweed, 15,000. You can imagine how weed seeds fill the soil.

Weed seeds can lie dormant underground for long periods of time. Most will survive for 10, 20, and even 40 years. Some weed seeds have life spans of many hundreds of years. These seeds germinate whenever conditions become favorable, such as when you bring the soil below up to the surface during the digging of your garden.

The skeptics may say that, eventually, turning the soil followed by surface cultivation should exhaust the weed seed supply. I don't think so. I dug and thoroughly cultivated one garden of mine for an eight-year period. After each turning of the soil, I was still rewarded with a thriving jungle of newly emerging weed seedlings.

The problem lies in numbers. First, most garden soil contains vast numbers of weed seeds, each with a long lifetime to wait for the right conditions to germinate. Second, no matter how thoroughly you cultivate, you will miss a few weeds here and there. Just a few missed weeds will add tens of thousands more seeds to the soil. Third, wind, animals, clothing, or soil on shoes can transport even more weed seeds into your garden. Finally, other seeds can arrive in mulches, manures, and even in bird droppings. So much for the value of digging garden soil to control weeds!

The best way to control weeds is to *not* dig the soil and to use shallow cultivation or a mulch. In this way the deeper seeds remain buried, never to germinate. Those weed seeds near the surface eventually disappear as they germinate. If the cultivation is shallow, no new seeds will make their way to the surface.

Drainage and Aeration

We've just seen that one of the traditional reasons for digging the garden each spring is not really valid. But what about the other two? Does cultivation improve drainage and aeration of the seedbed? Again, the answer is no. In fact, the reverse is true. Digging the soil ultimately brings about a deterioration of drainage and aeration, and I'd like to prove it to you.

Turning the soil brings organic matter in the root zone to the surface where the levels of oxygen are higher. This condition increases the oxidation, or breakdown, of organic matter, because the soil microorganisms that decompose organic matter are more active in the oxygen-rich surface layers of the soil. Studies show that soils under cultivation lose about 2 percent of their organic matter each year. These losses of soil organic matter result in poorer drainage, decreased aeration, and less ease of soil workability (tilth), as any good book on soils can inform you. Ultimately, continued loss of organic matter leads to increased water and wind erosion. The latter has become serious for U.S. farmers, since erosion is the leading problem in soil management for nonorganic farmers.

A second fact, revealed by Mark Kane in the September 1983 issue of *Organic Gardening,* is that tilled or dug soil is more susceptible to compaction. Compacted soils have poor aeration and drainage. Plant roots cannot get enough oxygen for good growth, and stunted plants result. The conversion of organic matter to humus also slows, since the needed microorganisms fail in oxygen-poor soils. In turn this curtailment decreases the levels of available nutrients supplied by the breakdown of organic matter. Nutrient storage is lessened and leaching increased, since humus helps to retain nutrients. The bottom line is less fertility and lower yields.

Al Trouse points out in Kane's article that slight pressures of 3.5 pounds per square inch will start to compact well-tilled soil. The simple act of walking on soil exerts far more pressure, perhaps as much as 25 pounds per square inch. When you dig and rake your soil into seedbeds, you produce a well-tilled soil which is easily compacted by even light foot traffic. (For the record, Al Trouse retired from the USDA's National Tillage Machinery Laboratory. He studied the development of plant roots in compacted soil, among other things.)

The problem of compaction involves soil structure. Turning the soil by vigorous digging has a detrimental effect on its structure. Essentially, disruption of soil crumbs and particles is caused first by the slicing and tearing action of the shovel or fork, and then worsened by force as the soil drops from the shovel or fork and hits the ground. Structure breakdown intensifies further as you bring the organic matter to the surface, where the newly exposed organic matter is lost quickly at the oxygen-rich, microbially active surface of the soil. Soils with weakened structures are more susceptible to compaction, have less ease of workability, and have poorer drainage and aeration.

Now are you convinced that digging your garden isn't necessary? As you can see, the digging of your garden actually damages your soil. You're probably ready now to throw away your spade and give up digging forever. But what do you do instead of digging soil? How do you control weeds? That's what Bill and I wondered several years ago. Although we solved the problem, it wasn't easy. But you can benefit from our experience. First, let's turn to the tools that will convert you from a hardworking soil buster to a no-dig loafer.

Tools for No-Dig Gardening

Do garden tools fascinate you? They fascinate me! When I buy a new tool for my garden, I feel like a kid opening a birthday gift. Once I have the tool at home, I can't resist admiring the complementary blending of fine wood and gleaming metal. And I have a lot of fun trying out the tool in my garden, where I look for good balance, comfort, and efficient function. A tool with these qualities, that is, one that works well and feels good in my hands, makes gardening chores go much more easily.

It was therefore with pleasure that Bill and I examined old and new tools for our no-dig garden. First, we had to shake our perceptions of the tools we traditionally relied on, the shovel or spading fork and the trowel. Sure, these tools can prepare a fine seedbed or plant transplants, but their use requires a lot of physical effort and time. And for what? The seeds or transplants fill only 10 to 20 percent of the garden area we struggle so hard to prepare. Once we saw the shovel, fork, and trowel in that light, Bill and I changed our rigid thought patterns and started looking for new tools.

Our new-found insight helped us to focus quickly on finding tools that would simply and rapidly prepare seed furrows or transplant holes in untilled soil without digging. When we discovered that Bill (who, remember, is in his 80s) found the tools we chose easy to work with, and my children could handle them with no trouble, the no-dig gardening method for all ages was born.

Tools for Transplants

First let's look at the tools for planting transplants. Bill and I had to decide whether or not one tool could handle all kinds of transplants, no matter how they were grown. As you know, you can grow or purchase transplants either in individual containers or as several plants in one container. The plants can be large or small. Transplants present a range of different situations for a single tool to handle. But we found two tools that could handle just about any kind or size of transplant.

Our first choice was a bulb planter. You may remember that I mentioned Bill's short-handled bulb planter earlier. However, we agreed that we needed one change. I suggested to Bill that a long-handled bulb planter would work better because it would provide leverage and we could stand upright while using it. The long-handled planter would be easy to use — all it requires is a firm push with your foot.

Although we initially had difficulty finding a long-handled bulb planter, we finally found reliable and respected mail-order houses that carried what we needed. (The Appendix lists these addresses as well as our other tool sources.)

Figure 1-1 shows our long-handled bulb planter. Although all metal, it's lightweight because it has a tubular handle. Don't let the light weight fool you, either. We have given our planter much abuse over three years, and it still looks almost new. This particular one came from A. M. Leonard, Inc., and retailed for around $15 at the time we purchased it. White Flower Farm sells a much heavier duty, sturdier version at over four times the cost. We rate the former as a "best buy."

Many of you probably already have a short-handled bulb planter. By all means, try it out in place of the long-handled one. Use the transplanting technique shown in Chapter 3. That way you can try out our method quickly and at no expense. You might even find that you like working with the shorter tool.

Our long-handled bulb planter is compatible with larger transplants, including those purchased in individual containers, such as broccoli, cabbage, eggplants, geraniums, melons, peppers, squash, and tomatoes. Transplants grown at home in individual containers also work out well.

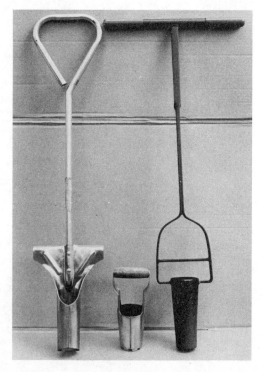

1-1 The lightweight aluminum bulb planter discussed in the book is shown at left. The heavy-duty carbon steel version on the right is available from Brookstone. The resharpenable cutter slices into the soil as you rotate the T-handle and apply foot pressure. If your soil is stony or heavy clay, this version at $25 is a good buy. A standard short-handled planter is shown for comparison.

Sometimes for reasons of economy or limited space, gardeners grow transplants in groups in flats or similar containers. Bedding plants such as begonias, coleus, marigolds, petunias, and salvia are often grown this way. Many people like to grow lettuce in flats, too. If you have an uncrowded flat and the transplants are medium sized to large sized, you can usually separate them with a reasonably intact soil ball. You can use the bulb planter for this task. If the transplants are small or have little or no soil ball, you will need another no-dig tool.

This additional tool is known as a dibble (Figure 1-2). Essentially, a dibble is a pointed stick with a handle. The better models have a metal-encased pointed end and a slightly rounded tip. Another name for the tool, particularly among gardeners in England, is the dibber.

When you're looking for a dibble, the question is whether to make your own or buy one. You can easily make dibbles from the broken handles of tools. The broken handle of a shovel or spading fork can become a short-handed dibble. A broken handle from a hoe, rake, or broom can be used to create a long-handled model. You don't happen to have any broken handles? Just buy a replacement handle for an outdoor push broom. A little whittling with a sharp knife and a touch of sand paper will give you a first-class dibble!

You can also buy some well-made dibbles for a reasonable price. One metal-encased short-handled version comes with a pistol-type handle, another with a "T" handle. Prices vary from $5 to $14, depending on the type of wood and metal used. These short-handled dibbles are all comfortable to use, regardless of handle shape.

The long-handled dibble is perhaps easier to make than to buy because it's not widely available commercially. However, Bill and I finally did find a company called Walter F. Nicke (see Appendix) that sells the makings of a long-handled dibble. For about $7 you can buy a steel dibble to attach to an extension handle. The handle can adapt to other tools as well, a subject I will cover later.

Should you go for the short-handled or long-handled dibble? The choice is not as clear-cut as it is with the bulb planter. The bulb planter, because of the size of the hole cut by it, requires more pushing pressure. You can more easily apply such pressure in a standing position. The dibble, on the other hand, requires very slight effort, so standing or stooping makes little difference. The choice really comes down to whichever you prefer. Between these two tools, you can tackle any transplanting task that arises in your no-dig garden.

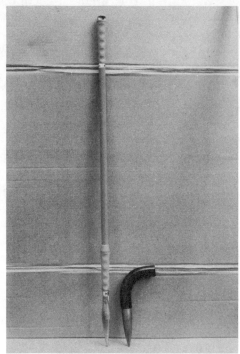

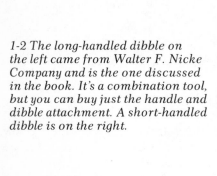

1-2 The long-handled dibble on the left came from Walter F. Nicke Company and is the one discussed in the book. It's a combination tool, but you can buy just the handle and dibble attachment. A short-handled dibble is on the right.

Tools for Seeds

OK, great, we've settled the matter of transplants, but what about seeds? How do you plant seeds without digging and preparing the soil? First of all, Bill and I found that we could plant some seeds, such as large bean or corn seeds that are planted in hills, with the bulb planter and dibble. Peas worked fine, too. (As an aside, these tools also made it easy to plant onion sets, garlic cloves, and seed potatoes.)

But suppose you want to plant seeds in rows. Although planting seeds was the toughest challenge Bill and I faced as we developed the total no-dig garden, we did find a tool that let us make seed furrows easily, without digging.

Our initial attempts concentrated quite naturally on hoes. At first glance the hoe looks ideal for creating a furrow as you draw it through the soil. But in reality, the labor involved in making a furrow with a hoe is comparable to an exercise workout. The problem with hoes is in their design. They are great for cutting weeds and disturbing soil in small amounts; however, cutting a furrow tends to build up a pile of soil at the blade front. This mound slows the hoe's movement and makes your muscles fight the hoe.

We quickly realized that what we needed was a hoe that behaved like a plow. This implement should cut through soil like a knife through butter, while throwing the removed soil to the sides of the furrow. Also, the tool should pull easily enough that anyone could use it.

We found such a tool in the furrower, also known as the furrow hoe, ridge plough, or hiller (Figure 1-3). This tool has just recently appeared in the United States but has been available longer in Europe. The wedgelike blade is polished steel, the edges are sharp, and the "wings" are angled. The blade's sharpness and wedgelike shape help it to sink into and slice effortlessly through the soil. The polished surface stops the soil from sticking, and the angled "wings" prevent soil build-up by throwing it to the sides. The furrower cuts neat, broad, vee-shaped furrows in depths from shallow scratches to several inches. My young children found it easy to handle, as did Bill. Prices vary considerably from as low as $15 to as high as $30. The main difference in price seems to be with the heft and blade dimensions. These two factors generally increase as the price does. (See the Appendix for a listing of mail-order sources.)

Whether or not you need the heavy-duty furrower depends on what you plant. If you plant only seeds, the lighter weight version is fine. The planting of seed potatoes requires the heavier model, which cuts the deeper furrow. However, keep in mind that you can also plant seed potatoes with the bulb planter and even the dibble. I favored the heavier

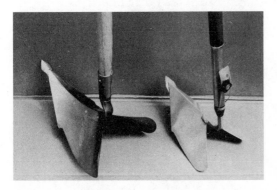

1-3 The larger, heavier Polar furrower on the left is the one I like. The lighter version on the right is actually one of the combination tools you make with the Gardena system. The tools came from Judd Ringer's and Smith & Hawken, respectively.

furrower because of its increased versatility, and I liked the way it felt when cutting a furrow.

At this point I'd like to mention a multi-purpose tool that can become, among other things, a furrower. Its brand name is Gardena. With the handle and the furrower attachment, it costs around $26. The cost places it at the top of the line, a few dollars away from the heavy-duty, one-piece furrower I favor. The Gardena furrower is of medium weight and size. The locking system is quite secure, giving this furrower the sturdiness of the one-piece unit. But the benefit of the Gardena is that you can convert the handle to make other tools. You can save money by changing tool heads instead of buying several individual tools. This approach works if you really need the other tools, which include rakes, cultivators, and various hoes. The decision about which tools you need is a personal one, but I don't feel that the rakes, hoes, and cultivators are necessary for the no-dig no-weed garden.

One other positive point, however, makes the Gardena furrower (or other tools) innovative. You can add on a second "comfort handle" for about $8. The comfort handle fits on the main handle and moves up or down until it is most comfortable for your less dominant hand. You can also position it for top or bottom grabbing. When you find the most comfortable adjustment you can lock the handle in place with a few twists.

The comfort handle makes the tool easier to use and allows you to cut deeper furrows with less effort because of your improved body symmetry and the more equalized pulling tension on both your arms and shoulders. Those of you who balk at the weight or effort with heavier furrowers would find this one far preferable. Bill prefers the Gardena furrower to a heavy-duty Polar furrower. My wife, Marian, thinks the Gardena is better for her. Although I like the heavier furrower now, I may change to the Gardena version as I get older. The only limitation with the smaller Gardena furrower is that it can't cut as deeply as the larger, heavier Polar one.

Bill and I have a final thought about no-dig tools for planting seeds. Suppose you just want to try the no-dig preparation of a seed furrow without buying a furrower. You can get a rough idea with a hoe.

Some hoes are better than others, but most will do the job. If you have one of the conventional square or rectangular blade hoes, just turn it on an angle so that the corner cuts into the soil. A gooseneck hoe with a triangular blade can also cut a furrow, as can the Southern Belle hoe. (Incidentally, the Gardena handle, when fitted with a single-share cultivator, is quite similar to a gooseneck hoe.) However, some hoes, such as the Action hoe, just cannot cut a furrow. Please keep in mind that the hoe is a poor substitute for the furrower.

Tools for No-Weed Gardening

As you know, this book is also about no-weed gardening. Why, you may ask, do you need tools if you're not going to do any weeding? Actually, you have a choice between doing no weeding whatsoever and doing very little weeding. If you prefer never to weed the garden at all, just use one of the permanent or temporary mulching systems discussed in Chapter 5. If you find you have the need to handle some weeds, Bill and I think we can surprise you at how easy it can be.

We examined and evaluated over a dozen different hoes for weeding, looking for the right one. Our goal was to find a hoe that cut through the soil with ease. As I explained earlier, most hoes pile up soil, thus increasing your workload. Others are blunt, thick, or heavy and hinder your effort. We also wanted a hoe that severed weeds effortlessly, not one that chopped like an ax. We finally found the ideal hoe. One company calls it an action hoe and another, an oscillating hoe. The mount of the cutting blade gives this type of hoe its name. The mounting allows the blade to move back and forth as you push or pull; hence, the blade has *action,* or an *oscillating* motion.

This hoe has several excellent features. First, the hoe is very light in weight, because the hoe blade is essentially little more than a cutting edge. The edge is knife sharp on both sides, allowing you to cut weeds on either the push or pull motion. The blade's thinness and sharpness allow you to move it through the soil just below the surface, cutting off weeds at the roots as you go. You do not have to chop or hack the weeds down. Because of the open tunnel design, no soil piles up and hinders the forward or backward movement of the blade. Finally, the blade-to-soil angle allows you to stand upright, placing no pressure on your lower back.

The action hoe is a pleasure to use and makes short work of weeds. Since the blade cuts near the surface, it does not disturb lower soil and bring new weed seeds to the surface. In a short time, your garden has only a few weeds, making it practically a no-weed one. Bill found he could handle weeds with the action hoe with no sweat or aches. He loves it, and I agree.

By the way, don't concern yourself with the blade's edge wearing out. A quick touch with an oiled whetstone keeps it cutting. An accidental nick or burr is quickly smoothed out with a file. This treatment holds the hoe through the gardening season. An annual sharpening with a grindstone, either at home or from a commercial sharpening service, will keep this hoe going for years.

You can find this kind of hoe at some garden centers and hardware stores. If you can't find one locally, see the Appendix under Smith and Hawken or A. M. Leonard, Inc. to order one by mail. Don't let those weeds get you down any longer.

Helpful Accessories

Some useful additional items can make the task of the no-dig gardener more comfortable and easier. Bill and I tried out several accessories along the way and believe that some of them are worthy of your consideration.

Regardless of whether you are young or old, the contact between your knees and the garden's soil is often uncomfortable. Soil usually feels hard after the first few contacts. Stones, twigs, and crop residues add to the unpleasant sensation. If the soil is wet or cold, the ache in your knees seems to go even deeper. Soils in the spring, being both wet and cold, can be enough to discourage planting sessions with bone-chilling promptness. What's a no-dig gardener to do?

Even a no-dig gardener must kneel sometimes, such as when placing transplants. But this communion between soil and gardener need not be an uncomfortable event. It can be a pleasant sharing of the plant's environment, an opportunity to get close to the soil with a sense of appreciation.

The difference between pain and enjoyment can be as simple as a pair of sponge rubber kneepads (Figure 1-4). At around $7 or $8 a pair, they are a bargain. My inspiration finally to get kneepads came from watching my children rollerskate. Sometimes they fell to their knees on the pavement but were unhurt because they wore protective pads. The light clicked on in my head, as they say. Working on my garden soil has become a pleasure, thanks to my gardener's kneepads.

You can also buy a kneeling pad for a few dollars less than the kneepads. The comfort level is the same, but I don't like picking up and carrying the pad every time I move elsewhere. The kneepads are no bother; you're wearing them, so they automatically go with you to the next area. However, a more sophisticated version of the kneeling pad should be considered if you appreciate a little help as you kneel or rise. The kneeling stool has a soft kneeling pad. In addition, two supports at the right and left sides provide arm-assisted kneeling or rising. If you get tired, you can flip the kneeling stool over to become a bench! When you finish, you can fold it for easy storage. At around $45, the kneeling stool is a blessing for senior or disabled gardeners.

Another quite useful gadget is a garden straightline, or row marker, which costs about $10. This unit consists of one stake with a windup top containing line attached to a second stake. You push the second stake into the ground and feed the line out to the desired length. Then, push the last stake into the ground. Now you have a way to make a nice, straight line. If

A

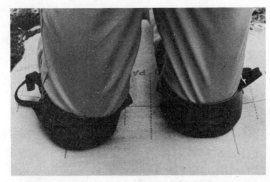

B

1-4 There are a number of available comfort aids that are great for your knees. You might try kneepads (A), a kneeling mat, or a specially designed kneeling stool (B) or bench.

you team up the straightline device with a furrower or bulb planter, you can make nice, straight rows.

I found yet another application that makes this gadget useful. If you have ever tried to lay black plastic mulch, you know that the trench into which the plastic edge goes must be true. If you prepare your trench based upon the garden straightline, you greatly simplify the installation of plastic mulches. Using a garden straightline and a spade, just try the easy one-two-three steps of placing plastic mulch that I mention in Chapter 5. I'm sure you'll agree the straightline is an indispensable accessory.

One last accessory deserves a mention. A row seeder can save you a lot of bending and stooping. Although most of us with smaller gardens do not really need one, proprietors of large gardens, or older or handicapped gardeners may find the row seeder to be invaluable. My advice is to avoid the smaller hand-held units with "click" features. These devices give good results if you are steady of hand and true of eye; however, your need for a seeder usually arises because you do not rate high in those traits. The better device is the wheel-type seeder with a long handle. You can push such units along with hardly any effort as you walk the row. As far as cost is concerned, I found three sturdy units that retail at around $13 to $17. These items, the Burpee, Plant-Rite, and Precision Row seeders, are listed in the Appendix.

Tool Simplicity

By now you have noticed that the no-dig gardener needs very few tools. If you are a gardener who works only with transplants, either purchased or home grown, you can make do with only the bulb planter. You might need an action hoe for weeds, but if you opt for our total no-weed approach described in Chapter 5, you won't need the hoe. Even if you like to grow plants that are not conventionally recognized or available as transplants, you still need but a few tools. If you plan to plant seeds, you will need the furrower.

At most, then, you will need two tools for the no-dig no-weed garden with full mulch. If you opt for no mulch or only a partial mulch, make it three. New gardeners need not invest a fortune. But established gardeners need not despair. Hang onto your tools. You may find new uses for them, such as using the spade to install plastic mulches. And don't forget, trees and shrubs will still need planting and lawns will need raking. Of course, you can always sell the dust collectors in a tag sale.

Chapter 2
Better Transplants— The Key to Success

You can't beat transplants when it comes to getting a head start in your garden. So why is it that we don't use more transplants? Several reasons may pop up in your mind. You've surely heard them all: "Some plants don't transplant well." "Growing transplants is too much work." "Transplants never take well in my garden." "I get quicker-growing, better plants with direct garden seeding." "Transplants cost too much."

Bunk and baloney! That's what Bill and I say to these arguments. Transplants are a great timesaver for gardeners. When they don't perform well, it's usually because the gardener doesn't fully understand how to handle transplants or is doing something wrong along the way. Let Bill and me tell you about our way to grow the best-ever transplants with little work. You won't need a greenhouse or a lot of money to follow our method. Yes, you will be able to transplant even the most finicky plant with our method. No transplanting shock or slow recovery will occur. Your transplants will grow as soon as they enter the soil, and you'll love the results. First let's look at why you should consider planting transplants.

Why Use Transplants?

Gardeners use transplants for different reasons. The most important reason they give is the head start transplants offer to the growing season. Transplants offer instant color with annual bedding plants like marigolds, petunias, impatiens, geraniums, and coleus. Of course, no tomato-lover would even consider direct sowing of tomatoes in the garden, since transplanted tomatoes yield fruit roughly two months sooner than directly sown tomatoes. This earlier and, hence, longer harvest is especially important to us northern gardeners because of our shorter growing seasons.

Another big plus for using transplants is that they allow for economical use of space in the garden. Because transplants are started outside your garden, plenty of garden space is available for direct seeding of fast-producing early crops. After the harvest of early crops, like peas, radishes, spinach, chard, and lettuce, you can fill in the garden space with transplants.

Another advantage of using transplants is the need for fewer seeds. Rates of seed germination are better indoors under controlled conditions, therefore fewer seeds are lost to the elements. Spacing becomes easier in the garden with transplants as opposed to seeds, because you can see just how much room each plant will need. With transplants there is no need for thinning, again due to more accurate spacing from the start. Seed packages seem to stretch further.

You can also use transplants throughout the season as reserves. As you harvest your crops, you can replace the old plants with new plants from your ongoing transplant nursery to fill the holes. Direct seeding during the hot, dry days of summer can be difficult, because the seeds need moisture and controlled warmth to germinate properly. On the other hand, transplant production can be a breeze at that time. (This topic will be covered in more detail later in this chapter.)

Another transplant plus is the significant advantage they offer in the fight against insects, disease, and unfavorable weather. The development of a plant from germination through seedling is a critical time. You must closely watch temperature and moisture conditions, and insects plus disease can knock out young seedlings very quickly. While you can control these problems outdoors in gardens to some degree, producing transplants indoors borders on luxury conditions. Each resulting vigorous transplant will have bypassed early problems and will now be at a stage and time where outdoor garden conditions will pose much less hazard.

This last reason for using transplants became very important to me. My garden, like most in the Northeast, was hit hard by a series of cold, wet springs in recent years, and most of my seeds rotted before they germinated. I resorted to sowing many more seeds than I needed and trying to wait out the weather. Needless to say, I was not a happy gardener. My brightest moments were with transplants, because they came through the miserable weather with flying colors.

I began to wonder if I could plant my entire garden with transplants, a reasonable thought considering the fact that I grow my own. Long ago I became displeased with commercial transplants and the very limited choices available, although I didn't blame the growers, who were forced to select cultivars based on salability.

Bill and I began to discuss the possibilities of producing transplants for any vegetable or flower. We knew that it was easier to produce transplants for some plants than for others, but we didn't know why. For example, why not produce corn transplants because I had many corn seeds ruined by weather and devoured by squirrels? We reasoned that the growing of some plants as transplants was not economically feasible, and the direct outdoor sowing of others gave satisfactory results. Some plants were thought to be difficult to grow as transplants, but were probably easier to raise if handled properly. Other transplants probably got the reputation for being difficult only through "hearsay evidence," while others were difficult to grow because of taproots.

Bill and I figured we needed to think beyond conventional approaches with transplants, as we did earlier with our no-dig techniques, but we knew that any new technique would have to satisfy certain conditions. The procedure would have to be inexpensive and easy, it could not require any special equipment, it would have to perform well under conditions available to the average gardener, it would have to produce transplants for any crop, and it would have to produce transplants that would not experience transplanting shock. You might say it was a tall order, but Bill and I have succeeded in satisfying all the requirements. Our method, like any other, utilizes containers, growing media, and certain cultural attention; however, some differences from traditional methods do exist.

You, the reader, now face a choice whether to finish this chapter or to skip to the next one. If you grow or want to grow your own transplants, read on. If you are a diehard buyer of commercial transplants, you just might want to grow your own after reading further.

Transplant Containers

The problem with transplant containers is that they serve only one purpose when they really should serve two. They serve to hold the soil and roots of the transplant in a nice, tidy package, but they fail to allow for the production of the kind of roots that help transplants recover quickly from the shock suffered when you remove them from the containers to plant them out. To the original designers of planting containers, roots were roots. Surprisingly little has been done to improve containers since those first designs. Yet Bill and I know that the container makes or breaks the transplant.

I'm sure you'll agree with Bill and me that transplanting success depends heavily on causing little or no damage to the root system. However, a second key point overlooked by early container designers is that root balls need to have many, healthy feeder roots on their surface. These feeder roots, essentially smaller roots with fine hairs, are extremely important to producing the best-ever transplants. You see, feeder roots are the part of the root system through which the plant takes up water and nutrients. Technically, plant scientists call such roots *root hairs*. You can find these small root hairs near the tips of actively growing roots. To the eye, root hairs give the root tip a fuzzy, white appearance. If a transplant has an extensive, fuzzy covering of feeder roots on the root ball, all the better. Feeder roots, being tiny and delicate, are good indicators to use in assessing root ball damage. If root hairs are present on the root ball when you remove it from the container, you know you have an undamaged root ball that will recover quickly after transplanting. Also, the feeder roots respond rapidly to water and nutrients in the starter solution, so the plant is off and running quickly. The fuzzier the root ball looks, the better the roots soak up water and nutrients from the soil.

The location of the feeder roots is also critical. If the feeder roots are not on the surface of the root ball, but mostly concentrated inside the root ball, the response of the transplant to planting will not be as good. The reason the transplant does not take as well as one having surface feeder roots may not be obvious but should become clear after our explanation. We based our information upon our own experiments with watering combinations of garden soils and growing media, and also upon the research of soil scientists.

If you've grown your own transplants in the past, you know that the soil in your garden differs from the material in which you grow your transplants. Mixtures for growing transplants are put together for one main purpose, that is, to produce better transplants than would soil. Therefore, these transplanting materials drain well, have excellent aeration, and are often rich in organic material. They look, feel, and weigh differently from the soil in your garden. Doesn't it follow, then, that when you put the transplant root ball into the garden, you join together two materials with different textures—soil and transplant growing mixture? Because of this texture difference, these two materials don't mesh together as soil to soil would. It's essentially like trying to mesh together two zipper tracks with different teeth spacing; they just don't go together. Scientists call the place where the two textures meet an interface.

Now let's add another element to the picture. Moving water seeks out the easiest path. Anyone who has a leaky basement will agree with this observation. The easiest path through the soil and the transplant root ball is at the interface. Many spaces and gaps in this area speed the water right on by; therefore, water and nutrients tend to flow over the root ball and spread out under it; less water actually enters the root ball (Figure 2-1). If the feeder roots are at the junction of the two soils, that is, the root ball's surface, they are in the water pathway. Their location, then, is ideal for gathering water and nutrients in the few critical days after the transplanting operation. Such surface-rooted balls give you a transplant that shows little or no wilting and rapid development in the garden.

Surface feeder roots promote not only initial growth but also later growth. Again we base our statement upon our personal observations and the comments of other gardeners. Transplants lacking surface feeder roots, when dug up at the end of the season, tend to show poor root balls. Roots are small and show very little outward spread from the original root ball. On the other hand, our transplants with lots of external feeder roots exhibit much larger root balls and greater spread. Better leaf and stem growth and higher yields go hand in hand with the bigger root ball. Such results are sure to bring smiles to gardeners' faces.

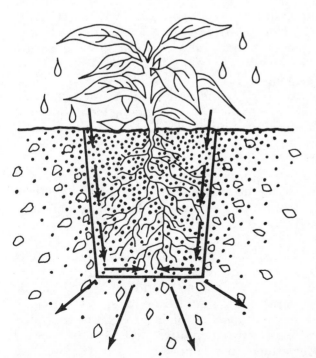

2-1 Water will flow rapidly along the path of least resistance, that is, the point where the transplant soil and root ball meet the surrounding garden soil. Only at the bottom of the root ball does water start to spread out. Roots at the sides and bottom surface of the root ball are the only roots situated for taking advantage of the passing water.

A similar, confirming situation is familiar to those of us who have planted container-grown shrubs and trees. To encourage root development outward, the gardener quarter-scores the root ball. Failure to do so usually results in a poorly developed shrub or tree that never reaches its potential, or even worse, dies. Upon digging up the shrub, the gardener would find limited development of the root system.

OK, you say, I'm ready to give it a try. How do I encourage feeder roots to form at the root ball surface? The answer is very simple: *localized aeration*, which translated means, give them air! Roots require oxygen to survive and to grow. Without oxygen, such as in overwatered soil, roots rot and die. They literally suffocate. Plants specifically need oxygen for a process called *respiration*, which is essentially the breakdown of food to supply energy for plant development. Roots tend to grow through the pore spaces in soil; the feeder roots form at the growing tips of roots where oxygen, water, and nutrients are present. In conventional containers, air enters through the surface of the growing mixture and spreads through the mixture. The roots in the center get first crack at using the air while they grow. By the time the air reaches the edges, little is left for the surface feeder roots.

Logically, we wish to increase oxygen levels at the junction between the growing media and the container. You cannot find this favorable condition in the usual nonbreathing (nonporous) containers used to grow transplants. Even if we switch from plastic to a more porous material, such as clay, the slight improvement is not enough to warrant the greatly increased container cost. So what kind of container is the right kind of container for growing transplants? Only one type will serve our purpose: Styrofoam coffee cups. Why? There are several reasons. Such cups are inexpensive, readily available, compatible with our no-dig technique, and are the easiest to modify for production of feeder roots.

What size cup do we need? Three sizes work out well with the no-dig hole left by the bulb planter, the 8-ounce, 10-ounce, and 12-ounce sizes. How can all these fit one hole? Quite simply, you just vary the depth to which you sink the bulb planter, putting a file mark on the bulb planter or drilling a small hole through it once you find the right depth.

The ultimate size of the transplant is a guide to cup size; for example, tomatoes, peppers, and eggplants do quite well in the 12-ounce cup and lettuce fits in the 8-ounce cup. (Our recommendations for sizes can be found in Chapter 8, along with many other guidelines for growing individual vegetables.) You can use the 12-ounce size for all transplants, providing you don't mind using a little extra growing mixture. You may have to grow some plants longer, such as lettuce, in a somewhat larger size cup than normal in order to complete external feeder roots, but the plants will still transplant easily. An alternative is to have two or three lettuce transplants in the large cup.

You can purchase the Styrofoam cups at many places, such as grocery stores, supermarkets, and discount stores. If you plan on using a large number of cups, or want to get the cheapest price, we suggest that you buy them in case lots. You can purchase cases by arrangement with supermarket or co-op managers or right off the shelf in the newer food warehouse operations. Restaurant and bar suppliers are also usually willing to sell cups by case lot to individuals.

Now let me explain the coffee cup modification or "secret" that produces tremendous surface roots. We suggest that you do this procedure in the winter months when gardening activities are not competing for your time. Actually, you will need very little time; one evening, afternoon, or morning should suffice. First, place three holes in the cup's bottom, such that they would form a triangle if connected (Figure 2-2). The holes must be ¼ inch to ⅜ inch in diameter to provide good drainage. You can use a drill bit, large nail, or even a screwdriver to make the drainage holes.

For the next step in preparing the cups you need a double-thickness hacksaw blade. I take a standard hacksaw blade, wrap it in a towel and break it in half. Next I glue the two halves together with a high-strength, fast-acting glue that works on metal. Be careful not to get any on your hands or elsewhere! Those of you who do woodworking can make some form of a wood handle for your homemade tool. I usually place the doubled blade in a vise to hold it steady while I guide the Styrofoam cups over it.

You may be tempted to use only a single blade, but Bill and I advise against it. We found that the root systems produced with aeration cuts done with the doubled blade were far superior to those done with a single blade.

Now take the doubled hacksaw blade, and starting at each hole, cut upward to just under the cup rim (Figure 2-2). This provides you with three slits. Now make a new cut halfway between each existing slit, starting just under the rim and stopping halfway down the cup. This last step gives the cup three long and three short slits. The air that enters the cup through these slits bathes the surface of the root ball with oxygen, producing the magnificent feeder roots shown in Figure 2-3. Incidentally, the root ball slides very easily out of this kind of cup.

You may be wondering how the cup can survive all of the cutting. The cup can take it and will not fall apart now or throughout the growing period. In fact, we found that we could reuse the cups for a second year; but we recommend against it because the leftover residues in the cup are not

A

B

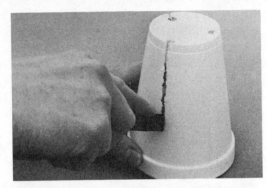

C

D

2-2 *Here's how to prepare Styrofoam transplant cups. A. Punch ¼-inch to ⅜-inch holes in a triangular pattern as shown with a file, screwdriver, or drill bit. B. With a double thickness of hacksaw blade or a keyhole saw, slice from the hole down just short of the rim. Make this cut at each hole. C. Halfway between each cut, put a new cut from just under the rim to about halfway to the bottom. You now have three long and three short alternating cuts. For a shortcut, put the six slits in first. Make sure the long ones cut into the cup bottom. D. Next make the bottom holes by pinching with your fingers.*

2-3 Transplants grow beautifully in the Styrofoam cups.
Here's a close-up of the root
ball on a tomato plant; note
the excellent development
of feeder roots.

easy to clean, thus posing a threat of seedling disease. You may also be wondering how the cup retains the growing media. Commercial growing media, or the growing medium that we use (see the next section in this chapter) will not leak out through the cuts or holes. Finally, we suggest that you use inexpensive plastic trays to catch the drainage from these cups. You can readily purchase these trays at garden centers and discount stores, or you can order them by mail (see Appendix for suppliers).

Remember one more important fact. While these changed containers are fantastic at producing feeder roots, they can't do their job if you skimp or cheat on the soil mixture. The soil mixture must have good drainage, aeration, and nutrient content. We will cover what makes a good mixture for growing transplants shortly; but before we do, I'd like to comment on producing transplants by other means.

In all honesty, a transplant produced in other containers by other methods, whether grown by you or purchased, will work with the no-dig method. However, these transplants will experience some transplanting shock and will get off to a slower start. For example, you might love peat pots. These pots fit nicely into the no-dig hole and produce transplants that show little or no transplanting shock; however, the plants that are produced in peat pots have fewer feeder roots and will not grow as quickly as plants started by our coffee cup method. You might like the ease and economy of growing marigolds or lettuce in conventional flats, but you should expect some shock and delay when you transplant the seedlings. Or perhaps you like the newer self-watering, greenhouse-type plastic flats. Whatever transplant container you choose, it will work with the no-dig method of gardening, as I will explain in Chapter 3.

Growing Media

You have two basic choices with growing media, whether to make your own or to buy commercial formulations. If you make your own growing medium, you know exactly what went into it. Homemade growing mixtures are also less expensive than commercial types. The drawback to making your own is inconvenience. Commercial mixes are convenient but more costly, although their prices are reasonably moderate. I'll cover both, and you can select the one that's right for you. Remember, we will introduce a modification to improve drainage and aeration over existing mixtures.

Homemade Growing Media

My experience with homemade growing mixtures is considerable. Over the years I have come to favor the following simple mixture:

$\frac{1}{3}$ sphagnum moss
$\frac{1}{3}$ vermiculite
$\frac{1}{3}$ perlite

Mix these three materials based upon parts by volume, not weight. For example, if you use a 2-quart container filled with sphagnum moss, you would also add 2 quarts of vermiculite and 2 of perlite.

The sphagnum moss should be the shredded or milled form commonly available as a germination material. Sphagnum moss has natural fungicides that fight the "damping off" diseases that attack seedlings. With reasonable sanitation and clean containers, you won't have to pasteurize your finished product. The vermiculite should be horticultural grade, preferably termed fine or number 4. Perlite should be coarse grade, with particles varying in size from $\frac{1}{16}$ inch to $\frac{1}{8}$ inch in diameter. The Appendix lists mail order suppliers of these materials.

I'd like to mention a few words of caution concerning the handling of these materials. First, perlite dust is a nasal irritant, and you should spray or wet it prior to handling. Secondly, some of you may have seen reports that sphagnum moss can carry a fungus known to cause sporotrichosis, a disease characterized by nodules and abscesses in the skin, just below the skin, and in surface lymph nodes. The infection occurs when the fungus enters a cut or abrasion on the hand. While the disease is quite rare, common sense suggests that you not handle sphagnum moss if you have any cuts or abrasions on your hands. If you are worried, wear gloves as a precaution.

Perhaps you are thinking of using peat moss or compost as a substitute for sphagnum moss. If you do, you will lose the natural fungicidal action of sphagnum moss. Also, the mixture will need pasteurization or treatment with a fungicide to avoid damping off diseases common to germinating seedlings. Secondly, substituting for the sphagnum moss doesn't necessarily mean you will avoid the problem of sporotrichosis, since the fungus that causes the disease can live on any organic matter, even garden soil. I don't intend to frighten you with this information, but I do want you to be aware of it. My awareness of the disease stems from a few cases reported and then overblown in the literature. The fact is that the disease is rare, with very few cases in the United States.

If you prepare your own mixture, based upon the earlier directions, you will need to treat it differently than the commercial mixture. You can prepare the homemade mixture ahead of time and store it in plastic bags in a dry place. When you get ready to use the material, you will have to make some adjustment of pH. Add dolomitic limestone, since sphagnum moss is acidic. Commercial mixtures don't need this step, because the manufacturer has already corrected any pH problems.

To add the limestone, take any plastic 1-gallon bottle with a handle, such as a plastic milk container. Carefully remove the bottom with a sharp knife or single-edge razor, and you now have a 1-gallon scoop. Each gallon of growing mixture requires slightly over ½ tablespoon of limestone (0.6 tablespoon to be exact). Three and one-half gallons of growing mixture would need about 2 level tablespoons of dolomitic limestone.

Both homemade and commercial growing mixtures need yet another addition. Bill and I found a material that promotes exceptional, rapid root growth through the ball. This material and the root mass help to hold the growing mixture together upon removal from containers and assure the quick appearance of feeder roots on the root ball surface. This "secret" ingredient that really excites the root system is none other than the Styrofoam "peanuts" usually found as packing material in packages sent through the mail. We save these packing materials in a large plastic trash bag as well as encouraging our friends to save some. If you know a storekeeper, perhaps the manager of a hardware store, he or she may let you cart these Styrofoam peanuts away for the asking. You may be wondering about the Styrofoam "chips" also seen as packing filler. These chips don't work well, probably because of their thinness.

We add the Styrofoam peanuts at a rate of 1 gallon (by volume) to 4 gallons of homemade or commercial growing medium. Their addition not only improves drainage but, more importantly, also increases the aeration of the growing mixture. The rooting results are dramatic, as you can see in the root ball section in Figure 2-4. The peanuts, coupled with the slitted Styrofoam cups, will let you grow the best-ever transplants, no matter what vegetable or flower you choose!

If you can't get the Styrofoam peanuts, you can substitute nylon screening cut into strips of 1 or 2 inches. Nylon screening is commonly available for window screen replacement and is easy to cut and economical.

A

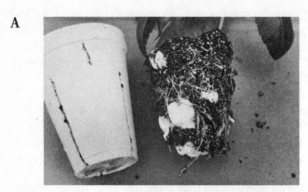

B

2-4 A. This photo shows a root ball with visible Styrofoam peanuts. B. Nylon screen is a good substitute, and helps to hold the soil ball together.

Rather than mixing the screen pieces into the growing mixture, put three to four pieces in each 12-ounce cup. The top edge of the screen should just break the surface of the mixture. The results are shown in Figure 2-4.

I just can't say enough about the combined aeration effect of the slit cups and Styrofoam peanuts or screen. The feeder roots on the surface and the interior root growth are impressive. Just look at Figures 2-3 and 2-4 again! The roots even grow right into the Styrofoam peanuts or through the screen, which really holds the root ball together. The feeder roots seem to thrive at the surface, most likely a result of excellent aeration and the diffusion of water and nutrients. Evaporation pulls the water and nutrients to the surface of the root ball. The slits admit air and help to increase surface evaporation on the sides of the root ball. You can't go wrong with our special cups and improved growing medium.

Commercial Growing Media

But suppose you wish to use a commercially prepared growing mixture rather than a homemade one. I have used commercial mixtures with fine results. Garden centers and many stores with garden supplies carry several brands of these growing mixtures. Also, seed companies such as Burpee and Park carry their own brands. One point to keep in mind is that some commercial mixes contain chemical fertilizers or fungicides, which you may want to avoid. Check the content before you buy a commercial brand. But now let's move on to growing areas and techniques.

Growing Areas

I know a lot of gardeners who would like to grow transplants but don't because they haven't got a greenhouse. Take heart! You can grow transplants without a greenhouse. I know, because I have produced healthy transplants for several years in my home. All you need is a brightly lit southern window or some fluorescent lights. Growing transplants is easy, and you can't go wrong using our altered cups and growing mixture, so why not skip that spring trip to the garden center and grow your own?

Indoor Growing Areas

Do you have a southern window? Is it bright and sunny most of the day? South-facing windows usually are aglow with sun, unless some obstruction is present. Sometimes a roof overhang, another building, or nearby trees and shrubs block the sun. If you can't avoid the obstruction, don't let the gloom at your window discourage you. You can still grow transplants.

You can produce excellent transplants under fluorescent lights. Since you don't intend your transplants to flower or produce vegetables but only to reach a reasonable size for outdoor planting, the choice of lamp is not critical. Any lamp will do. The cool white lamp used in fluorescent fixtures in homes or offices is a fine economical choice. Should you have other lamps on hand such as daylight or warm white, or lamps designed specifically for growing such as Gro-Lux Wide Spectrum, use them instead of buying cool white.

You don't need special fixtures, either. The best bet for growing plants is the fluorescent fixture with a hood that accommodates two 4-foot fluorescent tubes. These fixtures are commonly sold as workshop fixtures for the home and even come with fluorescent tubes and wire clips designed for hanging purposes. Since they are intended for work areas, they are not fancy or costly. These fixtures come complete for around $18 to $20; but if you watch for sales, the price may come down to $12 to $15. You can suspend the fluorescent fixtures by chains from hooks in the basement ceiling. You can raise or lower their heights by adjusting the chain.

Place an old table or door over two sawhorses situated under the lamp or lamps. Depending on how many transplants you need, you may want one, two, or possibly three fixtures. Each fixture serves a growing area of 4 feet by 1½ feet, or 6 square feet. Such an area accommodates up to 70 of our 12-ounce modified growing cups, if they just touch each other. If you use trays to hold the cups and allow for a little space around them, you will be able to fit about 60 cups under the lights. Eighteen standard plastic flats will fit into the area.

One fixture could easily supply the light for tomatoes, peppers, eggplants, and a few flowers for a garden. Two fixtures are probably adequate for growing enough seedlings for the average garden. However, if you like working with transplants, you may go for that third lamp! The space at your southern window may no longer look quite as inviting.

Outdoor Growing Areas

Under some conditions you can produce transplants directly outdoors. I experimented with raising seedlings outdoors over the last few years because of a succession of cold, wet springs that rotted many of my directly sown seeds (such as beans, corn, cucumbers, melons, and squash). Now I sow these seeds in our containers and germinate them indoors. I quickly place the new seedlings outdoors at normal outdoor planting time under a plastic cover, which sheds rain and warms the seedlings slightly but not enough to require ventilation. I staple the plastic cover onto a wood frame, which I can transport anywhere I want. Figure 2-5 shows a plastic cover in place in the garden.

Admittedly, I could start such transplants earlier and grow them indoors completely to have a head start. However, my way circumvents the wet, cold soil and doesn't tie up room indoors that I need for transplants such as tomatoes, where a head start is critical. The results I obtain are more favorable than having rotted seeds and offer a more timely harvest than would the later, direct replanting of rotted seeds.

2-5 Covers come in handy for starting seeds outdoors at normal planting times. Candidates for starting outdoors include crops like beans or squash, where early starts are not important and seeds are easily lost during germination in abnormally cold and wet springs.

The Greenhouse

Lastly, if you have a greenhouse, you are blessed with luxury quarters for growing transplants. I did without a greenhouse for many years and still grew great transplants. In fact, I only grew transplants for a few years in my present greenhouse before a large collection of cacti and succulents crowded them out. Now I use a little space in a greenhouse where I work; however, I still keep my fluorescent lights handy for the overflow. Who knows, they may serve fully again should I lose my present greenhouse space.

How to Grow Your Own Transplants, Step by Step

If you are ready, I'll take you through the steps for transplanting; but first I'd like to make a few comments. I will be using general information here on timing, the need for bottom heat, light requirements, and so forth. I will give more specific details for individual crops under their respective entries in Chapters 8 and 9 on vegetables and flowers.

First, make sure you order or buy your seeds as early as possible. You must start some seeds, such as seed geraniums (which are hybrids that grow easily from seed), as long as ten to twelve weeks prior to outdoor planting. Most plants need six to eight weeks of indoor growth before they're ready for transplanting, so I make sure I order my seeds by mail before the end of January.

Second, make sure everything you need is on hand. Nothing is worse than interrupting your planting to run off somewhere for whatever you forgot. Use the list below as your checklist.

Seeds	Labels
Growing media	Marking pen or pencil
Room-temperature water	Plastic food wrap or other clear
Modified Styrofoam cups or other	material
transplant containers	Tray(s) to hold cups

You need the plastic wrap to hold moisture during germination, because drying during that time is fatal to seedlings. If you have scrap pieces of window glass, pieces of rigid plastic such as acrylic or polycarbonate, or polyethylene plastic sheeting (used for storm windows or painter's drop cloths), you can use these materials instead.

The plastic trays catch the water that drains from your growing containers. You can buy plastic trays at garden centers or by mail (see Appendix). You can also recycle old dishpans, discarded baking pans, and cookie sheets to catch the water.

Preparing the Growing Mixture

The first step in preparing to plant your seeds is to wet your growing mixture. I prefer to wet it in a plastic bag, whether it be the one in which the mixture was sold or another. The amount of water needed varies slightly with the composition of the growing mixture. A good starting point is the ratio of 8:1, which works well with any of the mixtures described earlier in this chapter. Add one part of water to eight parts of dry growing mixture in your plastic bag; for example, 4 cups of mixture needs ½ cup of water, 8 quarts needs 1 quart, and ½ bushel (a common commercial size, 16 quarts) needs 2 quarts of water. I prefer to use lukewarm water for comfort and a somewhat easier mixing ability.

After you add the water, begin to knead the mixture like bread dough by alternately squeezing and releasing various parts of the plastic bag. Hold the bag closed, and turn or shake it a few times to assure that all the contents get moistened. Inspect the contents after a few minutes to see if all the material is wet. If it is not, continue kneading until the mix is moistened throughout. The mixture is wet enough if you squeeze it into a ball and it does not fall apart when you open your hand.

At this point I'm sure you have a few questions. What about pasteurization? If you recently made the sphagnum mixture or stored it dry in a plastic bag, chances are that you will not have to pasteurize it. Newly opened commercial mixtures or those promptly resealed after use should also be all right, assuming that you practiced normal sanitation: use of clean scoops for removal of mixture or direct pouring from the bag, no return of wetted mixture to the bag, and storage in a clean, dry place.

Also be sure to keep containers clean, because a dirty container could harbor the organisms which cause damping off of seedlings. If the containers are new, such as our modified Styrofoam cups, you will have no problem; however, do not reuse the Styrofoam cups unless you rinse them with warm, soapy water and soak them in a bleach solution. You can make the bleach solution with ¾ cup (6 ounces) of bleach to ½ gallon of room-temperature water. Soak the containers for five minutes and then rinse them well. Personally, I think the cost of the cups is so low that I don't bother to reuse them. If you are using any scoops, tools to make rows, or recycled plastic containers to start seeds, you should also treat them with soapy water and a bleach soak as described above.

Using the aforementioned precautions, you should have only remote chances of seedling diseases. I have not had any trouble as long as I have followed those guidelines. If you want an absolute guarantee of disease-free mixtures, you can pasteurize the mixture. Pasteurization of wet growing mix at 140°F for 30 minutes in an oven will destroy most disease problems.

2-6 I level the growing mixture in my flats with a homemade "T-bar." To make it, I took a wood dowel, slotted it, and glued in a wood slat. If you make the slat slightly narrower than a standard-size flat, you can use it to make rows for seed planting, too.

Alternately, you can fill shallow baking pans with dry growing mixture and cover them with aluminum foil. Pour boiling water into the pan through a hole in the aluminum foil, and then drain the pan and use the mixture when cool. Another choice is to water the unheated mixture with diluted seaweed extract before planting, which protects against seedling diseases.

Since you should not return excess wetted seedling mixture to the bag, you should only make enough wetted mixture for your immediate needs. But you may be wondering just how to determine the amount you need. Here's a rule of thumb to help you to gauge the right amount of mixture. Four cups (1 quart) of wetted mixture is enough to fill one standard 5½-inch by 7½-inch plastic flat or 3 of our 12-ounce modified Styrofoam cups. The standard size bag of commercial mixture, ½ bushel (16 quarts), will fill about 16 flats or 48 of our cups.

But now you may be wondering how many flats or cups you will need. First, if you use only our cups for the whole process of growing transplants, you will need one Styrofoam cup for each plant. Thus, if you want one dozen each of tomatoes, peppers, eggplants, and squash, you will need 48 Styrofoam cups. With smaller plants you can put more than one transplant in a cup, if you wish. For example, you can plant four lettuce or beet transplants in one Styrofoam cup. I have suggested specific numbers of plants per cup for various kinds of transplants in Chapters 8 and 9.

Suppose you want to start your transplants in standard flats and then transplant them later to the cups. You will usually need one flat for each crop, since the standard flat can accommodate 300, 200, and 100 seedlings from tiny, medium, or large seeds, respectively. These figures assume even broadcasting of seeds and transplanting once the true leaves (leaves that follow first seed leaves) of transplants touch each other. The use of rows in

A

B

2-7 Some conventional containers for transplant production. A. On the left and right are standard joined and single peat pots, respectively. The standard plastic flat is in the middle foreground and our specially modified Styrofoam cup stands behind it. B. A compartment tray, complete with plastic lid to keep moisture at correct levels for seeds, can start 72 transplants. C. A Styrofoam compartmentalized tray is also available with plastic lid and self-watering capacities. D. Paper pots allow transplants to be separated later. The tray shown in photo B is sold by Care Free Garden Products; tray and pots shown in C and D are available from The Gardener's Supply Company.

C

D

a flat cuts the number of seedlings it can accommodate by one-half to one-third. At the worst, each flat will accommodate 33 tomato seedlings — probably more than the average gardener wants.

The topic of using flats raises an interesting point. Do you really need to use plastic flats prior to our cups? Not necessarily, except in the case of very fine seeds, which can be easier to sow in flats. You may elect to raise transplants completely in flats, but I suggest not to do it. The no-dig transplant method works best with transplants that you grow in individual containers, although I do suggest a no-dig method for transplants from flats in Chapter 3. To repeat a point, the best and earliest crops come from single-container transplants. Difficult transplants, such as corn, fare very poorly in flats.

Let's move on now to the sowing of seeds to produce transplants.

Sowing the Seeds

Fill the containers you are using for starting seedlings to within ¼ inch of their top with growing mixture. Gently level the mixture with a flat stick that fits within the container, or gently pat the mixture flat with your hand (Figure 2-6). If you are using peat flats or pots, make sure you have moistened them first. Dry peat containers can act as a wick and suck moisture right out of your growing mixture. Figure 2-7 illustrates examples of both conventional and recent, innovative types of containers.

If you decide to make rows, use the eraser end of a pencil or a wood dowel (Figure 2-8). For example, in a standard flat (5½ inches × 7½ inches), run your rows starting about ¾ inch from one side and spacing them at 1¼-inch intervals. Depending on the length, you can have four long rows or six short ones. For larger seeds, you can also poke individual holes into the mixture with the pencil or dowel. I prefer to use this approach for tomatoes, eggplants, peppers, and marigolds. I usually make

2-8 My "T-bar" is great for making rows, or you could make rows with your finger or a pencil.

about one dozen holes for each flat or one hole for individual containers like the modified Styrofoam cups.

It's a good idea to sow more seeds than the actual number of transplants you want to produce, because some seeds won't germinate and you can always pinch out weak seedlings, leaving the best. I usually throw in two or three seeds per hole, and I still end up with leftover seeds. Save these leftover seeds for reserves in case of seedling failure; and if you have no problems, store them in a cool, dry place and use them to start next year's transplants.

Next, by pushing in the growing medium from the sides, cover each seed to a depth of one or two times the thickness of the seed. Do not cover seeds that require light for germination, such as begonia, coleus, and petunia, but rather press them gently into the soil. Spray the surface with a fine spray of lukewarm water. An old spray bottle from a kitchen cleaner will do nicely, but be sure first to rinse it very well.

An alternate way of sowing seeds instead of in rows is to broadcast them. Although I prefer making rows when I use flats, some seeds are too fine to be sown in rows. Broadcasting gives you a much better spread with fine seeds, such as begonia or petunia. I also suggest sowing fine seeds in flats and transplanting them to individual containers later rather than directly planting them in individual containers. You can cover broadcast seeds with sprinkles of dry growing mixture. Again some seeds, especially fine seeds, require light for germination; therefore, you should gently press them into the mixture. Make sure you lightly spray them with water to moisten the surface. Watch for dry areas if you used dry mixture to cover the seeds. The surface of the growing mixture should be evenly moist, but not wet.

You may be wondering what to do with pelleted seeds or seed tapes. Some fine seeds, such as petunia, are given a coating that produces an enlarged pellet that is easy to handle. Sometimes the pellet material has additives, such as traces of plant food or fungicide. The package usually lists such additions. Whether or not you need pelleted seed is a personal choice. If you dislike the task of working with fine seed and don't mind a slight price increase, go for the pellet. Plant the pellets like regular seeds, but do not cover them with growing mixture. Pelleted seeds already have their "cover," so just press them gently into the growing mixture.

Seed tapes are another device you can use for easy handling and, especially, to insure correct spacing of seeds. Seed tapes differ somewhat from pelleted seed, since you can find small to large seeds in the tape form. Again, the choice of whether or not to use seed tapes is yours. If you do use a tape, cut it to fit your rows and cover it with growing mixture as for seeds. Lightly spray the surface of the growing mixture with water. The tape will eventually dissolve and will not interfere with germination.

Next, label what you planted. Don't trust your memory, unless you plant only one package of seed. Plum tomato seedlings look just like 'Big Girl' tomato seedlings. Leaf lettuce looks just like Romaine lettuce when it's small. You can use your marking pencil to place the cultivar name and date of sowing on a label. Noting the sowing date will help you decide whether the seeds need more time for germination or whether you should suspect something went wrong. You will find the number of days required for germination of individual crops listed in Chapters 8 and 9.

I usually lay the label down in flats, because I will be covering them. But when I'm using individual containers, I label the plant name directly on the container. You will need to use two or more labels if you plant two or more kinds of seed in one flat. Be cautious if you do mix seeds; make sure they are compatible with one another in terms of light and temperature requirements, as well as days to germination.

Covering the Containers

Next, cover the containers (Figure 2-9) with clear plastic wrap, such as food wrap, or with scrap pieces of glass or rigid plastic. An alternative to these covering methods is to place the containers in a plastic bag. If you have several flats or lots of cups, you will find that the plastic bags that come with dry-cleaned clothes make good covers. To assure that the bag does not contact the growing mixture, place a few upright labels in each container or some bent coat hangers to hold the bag above the soil. Some of the newer containers, shown earlier in Figure 2-7, come with clear plastic lids that fit neatly over the container. You can cover seeds that require absolute darkness with several sheets of newspaper or scrap cardboard. Do not

2-9 Cover your trays or cups with clear plastic. Lay your labels on their sides for now. This step will greatly improve germination and eliminate watering for several days. The top of a refrigerator supplies warmth for faster germination. If you are in no hurry, a room at 70°F is fine.

neglect to cover the containers, because the seeds are critically dependent upon moisture during germination. Dryness at that time can kill or essentially result in a crippled seedling that never fully recovers. Also, watering at this point, unless done with care, can dislodge or uncover seedlings. We busy gardeners have enough to do without having to resow seeds. Fortunately, the clear cover over the container relieves the gardener of the constant worry and drudgery of checking for dryness.

Providing Warmth and Light

To use bottom heat or not, that is the question. Seed germination does depend upon temperature. Each seed has an ideal temperature at which germination occurs fastest. Temperatures above this ideal temperature result in no improvement, and temperatures below it slow germination. Of course, temperature extremes will kill the seeds. You can find the favored temperatures for each crop in Chapters 8 and 9. For economy of money and time, commercial growers of transplants usually use a soil-heating cable or mat to warm the bottom of their flats. But what's a private gardener to do? First, most seeds germinate in a reasonable time at 70°F, a temperature you can find in your home, especially in the kitchen. You say you lower your thermostat at night or when you're at work to save energy? No problem. The top of your refrigerator is always warm. Put a few sheets of newspaper on the refrigerator's top, and place your containers there. Do not put trays under the containers yet, because you won't need to water if you are using the plastic tray covers. The newspaper underneath the containers traps any slight traces of moisture or dirt but is still thin enough to allow heat transfer. The top of an upright freezer can also be warm.

Other warm places you may want to consider are near your furnace or water heater, but you must be cautious if you use one of these areas. Place your container nearby but not on top of or in contact with the furnace or water heater. Do not put newspaper or any flammable materials under the containers; actually, it's best not to put anything under them.

Above all, do not place your containers in direct sun at this time. The plastic will trap the solar energy and heat the growing mixture to temperatures fatal for most seeds. Only seeds that tolerate germination temperatures in the 80° to 85°F range will survive.

Another choice for providing proper germination temperature is to purchase a heating mat specially designed for germinating seeds. I recommend this purchase only if you are seriously interested in raising substantial numbers of transplants. Most gardeners can get by with the previously mentioned, less expensive options. (The Appendix lists sources for heating mats, under Propagation mat.)

2-10 *Use bottom watering for recently planted seeds prior to germination (left) and for small seedlings (right) that are not yet tough enough for overhead watering.*

Before we leave the subject of germination temperature, I should point out that a few seeds actually require cool temperatures for germination. The strawberry, for instance, has seeds that germinate best at 55°F. At 70°F, germination is not very successful. The best place to germinate seeds that need cool temperatures is a north-facing windowsill or the cooler concrete floor on the north side of your basement.

What about those seeds that require both coolness and light for germination? The sunny window is obviously out. Luckily, light needs for germination are nowhere near those for growing plants. Indirect light from a window, light from an incandescent bulb in a lamp or overhead, or a fluorescent lamp will all suffice. These lights need not be on at all times; you can turn them on and off to suit your daily routine.

You should check your containers once a day for dryness, mold, or seedling growth. If you spot dryness, water the growing medium right away; however, dryness is unlikely when using plastic cover. If dryness does occur, use bottom watering to correct the problem. Place the container in a tray of lukewarm water (water level below top of container) until the surface of the growing mixture appears moist. Remove the container at once, drain the water, and replace the plastic cover. Condensation on the cover is normal; therefore, you can ignore it (Figure 2-10). If mold appears, remove the cover once or twice a day for fifteen minutes.

Caring for Growing Seedlings

Once seedlings start to appear, you must move into action. Remove the cover and transport the seedlings to your light source. Remember, as we discussed earlier, the light source can be either a sunny southern window or fluorescent lights. Turn the seedlings every few days at the window to get even growth on all sides of the plants. Start your lights at a height of just a few inches over the seedlings, raising them as the seedlings grow. Don't worry about the closeness of the lights to the plants; heat from fluorescent lights is minimal. If the leaves curl downward, raise the lights; if the seedlings are thin and spindly or light green in color, lower the lights. Don't worry about temperature; ordinary room or basement temperature is fine, even if you drop the temperature at night to as low as 60°F.

Your seedlings will now need tender, loving care. Water and fertilizer will be the main concerns at first. As your seedlings grow, thinning or transplanting will also become important, especially for seedlings not in individual containers. But let's not get ahead of ourselves.

Watering the Seedlings

First, make sure your young seedlings do not dry out. At the first sign of surface dryness, use bottom watering as described previously. With some plants that grow fast, like marigolds or tomatoes, you will only need to use bottom watering for a few weeks. Tiny, slow-growing plants like begonias will need bottom watering for a longer period of time. Use bottom watering only until the seedlings develop enough of a root system that overhead watering does not uproot them. Overhead watering is usually safe when seedlings are 1½ inches tall, and are starting to develop their second set of true leaves. Now you will also need trays to collect the excess water as it drains from the plants. Be sure you discard the excess water. Letting the containers stand in a trayful of water could cause root rot. Trays also make it easier to carry flats or containers.

After a few weeks, allow the surface of the growing medium to dry out to a depth of ½ inch or so between waterings. The degree of dryness improves aeration of the soil, which in turn promotes root growth and helps prevent root rot caused by overwatering. Allowing some dryness to exist also helps to toughen up the transplant for the harsher outdoor environment in your garden. Of course, if you see the plants wilting when the soil surface is dry, water them right away.

The time of watering isn't too critical, as long as foliage does not remain wet through the evening. There is greater risk of disease when leaves stay wet at night. Let the water that you plan to use on your transplants sit overnight in clean gallon-size milk jugs or other containers. If you have city water, leave the caps off the jugs. Allowing water to sit brings it to room temperature. Water from the tap is usually too cold for the good of young seedlings; temperatures often range between 40° and 50°F. If you use water straight from the tap, the temperature of the growing mixture can easily drop 15°F, and several hours may pass before the temperature returns to normal. This temperature drop decreases root and

2-11 Once seedlings are well-established, you can use over-head watering.

shoot development, so your transplants grow more slowly. When you later transplant them into your garden, you will have lost some of your head start.

At this time I'd like to explain further my suggestion to keep the caps off bottles of city water. Recently several cities, some in the Northeast, experienced trouble with levels of certain bacteria. The response to the problem was to increase the levels of chlorine in the water, which can adversely affect some tender, young seedlings. Allowing the filled water bottle to sit overnight without a cap will allow some of the chlorine to escape. A simple step such as this protects the investment of time and money you have in your transplants.

Fertilizing the Seedlings

Besides water, your transplants need nutrients, so you'll need to add fertilizer soon after germination. (Remember, our homemade growing mixture does not include fertilizer.) The seed uses its nutrient reserves during germination; therefore, you must supply new nutrients for the growing plant. If you have a commercial growing mixture, the label will tell you if any nutrients were added. Some mixtures even have enough nutrients to last through the entire production of transplants. Whether you use a commercial mixture with no nutrients, small amounts of nutrients, or extended reserves depends upon your personal decision as an organic or conventional gardener. The nutrients in most commercial formulas are not supplied in organic forms.

When it's time to begin feeding the seedlings, organic gardeners will opt for organic, water-soluble fertilizer. My favorite is a product that combines fish emulsion and seaweed extract. (The Appendix lists sources for this product.) You can also buy fish emulsion and seaweed extract separately and use them side by side. The fish emulsion supplies nitrogen in suitable amounts but supplies only small amounts of phosphorus and potassium. The seaweed extract supplies suitable amounts of phosphorus and potassium.

Seaweed extract also has numerous trace elements of value to growing plants. It contains gibberellin and auxin, natural hormones in plants that promote growth. Indications are that seaweed extract may also work to keep seedlings from getting "leggy" and possibly may ward off spider mites. Some plants also show increased resistance to light frosts when treated with seaweed extracts. If you use seaweed extracts, perhaps you can worry less about that unexpected cold snap after you set out your transplants in your garden. Disease protection for seedlings is another plus offered by seaweed extract.

Whether you use a combined fish emulsion/seaweed extract or two separate products, apply it to the plant as a foliar spray, onto the leaves. The plant's uptake of fertilizer and the growth response of the plant occur more quickly using a foliar spray than when fertilizing through the root system. The fertilizer runoff from the plant foliage supplies enough solution for the root system. Adjustable leaf openings called *stomata* quickly take in the solution on the leaves. When spraying the plant, try to get some of the fertilizer on the underside of the leaf, which usually has more openings than the top surface. Essentially, foliar feeding is like intravenous feeding of nutrients to hospital patients; intravenous feeding makes the nutrients available more quickly than the patient's digestive system could.

Follow the route of more frequent but less concentrated applications of fertilizer. Transplants respond much better to this frequent but light diet. Follow the recommendations on the label, but double the dilution and frequency of application. Look for rates indicated for seedlings. If seedling directions are not present, use the directions for house plants or even flowers. Remember, use twice as much water, and double the frequency of use.

Whatever you do with your fertilizer, watch your transplants for signals that you may need to raise or lower your fertilization rates. For example, if the transplants are light green and spindly (stretched-looking), they probably need more light. If, however, the plants look sturdy but are light green in color, they probably need more nitrogen. Extremely dark green plants (leaves normal position, not curling downward as with too much light) could indicate excessive nitrogen. A lack of phosphorus usually shows up as red-purple color on stems, leaves, and veins, although you may have difficulty noting this condition with a reddish coleus or bronze-leaved wax begonia. Don't worry too much, though. I have never encountered problems with phosphorus or potassium and only on rare occasions with nitrogen. The beauty of using organic fertilizers is that extra, slow-release punch they provide that carries the plants through lean times!

Thinning and Transplanting Seedlings

Now on to the two Ts: thinning and transplanting (Figures 2-12 and 2-13). If you started your seeds in flats and do not intend to transplant the seedlings into other flats or individual containers, you will have to thin your transplants to a reasonable number; for example, a standard flat might hold four but no more than six tomato plants. Marigolds or peppers might approach eight to ten plants per flat. Actual numbers of plants per container depend on the size of the container, the size of the plants, and the amount of time they stay in the container. Remember, the more plants per container, the more tangled the roots and the more difficult the transplant. With individual containers, where your sowing produced more than one plant, thin out the plants to leave only the strongest. Should you want more than one plant, such as three lettuce plants, in one of our Styrofoam cups, thin the plants to the desired number.

A

B

2-12 A. Once seedlings touch, as these celosia seedlings do, you must either transplant or thin them. B. These thinned celosia now have a while to grow before they're ready for transplanting.

The next "T" is transplanting, which you won't have to do now, if you started with individual containers. You will need to transplant from flats once the plants' true leaves touch. You can transplant some of the extra seedlings into another flat or into individual containers, which we recommend (and discussed earlier). If you can transplant only some of the plants to individual containers, make those the vegetables that need an earlier start, such as tomatoes. Remember, once the true leaves touch, transplant soon; the neglected, crowded plants will soon become stunted or poorly developed and will result in poorer quality transplants.

Transplanting of seedlings need not be difficult (Figure 2-13). Of course, every individual container with which you started means less work now. Usually, the rule is to look for the stronger seedlings and discard the weaker ones, a rule that holds well for vegetables. An exception to the rule occurs with several annuals, such as begonias, coleus, dahlias (small, bedding types), impatiens, petunias, and snapdragons, where the weaker seedlings often have more unusual colors or forms not found with stronger seedlings. With mixed-color annuals, then, you might just want to include a few of the weaker seedlings for interesting variety.

Use the same growing mixture for your transplants as you did for your seeds. A teaspoon makes a fine tool for removing seedlings; remove medium to large seedlings with the spoon end and smaller ones with the handle. A small spatula or the end of a pointed label or Popsicle stick is also helpful when removing tiny seedlings. Handle the seedlings with care, and remove as much of the roots and growing mixture with each plant as possible. If you have to hold the transplant, pick it up by the leaves and not by the stem. A damaged leaf is a minor matter; a broken or bruised stem is usually beyond repair.

With a dibble or a spoon, open a hole in the growing mixture for your seedling transplant. Place the seedling and some growing mixture in the hole, and adjust the planting level; do not sink the seedling deeper than it had been planted in the previous container. Water the seedling with the dilute solution of seaweed extract mentioned earlier, and keep it out of direct sun for one day. If you use fluorescent lights, you can replace the transplant directly under the lights without a one-day wait. The seaweed extract will usually speed up the recovery of the transplant. Don't forget to label your new containers, and make sure you continue with watering and fertilization as explained before.

Moving Outdoors

You must now prepare your transplants for the move outdoors to the garden. An abrupt move from indoors to outdoors in the garden will most

A

B

C

2-13 These photos show how seedlings are transplanted into the special cups. A. These dahlias are ready for transplanting, as they have touching leaves. B. Cut or separate a good root ball with each plant. Put some growing medium in the bottom of the cup. Note the Styrofoam "peanuts." C. Place the transplant in the cup and fill in with growing medium. D. Label the cups.

D

likely kill your transplants. They will need an adjustment period of two weeks to toughen, a process we call *hardening off*. You are faced with two choices concerning where to harden off your transplants: the luxury approach, otherwise called the *cold frame*, or the economical way, called "making do with what you have." If you have a cold frame, great; your choice is made. Should you not have a cold frame, you could elect to build or buy one, or to do without. You can use cold frames for hardening off transplants, growing cool-loving transplants like cabbage and broccoli, and for providing salad greens into early winter. If your only interest is hardening off transplants, you probably should save your time and money.

You can purchase a ready-made cold frame with an automatic window opener for under $100. You can also buy the automatic window opener alone, complete with plans to build your own cold frame, for around $42. Scrap wood and windows or even purchased wood should give you a reasonably priced cold frame. Solar power (no electricity needed) activates the automatic window opener to open at 75°F and to close at 68°F. This device relieves you of the constant checking of temperature and window adjustments so essential to the success of transplants in a cold frame. Believe me, it's the only way to go! (The Appendix lists sources for the automatic window opener, or solar vent, and cold frame.)

Here's how to harden off transplants in the cold frame with the help of the automatic window opener. Place the transplants in the cold frame about two weeks before you plan to place them in your garden. Allow your transplants to dry out a little between watering, but watch out for wilting. Don't forget to fertilize your transplants. Don't worry about temperature and window adjustments except if frost threatens. If a frost looms, cover your cold frame with either blankets or straw. An alternative to covering the frames would be to bring the flats and containers indoors for the night. The odds of a frost occurring two weeks before it's time to set the plants in the garden are low in most areas, but nature sometimes does surprise us.

If you don't have a cold frame, you can use this "no frills" method to harden off your transplants. This is the method I use. I start on a Saturday about two weeks before the time I will be ready to place the transplants into the garden. I put the transplants in trays outdoors in a sunny area for three hours from 11:00 A.M. to 2:00 P.M.; then I bring them back inside. On Sunday I return them outdoors for about five hours (11:00 A.M. to 4:00 P.M.), and then bring them back inside. On Monday I take them outdoors before I go to work and bring them in on my return. On Tuesday, I take them out, and leave them outside for the rest of the two weeks, unless a frost or temperatures below 40°F threaten. If so, I bring them back indoors for the night. Don't forget to water and fertilize the transplants during this time. If you are lucky, rain will help you with the watering.

2-14 *My outdoor transplant nursery is a square wood frame with no bottom. I can put it in any unused corner of the yard and keep it filled with extra or ongoing transplants. The little stuffed animal in the foreground was placed there by my children, because they said a "nursery" must have toys.*

After hardening off your transplants, you can plant them in the garden. If your schedule gives you trouble, you can hold off planting after the two weeks of hardening off; however, don't delay beyond one or two weeks at most. Longer delays eat into your head start, and container limitations start to stress your transplants, causing further complications. The actual process of placing transplants into the garden using the no-dig method will be shown and discussed in the next chapter.

Growing Your Own Transplants Outdoors

Earlier I mentioned that I grew some transplants outdoors rather than direct-sowing seeds because of a series of cold, wet springs that rotted the seeds. The procedure I'm about to describe solved my problem of certain seeds rotting in the soil. I germinate the seeds of beans, corn, cucumbers, melons, and squash indoors in our modified Styrofoam containers using the same procedures described before for conventional transplants. The main difference is that I start these seeds indoors at their normal outdoor planting time. At the first sign of germination, I move the seedlings outdoors to the wooden frame with a plastic roof described earlier (look back at Figure 2-5). These seedlings develop normally outdoors, except that the plastic roof and frame sides protect them from wind and rain. Of course, I add water, fertilizer, and tender, loving care. When the transplants reach the proper size in two to three weeks, I place them directly into the ground with the no-dig approach. No more rotten seeds! Using this method, I have grown some wonderful melons after years of defeat by the cold and wet springs.

Bill and I also developed an outdoor transplant nursery. Essentially it's a simple, rectangular, wood frame that is portable (Figure 2-14). I usually place the frame in a corner of my garden and use it for all my leftover transplants. Yes, I always grow a few extra transplants just in case one fails or I want to give some to someone else. Besides, I don't have the heart to discard them. You can hold these plants for a few weeks to fill any holes that pop up when you have harvested earlier crops, such as radishes and peas.

I keep the transplant nursery going by planting a few seeds every once in a while, using the modified Styrofoam cups. Sometimes I'll plant one cup with several lettuce seeds and thin it to three or four plants. Others may hold individual squash, rutabaga, broccoli, bean, or beet transplants. This way I'm always prepared for any empty spaces that arise in the garden. Maybe you should become the parent of a transplant nursery, too. Instead of direct planting the midsummer crops that will produce fall harvests, such as broccoli or turnips, start them in cups in your nursery. It sure beats the hot, dry soil that gives summer germination a hard time!

You've waited long enough, patient reader. Now we will move on to no-dig techniques for planting and maintaining the garden.

Chapter 3
Planting the No-Dig Garden

Are you ready to say good-bye to that spade or digging fork, and your aching back and blisters? Once you become a no-digger, you'll wonder why you put up with the annual rearranging of your garden's soil. Perhaps you are about to become a first-time gardener and you're hesitating because of the thought of digging soil. Well, new and veteran gardeners, this chapter is for all of you.

Testing the Soil

I think the best piece of advice I can give any gardener, even no-dig gardeners, is to know your soil. Good soil is the foundation of a good garden. The one and only way to understand your soil is to study the results of a soil test and then make whatever soil corrections you need, such as adding fertilizer or lime. Before you do anything in the garden, and especially before you mulch or plant, take the time out for a soil test. It is a wise investment of your time, because a few minutes of testing can lead to a much more successful garden later.

You can conduct soil tests in two ways. The first method involves buying a soil-testing kit and testing your own soil. (You can find sources for these kits listed in the Appendix.) Home soil tests are similar to the sort of tests done with swimming pools. Basically you follow "cookbook-style" directions and you get a colored solution that you compare to color charts. From these colors it is a simple matter to decide what and how much of the various nutrients or limestone you need.

The second approach to soil testing is to send a soil sample to your local state agricultural experiment station or USDA state extension service office. You can find their address and phone number in the government section of your phone book. It's best to call first, because some of the agencies will supply you with mailing cartons or advise you as to what size container you should mail. You will also learn what information they need from you and how much the tests cost. Usually the charges are quite modest. The soil testing laboratory will mail you a report on the analysis of your soil and tell you what steps to take to correct soil deficiencies. Usually the report indicates what kind of fertilizer to add in pounds per 1,000 square feet and the amount of limestone the soil needs. The report frequently includes an indication of organic matter levels and needs. If you mention with your soil sample that you are an organic gardener, you may get fertilizer needs stated in terms of organic fertilizers. If you don't receive organic gardening results, don't despair. I will translate chemical fertilizer suggestions into organic ones in Chapter 4.

Which method is the best for you? Some gardeners use both kinds of soil tests and compare the results to check whether or not the tests are reliable. Some gardeners do a few soil tests of their own later after they receive the state report to check their soil's progress and find out if the soil needs additional correction as the plants grow.

What's the best time to remove a soil sample and send it in for analysis? Your best bet in terms of promptness of reply is to sample in the early fall. If you delay until the spring, it may take weeks to receive your results, because gardeners preparing their soil for planting swamp the station testing laboratories with soil samples at this time.

The key to a good soil test is to obtain a soil sample that adequately represents the root zone area in your garden. To do this you must prepare a composite sample from several different places in your garden, assuming your garden is reasonably uniform in soil features. Should you have distinctly different areas, such as a damp, low-lying area versus a high, dry area, it's best to prepare separate composite samples.

Although you can utilize soil sampling devices, you can also make do with a trowel or spade. A soil sampling device (auger) is essentially a sharpened pipe with a T-bar handle that is driven into the soil to remove a soil core. Make sure the soil is neither bone dry nor soaking wet when you sample. Moderate wetness is best for sampling. With your clean trowel, spade, or auger, remove a soil slice or section from the surface to a depth of

12 inches. This depth will give you an adequate sample of the soil through the root zone. Place the sample in a clean plastic bucket and repeat the procedure at five to seven other scattered locations in your garden. Mix the samples thoroughly in the bucket. Don't use a metal bucket for mixing soil, because contamination from rust or flaking metal could alter the test results.

Now remove about 1 pint of soil or whatever other quantity the testing laboratory specifies. Be sure to supply all information the laboratory requests. If you are unsure about what information they need, I can tell you that the desirable information includes the crops you will be planting (vegetables or flowers or mixed crops), what you planted last year, previous liming and fertilizing history if known, and any indication of problems or unusual conditions you have noticed in your garden. It also is helpful to indicate that you are an organic gardener.

In a few weeks you will receive the results of your soil test. My test information will most likely be similar to yours, if you submit a sample to an agricultural experiment station. First, the report describes the soil texture, which is useful in itself. For example, my soil is a sandy loam, which requires more frequent watering during droughts and loses nutrients more readily by leaching than does a loam soil. (A loam soil is the ideal garden soil. If you have it, you're lucky.) However, sandy soils are quick to warm up for planting in the spring. Soils whose textures are described with the words clay and/or silt hold moisture longer than sandy soils and lose fewer nutrients by leaching. Such soils also tend to stay cooler longer in the spring, thus delaying planting.

Next the report lists the organic matter content, the soil pH, and the levels of several nutrients. The nutrients listed include nitrate nitrogen, ammonia nitrogen, phosphorus, potassium, calcium, magnesium, aluminum, and manganese. The report indicates the levels of each as VL (very low), ML (medium low), L (low), M (medium), H (high), or VH (very high). Next to these levels you may see another letter, which indicates that a problem exists. The letters are D for deficient, d for probably deficient, e for probably excessive, and E for excessive. At the bottom of the report are recommendations for limestone, fertilizer, and organic matter amendments. The report offers these suggested treatments in pounds per 1,000 square feet. I will discuss how to incorporate fertilizers, limestone, and organic matter the no-dig way in the next chapter. Right now I'd like to tell you how to prepare your garden for planting.

Preparing the Garden for Planting

I will explain how to prepare for no-dig gardening in several different garden situations, so skip to the one that best describes your case. I will look first at established gardens, then new gardens, and finally problem gardens. This last category includes gardens with soil so compacted that it seems like concrete, soil so rocky and stony that you could open a quarry, and soil with hardpans (compacted, often clayey, layers of soil that are impenetrable by roots), or such poor drainage that the garden becomes a pond after the slightest rain. If your garden soil has one of these problems, go directly to the section on Problem Gardens, on page 56.

If you're not sure if you have a problem, consider these two questions. Can you drive the bulb planter into the soil and remove a soil core? Does the furrower scratch into the soil? If you answered yes to both questions, then you don't have a problem garden. Even if some stones interfere so that your bulb planter makes a slanted hole or you have to move it around to a slightly different location, you still probably have a garden that is not a problem.

Preparing Established Gardens for No-Dig Planting

Any established flower or vegetable garden that you have dug or tilled and cleaned up the previous year, whether it's an organic garden or not, can easily become a no-dig garden. Most of you reading this book probably have gardens that fall into this group. These gardens will be transformed into no-dig gardens quickly and easily. How you go about achieving a no-dig garden depends upon how your garden looks now. Take a good look at it. Did you clean up the plant remains from last year? Was your garden relatively weed free last season, that is, were the weeds controllable with only sporadic weeding? If you answer yes to both of these questions, go directly to the section on no-dig planting techniques, beginning on page 61. Did you answer no to the first question and yes to the second? If so, first clean up your garden by cutting and raking off last year's debris, then skip to the no-dig techniques. Perhaps you answered no to both questions. Well, clean up your garden and continue reading here. And if your garden needed more than sporadic weeding last year, read on.

Weeds got you down? If that's all that stands in the way of your no-dig garden, don't despair. This year you will destroy weeds and weed seeds in the top few inches of your garden soil, either mulching or weeding. If you opt for mulching, make sure you read Chapter 5 to learn how to mulch the easy way using black plastic. You can apply black plastic or organic mulches either before or after you plant, although applying them before is probably better because your crops will not need weeding before you mulch (as they would if you laid down the mulch later on). Before you lay down any mulch, it will be important to have your soil tested, as I described earlier in this chapter. Also, be sure to apply your fertilizer and/or limestone (as described in Chapter 4) before you mulch.

If you want to mulch at conventional times, that is, when the plants are several inches tall, you'll have to use your action hoe to keep weeds under control before the mulch takes over. Of course, you can also control weeds throughout the growing season with your action hoe. The severity of your weed problem will dictate which method of weed control is best for you.

Keep one thought in mind. Weeds, once controlled with black plastic, organic mulches, or action hoeing, will probably become a thing of the past. Remember, our no-dig techniques do not disturb soil; therefore, no new weed seeds are brought to the surface. Once those top few inches of soil are weed free, half your work is done!

Preparing New Gardens

Are you planning a first-time garden? Did you skip gardening last year but decided to give it another try this year? Either way, whether the site was never a garden or was once a garden, you should treat the plot as a new garden.

Most likely some plants, either green or dormant brown, cover the garden-to-be. The area may be grassy, perhaps even part of a lawn. Maybe the overgrowth is weedy, like an abandoned lot. The first step to preparing your new garden is a manicure. Use your lawn mower on its lowest cutting level and go over the area well. If the overgrowth is too high for your mower, first cut it down to size with either a power "weed whacker" or hand sickle, and then go over it with your mower. Make sure you wear appropriate clothing (high-top work shoes or boots with nonslip, ribbed bottoms and sturdy work jeans) and exercise caution. Wear safety glasses, especially when using the weed whacker.

Now you have a choice to make, assuming your garden-to-be is not a problem site. You must kill the remaining roots and stubble of the mowed plants so that they do not compete with your crops. There are two ways to solve the problem. First, you can rent a rotary tiller or hire someone to till under the surface vegetation. This digging step will be the first and last time you will have to dig or till your garden. If the area is bumpy and requires minor leveling, you can easily level the turned soil with a rake.

Your other choice for killing the roots and stubble is to use black plastic or other mulch, which you must apply before you plant. You can quite easily do the actual planting directly through the mulch for transplants or seeds, using the bulb planter, dibble, and furrower. I will cover the technique for direct planting through mulches later in this chapter.

If you apply loose mulches to the garden too early in the year, the soil may be slow to warm up, and planting times will have to be delayed. You will not have this problem if you mulch with black plastic and apply it shortly before normal outdoor planting times, because the black plastic absorbs heat and transfers some of it to the soil. You can actually measure this heating characteristic with a soil thermometer, which I did. I saw no delay in the warming of the mulched soil; if anything, the soil was slightly warmer than normal. In fact, the melons I planted directly through black plastic were earlier and larger than those planted in bare soil.

Preparing Problem Gardens

In this section you will learn what to do if you couldn't get the bulb planter to work in your garden because the soil is severely compacted or you hit rocks wherever you tried to push in the planter. This section is also for you if you could get the bulb planter into the ground but drainage problems from underlying hardpan kill or cripple everything except water lilies or marsh grass. If your furrower made only a scratch in the garden soil after lots of hard work on your part, well, you do have a problem garden, but Bill and I have solutions. Let's look at them and help you pick out the right one for you.

Compacted Soil

Let's examine the problem of compaction first. Soils that you dig up, as we saw in Chapter 1, are susceptible to compaction by ordinary foot traffic. Heavier traffic, such as tillers or wheelbarrows, makes the problem even worse. Compaction hinders root development, because there are few air spaces between soil particles for roots to grow in and roots are deprived of oxygen. Consequently, crop yields go down. Continual traffic at the same depth, such as occurs when you use a tiller year after year, can eventually produce a hardened, compacted soil layer, which we call hardpan. Roots cannot grow through hardpan, and water drains through it very slowly. If you see standing water after a rain and your crop harvests aren't good, you probably have hardpan. A quick soil check can confirm the problem. Slowly push a pointed metal rod about 3/4 inch in diameter into the soil until you feel slight resistance. Note the depth, and repeat the test in several different spots. If you come up with resistance at about the same depth everywhere, you have hardpan. If you find no resistance down to 24 inches, you can count your blessings.

We have two possibilities that could be the cause of resistance. Either you have soil compaction but no hardpan yet, or you have compaction to the point of hardpan. Let's look first at compaction. How bad is your compaction? Does your soil drain reasonably well and are your harvests respectable? Can you push in the bulb planter or open a furrow with the furrower? If your answers are yes, your compaction problem is not serious, and you can go ahead and follow the planting directions on page 61. I would suggest that you restrict traffic in the garden to small paths only, and use raised bed or band plantings as described later and in Chapter 7. Remember, no-dig procedures do *not* cause compaction. You will also be adding organic matter to the garden (see Chapter 4), which will gradually reduce the slight compaction in your garden.

If your soil drains poorly, your harvests are poor, and you found it difficult to push the bulb planter into the soil, you need to take steps to correct the compaction problem before you become a no-digger. The best way to alleviate compaction is to work a considerable amount of organic matter into the soil with a rotary tiller. This garden tilling will be a one-time event and will soon be only a memory when you become a no-dig gardener. Believe me, the work you will save with the no-dig method will be well worth a bit of extra effort to correct the problem now. The kind of organic matter you work into the soil is not important. You can use whatever you have or can get easily: manure, leaves, peat moss, or compost. However, for reasons of economy, you might want to consider my choice: leaves. My garden had somewhat compacted soil from years of traffic and rotary tillers. The fall before my "no-dig spring," I spread 2 to 3 inches of freshly fallen leaves all over my garden. I turned the leaves into my garden with several increasingly deeper passes of the rotary tiller, until I reached the tiller's depth limit. In went the leaves, out went compaction. Tilling leaves into soil effectively lightens its texture. Just don't do it on a windy day! A soil test in the spring is especially important here, because the decaying leaves will use some of your soil's nitrogen reserves.

If you have soil compaction with hardpan, you may have one or two problems to correct prior to becoming a no-dig gardener. If your hardpan is 12 inches down or deeper and is not causing a drainage problem, you can ignore the hardpan and correct for compaction with organic matter as I just explained. But if you have serious hardpan woes, you must disrupt the hardpan layer or rise above it. The best way to disrupt hardpan is through subsoil tillage. Generally, a subsoil chisel is used to cut up the subsoil to a depth of 16 to 30 inches. If you have a large garden, you may be able to rent a subsoiler or hire someone to do this for you. Again, this step is a one-time correction, because no-dig procedures will not cause compaction and hardpan problems.

Other ways to correct hardpan include constructing raised beds (which I will cover in a moment when I discuss stony or rocky soils) and growing alfalfa in sections of the garden. Alfalfa has a deep, strong taproot, which will help break up the hardpan. At the end of the season, turning under the alfalfa will increase soil's organic matter and nitrogen content. Raised beds, while more work, are a quicker option for small gardens. Also, you don't lose any of your gardening space or time with raised beds as you do with alfalfa.

Stony and Rocky Soil

Another problem you may have in your garden is stony and rocky soil. Most New England gardeners (including me, here in Connecticut) know this problem only too well. No-dig gardening can work in such gardens, depending on the severity of the problem.

I can use the bulb planter in my stony soil, although sometimes I may have to give up on one hole and try a new one close by. Sometimes I can slant the bulb planter on an angle and bypass the stone. The transplant may have a funny angle for a while, but it does eventually grow straight. My furrower also works fine. Sometimes I simply draw the furrower and it pulls out the smaller rocks, while other times I may have to zig or zag. These minor problems are nothing when compared to the back-breaking, wholesale digging I used to do.

However, I will admit that at some point a soil can be so stony or rocky that it interferes with no-dig gardening methods. Should you have this problem, you may have solved it already with raised beds. If you don't have beds, you can construct some right on top of your present garden and never have to worry about rocks again. You will fill the raised beds with a fine, rich soil mix that will produce beautiful crops for you. No-dig gardening works just fine in raised beds. We'll examine two ways to make raised beds; you can think of them as "economy" and "luxury" models. Keep in mind that the length of your raised beds is your choice, but the width should be such that you can reach the middle easily from the side. A good width is 4 feet.

Bill and I found that it's easy to make raised beds with inexpensive wire border fence and newspaper (the economy-model beds). Usually this

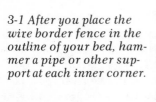

3-1 After you place the wire border fence in the outline of your bed, hammer a pipe or other support at each inner corner.

3-2 Instead of newspaper, I lined this bed with sides from cardboard cartons for longer life.

kind of fencing comes in folding sections 12 inches wide, of various lengths, and about 18 inches high. You can join these fences together to create whatever lengths you need. To make our simple beds, first, push the wire border fence into the soil to form the outline of the raised bed (Figure 3-1). Pushing the wire legs into the soil anchors the fencing nicely. Next, take several thicknesses of newspaper, around ten to twelve sheets, and line the inside of the fence with them (Figure 3-2). Do not use any newspaper with colored inks, because there may be lead present in some of them. Now fill in the bed with your soil and you have an economy-model raised bed. (Where did the soil come from? We'll get back to this question in a moment.)

Admittedly this bed is not permanent. It will last one year at least, perhaps two, depending on weather conditions and the treatment that the bed gets; however, such a bed costs little and gives you the opportunity to observe its results. Chances are that the raised bed will outperform your problem garden soil severalfold. If you like the bed idea, you can always replace the sides with more permanent materials at the end of the season.

You may, however, want to start off with one of the luxury models of raised beds, or at least consider them later. For the sides of these raised beds, you may choose to use railroad ties, planks, or cinderblocks. Be careful when using wood, though, and especially with the railroad ties. Sometimes wood is treated with preservatives, such as creosote, that are toxic to growing plants. If you are unsure or can't find out what preservative was used, buy untreated wood; then you can treat the wood yourself with a safe preservative, such as linseed oil or special commercial formulations for plants. Cuprinol formula (#10, #14, or #20), for example, contains a special wood preservative (copper naphthenate) that is safe for use with plants.

You can hold the wood ties or planks in place by nailing them to wood stakes or attaching them to pipe stakes with screws and U-brackets. The height of the bed should be at least 12 inches, but 18 or even 24 inches is better. In most cases, the amount of available soil will probably determine your bed height.

Now to get back to an earlier question, where will you get the soil to fill the raised beds? It's not an unreasonable question, since your soil was a problem from the start. Well, only two courses of action are possible; you can buy the soil or make it. If you buy topsoil, you will obviously save some work, but it will cost you dearly. Make sure it's good soil, and if at all possible, try to get samples and have them run through a soil test. Your other choice is to make your own soil mix. Blending an improved soil for use in your beds involves a fair amount of work. But sometimes it's the best way to insure an excellent growing medium for your plants. Consider, too, that you don't need to make enough soil to fill a garden, just enough to fill one or more raised beds. The richer soil in the beds will let you plant intensively. You will be able to grow as much in these raised beds as many gardeners do in conventional row gardens two to three times larger!

To make your own soil, you can either start with some lower quality, existing soil and add ingredients to it to make it better, or you can start with basic ingredients and build a soil (actually a soil substitute) from scratch.

If you're lucky, you may have an area, such as a hill or low knoll, from which you can remove some soil, or you may be able to get a truckload of inexpensive, lower quality soil. To this soil, add an equal volume of a mixture composed of 50 percent builder's sand and 50 percent compost. If you don't have compost, you can substitute leafmold or peat moss. Mixing everything by hand will probably be quite a chore, so I suggest that you rent a cement mixer for the day. You can mix the materials while they are moist; but if they are too wet, you could damage the soil structure. Don't overmix, either. When the ingredients are evenly combined, fill your raised beds. Save some soil for a soil test, which we covered earlier in this chapter.

How much soil do you need? If you multiply the width times the length of your raised bed and then multiply this figure times the desired soil height, you get the volume of the soil you need. For example, a bed that measures 4 feet by 8 feet by 1 foot needs 32 cubic feet of soil. Using the recipe given above, you need 16 cubic feet of soil to which you add another 16 cubic feet of the sand/compost mixture.

To prepare soil substitute from scratch to fill the same bed, you need enough materials to make 32 cubic feet. Some measuring containers will be most helpful when you're mixing up a batch of soil substitute. A bushel basket holds about 1.3 cubic feet, and a standard 5-gallon pail with handle holds 0.3 cubic foot of dry material. You can make a soil substitute from scratch with peat moss and vermiculite (horticultural grade, either number 2 or 4). Mix 12 bushels of each with 5 pounds of dolomitic limestone and 5 pounds of an organic fertilizer containing nitrogen, phosphorus, and potassium. This formulation gives you about 32 cubic feet of soil substitute. Don't worry about which fertilizer to use. Any of the general-purpose organic fertilizers described in Chapter 4 will be fine. Incidentally, a 2-pound coffee can will hold about 5 pounds of limestone or dry fertilizer.

And now here's a last option for correcting problem soil. Although your soil may be stony or have hardpan and be difficult to work using no-digging methods, it may still be tillable with a rotary tiller. Your best bet is to rent a tiller or hire someone who owns a rear-tine tiller to do the job for you. You can then create raised beds quickly and easily with the tiller, using your existing garden soil enriched with sand and compost. Once you have finished the beds, you can wall them in and become a no-dig gardener.

You even have a choice on how to make raised beds with a tiller. One approach is to till your soil to the maximum depth of the tiller. This depth varies with tillers, but 11 inches is possible. Next shovel and rake the loose soil from areas that will be paths between beds. Heap the loose soil on the beds-to-be. You will get raised beds nearly 15 inches high, assuming you use 4-foot-wide beds with 18-inch paths between beds.

Another technique for making raised beds with a rotary tiller is to till as deeply as possible, and then replace the tines with a hiller attachment, which is a shovellike device used to direct soil. This method depends upon being able to find a rental place or a tiller operator who has a hiller attachment.

Now that the soil is in good shape, you're ready to plant.

Planting the Garden

Planting time is the best time of year for gardeners. There's nothing like the happy, hopeful feeling you get as you tuck the young plants into the ground at the start of a brand new growing season. Besides, it's spring and it's just plain wonderful to get outdoors in the warm sunshine. Planting times for crops in your no-dig garden will be much the same as in a conventional garden. If you have put down a black plastic mulch, you may be able to plant a week or two earlier. You will find recommended planting times for specific vegetables and flowers in Chapters 8 and 9. Those chapters also have information on plant spacing and placement in the garden. A good way to test whether your soil is dry enough to plant in is to scoop up a handful and squeeze it into a ball by clenching your fist. As you release your hand, the ball should crumble and fall apart. If it sticks together, the soil is too wet and probably too cold to plant anything in it. You should figure out where all your crops are going to go before you start any planting. Some gardeners like to draw a garden plan on paper, and others prefer to plan the garden in their heads and get out there and plant. Whichever way you choose, just make sure you know where you want to plant what when you step into the garden.

When planting day arrives your first instinct, especially if you've gardened before, will probably be to look up in the sky and see if the weather looks right for planting. If you grew your own transplants using the method I described in Chapter 2, you don't need to worry too much about the weather. Our method produces strong, well-rooted transplants that are tough enough to go into the garden without danger of transplant shock. If the weather is more or less normal for this time of year, you don't have to wait for an ideal day to do your transplanting. However, if you purchased transplants or grew them by methods other than ours, you should transplant on a cloudy, calm day to lessen transplant shock.

Now we are ready to pick up our tools. Let's look first at the bulb planter. The first thing a transplant needs is a no-dig hole which you will make with the bulb planter. You can either prepare all the holes and then place the transplants in these holes, or you can make one hole, put in the plant, and then repeat the process. Bill and I tried both methods and we thought it was easier to make all the holes in one continuous standing movement. After all, when you're on a roll, why stop? When we were putting the plants in the holes, we found that one stoop usually brought us into the reach of around four holes. At this rate we figured the method of preparing all the holes at once had about one-fourth of the stoop-and-stand action as did the method of making one hole at a time. The continuous up-and-down motion of the latter method tired us out more quickly.

Transplanting with the bulb planter is as easy as one, two, three. Take a look at Figures 3-3 through 3-9 starting on page 63; they show the no-dig transplanting steps. First place your long-handled bulb planter on the soil where you wish to put in a transplant. While holding onto the handle, firmly push the bulb planter down into the soil, with your right foot. Let the planter sink down until the hole is as deep as the height of the Styrofoam cup or other container that holds the plant. If you encounter a rock, tilt the bulb planter and angle past it. Don't worry about the slanted hole; the transplant will straighten up in a few days. Large rocks pose no problem, if you move the hole to any side. Pull the bulb planter out of the soil.

3-3 The aluminum bulb planter cuts right through soil or black plastic mulch with simple foot pressure.

Suppose you had decided to put down black plastic early to kill extensive weeds or sod, as mentioned earlier in this chapter. Just place your bulb planter on the plastic mulch and firmly push it with your foot right through the plastic. The bulb planter will neatly slice a hole through the plastic and into the soil (Figure 3-3). If you have an organic mulch on the garden, just push it aside and sink the bulb planter into the soil.

Removing the soil plug should pose no difficulty, if you are doing your planting at the proper time of year. If you try to transplant too early, the soil will be too wet and will stick, causing you some annoyance. Remember the squeeze test for determining when soil is ready for planting. To get the soil plug out, just turn the bulb planter upside down and grasp the outside of the metal corer section containing the soil plug. Rap the handle of the bulb planter on the ground. The soil plug will fall out cleanly onto the ground without hitting your hands or feet. Once in a while I have to give a hesitant soil plug a little push with my free hand. By the way, don't worry about the mound of soil. Leave it and move on to the next position to make another hole. If you can't make straight lines by eye, you might want to use the line guide mentioned in Chapter 1.

3-4 After you make a no-dig hole, fill it with organic rapid starter solution.

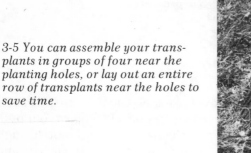

*3-5 You can assemble your trans-
plants in groups of four near the
planting holes, or lay out an entire
row of transplants near the holes to
save time.*

The next step is to pour an organic rapid starter solution into each
hole, filling it up to the top (Figure 3-4). Organic rapid starter solution
contains kelp and fish emulsion (as described in Chapter 4), and it will give
your transplants a quick start. If you grew your transplants our way, as
discussed in the previous chapter, you will get a double quick start! Unlike
conventional transplants, ours have lots of super-strong feeder roots to
take up the organic starter solution ever so quickly.

Now gather up your transplants and place them near the planting holes
(Figure 3-5). You should use recently watered transplants, so the root balls
are moist but not soggy. Bill and I like to place them in groups of four in
positions from which we can reach four holes. Do you plant in a squatting
or kneeling position? We find a kneeling position most comfortable for
planting, especially when we wear a pair of foam rubber kneepads. If you
grew your transplants as described in Chapter 2, take the Styrofoam container in your working hand; then place your other hand over the cup,
keeping the plant stem between your fingers. Invert the container and give
the bottom a gentle rap. The soil ball should easily slide from the cup
(Figure 3-6), as our seedling growing mixture allows for easy removal.

3-6 To remove the transplant from the cup, place the stem between your fingers and invert the cup. The transplant will usually slide right out and the soil ball remain intact. Tap the cup bottom or gently squeeze the sides if a transplant seems stubborn.

You may be tempted to remove some of the drainage and aeration materials from the root ball, but don't! You will damage the roots if you do, and besides, these materials will go right on improving drainage and aeration in your garden soil if you allow them to remain on the root ball.

Planting Home-Grown or Purchased Transplants

If you grew your transplants by some method other than ours or if you purchased them and the transplants are in individual containers, you can treat them the same way as described above for our transplants. If your transplants are in paper or peat pots, you have to take one precaution. Make sure none of the paper or peat pot is above the soil line when you set the transplant in the hole. If it is, the pot edge can act as a capillary wick and evaporate moisture from the root ball, which can lead to slowed recovery, slowed growth, and even death for your transplants. I usually feel better when I remove the top inch or so of a paper or peat pot before I bury it.

If your transplants are in flats, take a sharp knife and cut the soil into cubes, with a plant at the center of each cube. If you are careful, you can

A

B

3-7 Plants grown in trays or flats can also be transplanted into no-dig holes. When planting a transplant from a plastic compartmentalized tray, like the squash plant in photo A, add soil to fill in gaps around small root balls or round off the edges on larger soil squares. To transplant from a flat, first remove the soil block from the tray, as shown with the marigolds in photo B. Next use a knife to cut the soil block into cubes that will fit the no-dig hole (C).

C

also break the soil mixture apart by hand. The cube's length or width should not be any larger than the diameter of the garden hole, but it can be smaller. Remember, if the transplants look quite small when compared to the hole, you should probably make your planting holes with the dibble, as I will explain later.

Next, place the transplant's root ball or the cut cube of soil into the hole. If you used our method for growing transplants, you'll find that the root ball fits perfectly in the no-dig hole (Figure 3-8). If you have other

A

B

3-8 When you prepare a no-dig hole for a transplant, make it as deep as the container with the transplant. One exception is with transplants in peat pots, where you want the hole to be 1 inch deeper. This extra depth allows you to cover the rim of the peat pot with soil, which will prevent it from "wicking" away soil moisture and fatally drying out your transplant. Plants from our Styrofoam cups fit perfectly into no-dig holes, as shown with this pepper plant (A) being planted through black plastic. If you cut the hole to the right depth, the plant will fit in just right. You can also use no-dig holes for either circular or square (B) peat pots. If the square pot fits poorly, "round" it by squeezing carefully with your hand or stretching the sides of the hole with your hands.

kinds of transplants, you will probably need some soil to fill up the hole. You can use the soil plugs left nearby from the no-dig holes, you can push in soil from around the hole's edge, or better yet, you can fill in the hole with our special mixture of soil and compost, called seedling helper (see page 93). You can keep a bucket of this mixture close at hand for filling the holes. One final note: If the soil cube or root ball is a little wider than the hole, just place your fingers on the inside of the hole and pull to stretch the hole a little larger. At this point you will notice that you did half as much work in half as much time as compared to when you transplant with a trowel.

I'd like to give you a word of caution here. When the transplant is safely in the hole, resist the urge to press down on the root ball or the soil around it and do not water the transplant. Pressing causes compaction, which reduces the drainage and aeration of the soil. In turn, the compacted soil results in poorer root systems and slower growth.

As far as watering transplants, if you think back to the start of this section, you'll remember that we said to start with *recently watered* transplants, so the root ball is wet already. If you add more water, the root ball will be

3-9 Use the bulb planter to make one or more holes around your transplants and fill with enriched organic matter, such as this leaf compost mixed with organic fertilizer. The edge of the organic oasis should start roughly 4 inches away from the transplant. Use one oasis for each transplant in average garden soil, more if the soil is poor and neglected.

soggy and wetter than the surrounding soil. This condition defeats the purpose of putting our starter solution in the hole before planting the transplant. We want the soil around the root ball to be wetter than the root ball itself so the the feeder roots will be encouraged to grow outward into the garden soil, seeking out the water. Of course, if the root ball dries out over the next few days, by all means water it then and afterward as needed.

If your garden soil is in excellent organic health, you are done. The organic enrichment methods I'll explain in Chapter 4 can speed you to this goal. However, if you are still working on getting your soil in top condition, you can assure a bountiful harvest from the transplants with one last simple step (Figure 3-9). Use the bulb planter to make a no-dig hole about 4 inches to the right or left of each transplant. Dump the soil aside as before. Fill each hole with some garden compost or leaf mold amended with organic nutrients. Bill and I suggest you try our recipe in Chapter 4 for organic oases. These organic oases will be a favored watering hole for your tranplants' root systems after they deplete the starter solution. If your soil is in poor health, you might want to put two, three, or even four organic oases around each transplant.

If you have any leftover soil plugs when you have finished planting, you can just leave them or, if you plan to lay down a plastic mulch to keep away weeds, scatter the soil plugs with your foot or a rake.

Planting Smaller or Leftover Transplants

How can you handle those much smaller transplants in flats or the transplants that arise when you thinned extra seedlings from the containers? Using a sharp knife, cut the root ball into little cubes, with one plant at the center of each cube. Next make a series of holes in the garden with your dibble. Make sure the holes are a little larger than the soil cubes. Rocking the dibble back and forth enlarges the hole (Figure 3-10). Now add the same kelp/fish emulsion starter solution recommended before with the larger

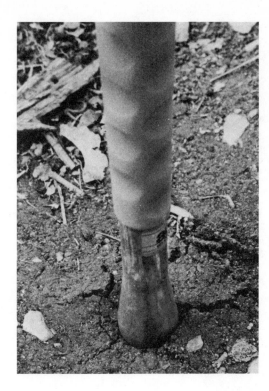

3-10 To plant small transplants, first place the long-handled dibble as shown in the soil or plastic and rock it back and forth to create a transplant hole. Fill the dibble hole with organic rapid starter solution twice. Place the transplant in the hole and push in soil as needed to complete the transplanting operation.

transplants. Fill the hole twice, since its volume is small. Now place your transplant cube or your seedling in the hole. Put a little compost amended with organic nutrients or a little soil in each dibble hole so that the cube's top is even with the soil line when you place it in the hole. Fill any gaps with the same mixture. Again, do not press on the soil or water the new transplant until the soil around it starts to dry out. If your soil is not in good organic health, amend it for the short term with the organic oases used with the larger transplants.

Other Uses for the Bulb Planter and Dibble

The bulb planter and dibble have other uses as well (Figure 3-11). The dibble is fine for planting onion sets, onion transplants, garlic cloves, and small seed potatoes. You can use the bulb planter to plant larger seed potatoes. By cutting a bulb planter hole or dibble holes to the proper depth, you can also plant some large seeds, such as beans, corn, cucumber, melon, and squash, in hills or groups. Of course, you can plant all of these equally as well in a row made by the furrower, which we will be discussing next.

Let me remind you that you don't *have* to use a bulb planter or dibble to plant onions (sets or transplants), garlic cloves, seed potatoes, or large

A

B

3-11 The bulb planter, when sunk just 1 or 2 inches into the soil, can be used to plant larger seeds in soil or black plastic (A), as can the dibble (B). Seed potatoes, onion sets, and garlic can be planted with either tool.

seeds. You could use the furrower instead, if you prefer. There is, however, one case in which a bulb planter or dibble will indisputably offer the greatest convenience.

If you have a black plastic mulch in place, it's easier to plant large seeds or various bulbs with the bulb planter or dibble. These tools slice nicely through plastic, but other tools, particularly a furrower, would only tear it. There *is* a way to plant rows with the furrower and still use black plastic mulch, but we'll cover that later on.

How to Use a Furrower

The other tool you need in the no-dig garden is a furrower. This tool, as you recall, is what you use to plant seeds of fast-maturing crops directly in the garden. How do you use it? First place the point downward and work it into the soil. The angle made by the soil surface and the handle determines the depth of the furrow. Standing upright will let you create the largest possible angle and the most shallow furrow (Figure 3-13). As you bend at the waist, the angle decreases and the furrow cut goes deeper. Walking backward, draw the furrower toward you. If you have a good eye for rows, you will get a nice straight furrow; if you do not, use the row guide discussed in Chapter 1. Make sure you cut the furrow 1 to 2 inches deeper than the required seed planting depth. You can easily cut a deep furrow in one pass. If, however, you find this furrowing too strenuous, you can make the task easier by cutting the furrow increasingly deeper using two or more passes with the furrower. The depth for seed potatoes, for instance, might require more than one pass for some people.

To prepare your furrow for seeds, place enough soil mixed with compost and organic nutrients in the bottom of the furrow to decrease the

3-12 If the garden area is not already clean, you should remove the weeds with the action hoe (shown here) and rake before planting seeds with the furrower. Or you could just cover the area with black plastic and furrow through it.

A

B

3-13 Depending on the depth you wish, adjust the furrower angle. A large angle between the handle and soil (A) gives you a shallow furrow, while a smaller angle (B) gives you a deeper furrow. Draw the furrow toward you by eye or guide it with the garden straightline for easy seed furrows (C).

C

depth to that which is needed for the seeds (Figure 3-14). You can use the outdoor seedling helper recipe in Chapter 4, or you can buy ready-made mixtures. This material will help the seedlings get off to a great start.

Now you are ready to put the seeds into the furrow. If you are a kneeler and like to get close to the soil, please remember to be kind to your knees. Kneepads (discussed in Chapter 1) will be a great help. Not only are they comfortable, but they stop the chill and dampness that arise from contact with spring garden soil. Or perhaps you like to stand. I know that I can

3-14 Add the seedling helper to the bottom of your furrow. Put in enough so that your seeds will sit at the proper depth.

stand and drop large seeds, such as corn and beans, quite neatly into open furrows, but small seeds give me trouble. One puff of wind and I find that my straight line looks like a path through a maze. For small seeds, you might want to use a mechanical seed sower. Some of the seed sowers we covered in Chapter 1 fit the bill, in terms of both sowing ease and cost.

Now you can sow your seeds using the method of your choice (Figure 3-15). Of course, you can also plant onion sets and plants, garlic, or seed potatoes in your furrow. Next cover the seeds. *Do not* use the soil on the sides of the furrow unless it is friable (easily crumbled) and in good organic health. Left in place, this little ridge of soil will also trap and retain rainwater in the furrow. If your soil is not up to par yet, you can cover the seeds with a soil and vermiculite mixture called soil helper. You can find the recipe for this soil helper in Chapter 4.

Do you want super seedlings in a hurry? If you are like Bill and me, you do. Take your watering can and fill it with our rapid starter solution of kelp and fish emulsion for seeds (see Chapter 4). Now sprinkle your freshly

3-15 Sow your seeds on top of the seedling helper.

covered seed furrows. The nutrients and growth promoters in this solution will improve both germination and seedling growth. A head start is a
good start! Later when these quick-acting nutrients have gone, the slow-
release nutrients in the soil/compost supplement (or seedling helper)
underneath your seeds will continue feeding the growing seedlings.

What if you want to use black plastic or other mulches, but still use the
furrower? With loose organic mulches, the furrower will work just fine.
You can cut right through the organic mulch and into the soil, like a hot
knife through butter. Black plastic, on the other hand, requires a somewhat different approach. One way to solve the problem is to leave roughly
12 inches of space between each sheet of black plastic. Use these earth
strips for your seed rows. This method, however, has two disadvantages.
First, I find it difficult sometimes to plan ahead for row placement. My
ideas change or a new pack of seeds comes my way. The other problem
concerns the width of the plastic mulch versus the distance I want between
rows. The two sizes are hardly ever the same, thus I end up trimming
plastic and installing far more edges than I really need.

The better way to install black plastic involves using the widest available width. This approach helps cut down the number of edges you need to
install. Butt each of the edges up close together, leaving very little soil
showing between sheets. Wherever you need to place a seed row, slit open
the plastic (stop short of buried edges) with a knife or scissors (Figure
3-16). Now draw your furrower through the soil exposed by the slit. Don't
worry about the plastic edges. The soil thrown to the sides by the furrower
will bury the plastic edges as you make your furrow. If you are unhappy
with the edge burial, you can pin down the edges with U-shaped pieces of
coat hangers, or place a few rocks along the edges. Make sure you use the
same procedure for furrowing and sowing as described earlier for bare
soil; that is, cut a deeper furrow than needed, place some seedling helper
below the seeds, put in the seeds, cover them with soil helper and water
them with rapid starter solution.

*3-16 If your garden is mulched
with black plastic, you can plant
seeds if you slit the plastic as
shown and then cut a furrow
through the slit. The soil thrown
to the sides holds the cut edges of
the plastic down. Of course, you
must cover the seeds with some
fresh soil or soil and vermiculite.*

Raised Beds, Hills, and the No-Dig Method

If you have raised beds, the no-dig method will adapt readily when you plant the beds. If you want to plant your seeds in rows, use the furrower. If you are planning to plant transplants, use either the bulb planter or the dibble. You can also plant larger seeds using the dibble to make individual holes. You can find more information on these special cases under the various vegetables and flowers discussed in Chapters 8 and 9.

Perhaps you plant most of your crops directly into the existing garden soil but you still like to plant a few special crops — like corn — in hills. The no-dig way of gardening works just as well with hills as with raised beds. It doesn't matter if your hill is just a simple mound of soil or a more formal raised mini-bed. Choose the dibble if you plant seeds for your hills of corn, squash, melons, or other plants. If you have transplants, use the bulb planter. Just follow the steps given on page 61.

You may want to make some formal mini-hills like Bill and I use. We love using them because our hills, combined with black plastic and cloches (transparent plant covers), give us extra-early melons or squash. Gardeners in the South may not care about this result, but we northern gardeners are very happy to get early crops. Here's our method.

First, prepare 36-inch-square frames from pine or particleboard shelving. You can buy this board 6 feet or 8 feet long by 12 inches wide by 1 inch thick. Actually, the true dimensions for the width and thickness are more like 11 inches and 3/4 inch, respectively. If you wish to reuse this frame for many years, stain it with a wood preservative that's safe for use with plants. For example, Cuprinol markets a formulation (#14) for use with wood greenhouse flats. Building this frame is a good winter task, when the call for garden work is minimal.

When spring arrives, you can put the mini-hills wherever you want them in your garden. I suggest that you drive in a wood stake or metal pipe at each inside corner of the frame. This step will securely anchor the hill frame. Now fill the mini-hill either with soil or the soil substitute described earlier in this chapter. At planting time (Figure 3-17) you can use the dibble for planting seeds or the bulb planter for planting transplants. Make sure you read about the use of the milk bottle fertilizer feeders for hills and raised beds in the next chapter. And don't forget to check out early hill crops with black plastic and cloches, which I will discuss in Chapter 7.

Before we leave planting techniques, let's talk about planting patterns. The old standby is single row planting. The bulb planter, dibble, or furrower easily makes a single row of holes or a single (row) furrow. However, if you

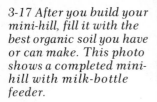

3-17 After you build your mini-hill, fill it with the best organic soil you have or can make. This photo shows a completed mini-hill with milk-bottle feeder.

want greater yields from the same area, you are better off with beds and bands. These planting patterns give increased yields because they use space more efficiently and cause less yield-robbing soil compaction.

You can plant beds with any of the tools, depending on whether you are using transplants or seeds. Beds should be 4 feet wide so you can easily reach plants in the center from either side, and be any length you want. Space the no-dig holes or the multiple furrow rows at the closest allowable distance (see Chapters 8 and 9) for intensive planting. You can place the transplants side by side or thin seedlings to the same pattern, essentially a compressed row concept. However, if you stagger the plants in the alternate rows (see Figure 7-4 in Chapter 7), you get even more plants in the bed than with row-type patterns.

Bands are somewhat narrower than beds (see Chapter 7) and perhaps more suited for smaller, intensive plantings like lettuce or carrots. Here, too, you can prepare transplant holes or multiple, tightly spaced rows with the bulb planter or furrower. Another no-dig approach with bands for small seeds is to rough up the surface of the soil with either a rake or action hoe. Next broadcast or scatter the seeds and cover them with a light sprinkling of soil. Later on you can thin the seedlings to the efficient pattern and spacing of your choice.

Well, dear reader, I hope you are as excited as Bill and I are about the ease and versatility of no-dig gardening methods. You undoubtedly want to skip right to Chapters 8 and 9 now, but try to resist the urge. Our next chapter on fertilizing and adding organic matter to your no-dig garden is important. Remember, healthy plants and wonderful yields depend on organically enriched soils; no-dig gardens are no exception.

Chapter 4
Feeding the No-Dig Garden

Many gardeners don't realize that digging the soil is the key culprit in the loss of organic matter. Digging brings deeper organic matter to the soil surface. There air-loving microorganisms quickly break it down, wasting much of the soil's organic matter before plants can make use of it. Of course, this sets off a whole chain of events that eventually ruins your soil as we already discussed in Chapter 1. No-dig techniques, however, conserve organic matter, so much so that you can maintain levels simply by leaving roots from previous crops in place and perhaps occasionally adding an organic amendment to the soil. Naturally this statement assumes your soil already has an acceptable level of organic matter, which is probably not true of many gardens with a history of heavy digging and cultivation. But don't worry. If your soil test indicates low organic matter content, there are ways you can quickly improve it (I'll offer some suggestions later in this chapter). Once you have improved your soil, it will be easy for you to maintain the level of organic matter in the no-dig garden.

A no-dig garden also requires less supplemental feeding of nutrients than other gardens do. In plain English, your fertilizer dollar gets a lot more mileage in the no-dig garden. Part of this savings relates to organic matter. Any fertilizer, even organic fertilizer, has some part of its nutrient pool in a water-soluble form. This nutrient amount may be small, as with organic fertilizers that release nutrients slowly, or quite large, as with water-soluble chemical fertilizers. Plants can use only a certain amount of water-soluble nutrients in their day-to-day development; therefore, some excess nutrients are present. True, with organic fertilizers the amount of excess nutrients is reasonably small; still the soil can either waste or store the nutrients not needed by the plants. What happens depends heavily on how much organic matter is present in the soil.

Organic matter has the ability to capture and hold nutrients until the plants need them, a process scientists call *chelation*. If organic matter is not present, water carries the nutrients downward into the water table where they are lost to plants. This process is known as *leaching*. The no-dig garden has higher levels of organic matter; therefore, the no-dig garden soil has superior ability to capture and hold nutrients. Nutrient losses through leaching are minimal; therefore your fertilizer goes further and you need less.

Certain practices associated with our no-dig garden methods also greatly improve fertilizer efficiency. Normally you apply fertilizers by broadcasting or evenly scattering them over the garden before you sow seeds or place transplants. This approach to fertilizing is inefficient, or nutrient wasteful, for a number of reasons. One, a lot of nutrients end up in areas where the plants won't be able to use them. For example, the nutrients in the fertilizer that fall on the paths will probably be lost by leaching. Even if the soil stores the nutrients there, the degree of compaction present means the nutrients will probably never be used by plants. Foot traffic on the paths compacts the soil, driving out air and destroying soil structure to the point that roots will not grow into the soil in the path areas. It's not hard to see that if there are no roots, there will be no need for nutrients, and they will be wasted.

Timing is also an important factor in fertilizer efficiency. Some nutrients land in good soil, but it is soil where the plant roots are not yet present. By the time the roots arrive in that area, leaching will have robbed the soil of some of its nutrients. The plants will eventually use the nutrients stored in the organic matter, but any nutrients outside of the organic matter holding area will disappear.

So what's a gardener to do? You should apply fertilizer at the right time and place so that you are sure you have utilized it as efficiently as possible. Bill and I use localized, intensive fertilizer applications, which I will explain. If you recall the transplanting procedure outlined in the previous chapter, you'll remember that we used an organic rapid starter solution. This starter solution goes directly into the transplant hole, so we localize the nutrients where the feeder roots can absorb them quickly. The solution quickly releases some of the nutrients for immediate use, while it releases other nutrients more slowly for later uptake; thus, we have an intensive availability of nutrients for the transplant. A somewhat similar situation occurs when we use the rapid starter solution with seeds.

Bill and I use this same idea of localized, intensive applications as the plant develops from either a seed or transplant. We localize the fertilizer application by using foliar feeding, and the leaves then directly absorb the nutrients. Any runoff at the plant's drip line also goes right to work, because this is where the feeder roots are found. The feeder roots capture the nutrient runoff, so the plant is actually fed twice. This is another kind of intensive fertilizing.

Of course we do use some slow feeding techniques, too, such as the seedling helper or the organic oases I mentioned in Chapter 3. These techniques, which I will describe in detail later in this chapter, help to maintain a steady, slow stream of nutrients to the plants.

Let's turn now to fertilizers and fertilizing techniques for your organic no-dig garden.

Water-Soluble Organic Fertilizers

I have settled on two products as the mainstays of my foliar feeding program: fish emulsion and seaweed extract. You can use them combined or separately, and you will find them to be readily available (see Appendix). Their price is right, they go a long way, and they produce remarkable results. I use them on everything—vegetables, flowers, fruit trees, and shrubs. First, let's look at the products themselves.

My favorite water-soluble fertilizer is a commercial blend of liquid fish and seaweed extract (called Sea Mix) that is readily available to consumers (see Appendix). It contains 3 percent nitrogen, 2 percent phosphorus, and 2 percent potassium. The seaweed portion also contributes all the trace elements plants need, as well as a few growth-promoting hormones.

One quart costs about $6 to $8 and provides you with quite a lot of fertilizer. The dilution rate for gardens is 8 teaspoons to 1 gallon of water. Since 6 teaspoons equals 1 ounce, 1 quart equals 32 times 6, or 192 teaspoons; therefore, 1 quart of Sea Mix will make 24 gallons of fertilizer.

Two gallons of fertilizer is enough to thoroughly spray all the plants in a garden of 800 to 1,000 square feet. If you sprayed every three weeks, your bottle of Sea Mix would last for 36 weeks, or roughly nine months. Even if you have a very large garden that requires 4 gallons of fertilizer per spraying, you can feed your plants for four and one-half months. Most gardeners find that 1 quart is enough for one gardening season. Those of you with very large gardens might want to consider the 1-gallon size of Sea Mix, which will save you roughly 30 percent over the quart price.

While less convenient than the combination fertilizer, you can also buy separate bottles of fish emulsion and seaweed extracts. You then have the option of mixing your own combination (1-1) or using them separately at staggered or simultaneous intervals. Even though I use Sea Mix, I still keep a bottle of seaweed extract on hand for the times when I want to take advantage of its growth-promoting, insecticidal, or other properties. Then I apply it diluted per the bottle's instructions, which gives me an effective concentration double that of the seaweed extract present in Sea Mix.

We keep coming back to seaweed extract and its value beyond that of a fertilizer, so let's talk about it now. First, the easiest commercial brands to locate are Maxicrop and Seacrop. The former comes from England and the latter from Maine. Although you may get arguments from each manufacturer that theirs is better, I rather doubt that much difference exists. The only difference may well be in English versus American seaweed. Your best bet is to let your pocketbook decide for you or to go for whichever brand is available. Incidentally, the people that make Seacrop also make Sea Mix. You can also buy seaweed in a soluble powder form to which you add water and make up your own seaweed extract.

So what's so wonderful about seaweed extract? Well, it contains nitrogen, phosphorus, and potassium, as does fish emulsion; however, seaweed extract contains more phosphorus and potassium, and fish emulsion contains more nitrogen. That's why we mix them together; each complements the other to give you a balanced liquid fertilizer. Seaweed extract also contains all the trace elements plants need, which include calcium, magnesium, sulfur, boron, chloride, copper, iron, manganese, molybdenum, and zinc. Recently, plant physiologists found that plants also need very tiny amounts of nickel, yet another trace element that seaweed extracts provide.

Besides providing your plants with a complete diet, for what other purposes can you use seaweed extract? You can use seaweed extract as a foliar spray, a seed treatment, and a rooting solution. There are numerous claims being made for it. It reputedly improves plants' resistance to disease, insects, and frost. As if that weren't enough, seaweed extract supposedly improves mineral intake by plants and enhances fruit set.

Foliar Feeding

But let's take an even closer look at these claims. I mentioned that I use seaweed extract for foliar feeding. But is there a scientific basis for its use? Plant physiologists don't agree as to exactly how nutrients in solution penetrate leaves. They may enter through the adjustable pores in leaves (called stomata), the leaves' waxy cuticle layer, or both. But scientists do have proof that nutrients do enter leaves in water. Nutrients also leach out of leaves during periods of heavy, continuous rain, but these nutrients eventually enter the plant through the root system. Foliar feeding is, then, indeed efficient.

There are many other pluses to foliar feeding. If the leaves, rather than the roots, take in the nutrients, the beneficial effects to the plant occur more quickly. Foliar absorption can be up to twenty times faster than root absorption, and nutrients entering through the leaves produce beneficial results with a smaller amount of nutrients than when they enter through soil routes. In some instances with trace elements, foliar feeding may give quicker but similar results at feeding rates as low as one-twelfth the rate of soil feeding. This last point is especially important. It's the heart of our localized, intensive feeding program and explains further why we use so much less fertilizer than gardeners who use conventional fertilization. The nutrient levels in Sea Mix may seem low at 3-2-2, but the *efficiency* of foliar feeding may make it the equivalent of a 10-10-10 fertilizer in the soil. The enhancement effect of foliar feeding is real, but a few reasons might better convince you.

For example, let's look at phosphorus. We're always adding phosphorus to the soil, so it seems as though most soils must be deficient in phosphorus. Wrong! Most soils have plenty of phosphorus, but it isn't available to plants because soil chemistry tends to keep it locked up. With foliar feeding, we can bypass this chemical lock; therefore, we need much less phosphorus. In effect, much of the phosphorus put into the soil is in an effort to get past the chemical lock, so that only a little of what we add goes to the plant. This problem of soil chemistry also affects trace elements added to the soil; most become unavailable to the plant because of chemical attack in the soil. But foliar feeding provides as excellent bypass route.

Let's look at another aspect of foliar feeding versus conventional feeding: competition. The nutrients we add to soil don't always get to the plant. Microorganisms in the soil and weeds steal some for their needs, and some nutrients leach downward to the water table. Conventional feeding is certainly inefficient, since we have to add extra nutrients to compensate for losses. Direct feeding through leaves bypasses these problems and results in more efficient feeding from a smaller amount of fertilizer.

One last point deserves a brief mention. When you encounter an unseasonable period of dry weather, it's impractical to apply fertilizers to soils, because the nutrients must be dissolved in water in order to enter the root system. Foliar feeding works even when the soil is dry. Again the foliar feeding solves a gardening problem.

The Many Uses for Seaweed Extract

How about the use of seaweed extracts for seeds and transplants? How can this work? The key to this use of seaweed extract is its chemical composition. First, seaweed extracts contain certain hormones that control plant development. These hormones, called auxins, cytokinins, and gibberellins, are mixtures of chemically related compounds. Some forms are like those hormones found in plants, and some parts of the mixture are somewhat different from their counterparts in land plants. Auxins promote rooting in cuttings. In fact, one well-known rooting aid for cuttings is a synthetic auxin. Auxins in seaweed extract could conceivably promote rooting of recently planted transplants. Auxins, cytokinins, and gibberellins work together to increase cell division and cell size; therefore, their presence in seaweed extracts might improve seedling and transplant growth. This theory hasn't been entirely proven, but it is true that large numbers of gardeners who treat their seeds and transplants with seaweed extracts notice enhanced growth. Perhaps plant hormones in the seaweed are the reason.

There is a limit to the scientific evidence for the effects of adding seaweed extract, but what does exist is certainly encouraging. Some scientific studies with seaweed extract suggest possible yield increases in several crops, including black currants, Brussels sprouts, cauliflower, leeks, lima beans, peppers, poinsettias, potatoes, sweet corn, soybeans, tomatoes, and turnips. Gardeners and farmers have reported that even more crops respond with earlier growth and yield increases. Those of you who have an interest in learning more about the scientific studies should read W. A. Stephenson's book, *Seaweed in Agriculture and Horticulture* (Wakefield, England: E. P. Publishers, Ltd. Second edition, 1973).

Studies by scientists and gardeners also suggest that both the overall germination rate and the speed of seedling emergence increase if the gardener uses seaweed extract. Again, this possible effect strengthens the case for following our advice and using our rapid starter solution, which contains seaweed extract, when you plant seeds. Seaweed extract also encourages cuttings to root better. How can you go wrong?

But wait, there's still more. Seaweed extracts also improve soils. The runoff from foliar feeding enters the soil, and the seaweed nutrients stimulate the growth of beneficial microorganisms in the soil. These creatures are the ones near and dear to the hearts of organic gardeners, because they are able to make locked-up nutrients in the soil available to plants. Of course this release of microorganisms also affects the small amount of slower, locked-up nutrients in the seaweed extract itself. While most of the seaweed's nutrients are available immediately, a small fraction is not, but becomes available later in the soil. A similar situation holds true for the fish emulsion in that a small amount of nutrients becomes active later after action by soil microorganisms stimulates it.

Seaweed extract also contains alginic acid, which is reputed to act as a soil conditioner. The noted benefits of alginic acid include improved soil structure and water-holding capacity. The exact way in which alginic acid accomplishes these tasks is not clear.

Extracts of seaweed also contain chelating agents, natural chemicals in the seaweed that improve the availability of certain trace elements to plants. How can that be? The answer lies in solubility. All nutrients must be soluble to enter the root system, but certain minerals, such as iron, are not very soluble in soil water; therefore, iron deficiency can occur in a plant, even when sufficient iron is present in the soil. The problem is iron-poor solutions. Here in New England we often see iron deficiency, or chlorosis, in rhododendrons, mountain laurel, and other broadleaf evergreens. Chelates have the ability to enfold or trap iron within themselves. Chelates are highly soluble in water, so the iron or other element is now in solution. Eventually the chelate will release the iron near the plant roots for entry. In some cases both the chelate and iron will enter the roots together; so seaweed extracts have the potential to improve mineral uptake by crops. Of course these chelates also improve trace element uptake and utilization during foliar feeding.

Seaweed extracts might possess antibiotic properties as well, according to Stephenson in his seaweed book mentioned earlier. While we do not know the exact nature of these antibiotics, we can see their effects on plant health. Let's take seeds, for example. As most of us know, germinating seedlings are susceptible to damping off. I discussed this fatal disease in Chapter 2. Perhaps we can reduce this problem if we water the soil or other growing mixture with diluted seaweed extract at seed sowing time.

Stephenson in his book also implies a pest-deterrent effect. Apparently spider mites don't like seaweed extracts either. The use of foliar feeding with seaweed extract has been observed to knock spider mite populations for a loop. Whether the material acts as a pesticide or a repellent or interferes with their life cycle is unclear, but it does keep the mites away from plants.

Can this antibiotic action relate to reports from nurserymen and one scientific study that seaweed extracts improve frost resistance? While I have no proof of how this happens, I think I can offer a possible explanation. Recently scientists discovered that a certain species of plant bacteria acts as a collector or trap for bringing together ice crystals. Once these crystals start forming, a layer of frost quickly appears. If the scientists remove or destroy the bacteria, light frost does not damage the plants. Could it be, then, that the antibiotic effect of seaweed extract keeps these bacteria at bay and, hence, improves frost resistance? Perhaps some researcher will answer the question someday.

One final quality of seaweed extract to examine is how it may improve fruit set. Well, there is a commercial product available that when sprayed on tomato blossoms improves fruit set. The effective ingredient in the product is a plant hormone, gibberellin. Seaweed extract, as indicated earlier, contains several hormones, including gibberellin. The reports that seaweed extract improves fruit set on crops therefore seem to have a basis in fact.

I hope all these beneficial effects of seaweed, as reported by Stephenson in his book, a few researchers, and many gardeners, are true. Whether the claims turn out to be true or only partially true, one thing is clear: Seaweed extracts do contain nutrients and many trace elements which do promote plant growth. I have used seaweed extracts and like the results in my garden. So why not give the seaweed extract a chance in your garden and see what you think?

I do caution you, though, not to go overboard with your applications. Too much seaweed extract can be counterproductive, as can using seaweed without balancing it with fish emulsion. Later on we'll look at how much to use and how to apply it. As wonderful as seaweed extract is, you still need the complement of nitrogen, phosphorus, and potassium present in the fish emulsion. Together they are a dynamic duo. In fact, most of the studies I've seen found that the presence of other fertilizers enhanced the action and benefits of seaweed extract.

Can you carry an entire garden on fish emulsion and seaweed extract? Yes, if it's a no-dig garden and you already have moderate levels of nutrients and organic matter in your soil. If you're there, great! If not, don't worry; we'll get you there later on in the chapter. Once you have a base of soil nutrients and organic matter, seaweed extract and fish emulsion will be all you need to feed you garden year after year.

Solid Fertilizers and Soil Amendments

I would now like to consider a few solid fertilizers. You may need them if your soil test shows that your soil isn't up to par; however, you may only need them for a few years, until you put your garden on an exclusive seaweed and fish emulsion diet. I'm recommending solid fertilizers on the basis of their effectiveness and availability. In the past, organic gardeners placed a lot of emphasis on rock powders such as granite dust. These products are hard to find, so I'm suggesting others instead.

Seaweed Meal

First let's turn to seaweed meal or, as it's sometimes called, kelp meal. Don't confuse seaweed meal with the previously discussed liquid or powdered seaweed extract. The extracts, whether in liquid or solid form, are hot-water or alkaline extracts of seaweed that are highly water soluble and have immediately available nutrients. Seaweed meal is not an extract, but is ground-up seaweed itself. It differs somewhat from the extracts.

One way in which seaweed meal differs from seaweed extract is that its nutrients are not readily available to the plant or soil. Microorganisms must first break it down to release its nutrients slowly. Unfortunately, if nitrogen levels in the soil are low, some nitrogen robbing from plants could occur initially; however, the nitrogen will eventually return.

One advantage of using seaweed meal is its residual effect: The nutrient release and growth enhancement effects go on for two or even three years. A second advantage is that it acts as a soil conditioner. Seaweed meal improves water retention and soil structure to a greater degree than do extracts. If your soil isn't up to organic expectations, a one-shot treatment with seaweed meal may be just the right ticket!

Homemade Fertilizers

You can also make your own organic fertilizers in various strengths. An easy one to make is a mixture of coffee grounds, bone meal, and wood ashes in a proportion by weight of 4-1-1. This mixture will have an N-P-K (nitrogen-phosphorus-potassium) ratio of roughly 2-4-2. While this N-P-K rating may sound low, it's probably equivalent to a 5-10-5 chemical fertilizer. Remember, because the mixture is an organic fertilizer, it will release its nutrients slowly over a period of time.

Another fertilizer you can make consists of dried blood, bone meal, and wood ashes in a 2-1-4 ratio. This mix has an N-P-K value of 4-4-4 and might be similar to a chemical 10-10-10 fertilizer.

Commercial Fertilizers

You can also buy organic fertilizers. One popular brand is available in several forms (see the Appendix listing under complete powders). One type of commercial fertilizer for rejuvenating poor soils in a hurry is an organic blend rated at 4-2-4. The cost is roughly $10 through mail order for 50 pounds, which will fertilize roughly 2,200 square feet. For example, a garden 50 feet by 44 feet needs 50 pounds of fertilizer. If you do order through the mail, the shipping cost will run you another $10, but $20 is a reasonable price to pay for the restoration of your soil. Remember, this treatment is probably a one-time procedure. Once done, you can get by with fish emulsion and seaweed extract.

Another interesting product, worm castings, is available commercially. Essentially the product comes from worms, which digest horse manure, peat, and minerals. The cast-out material, worm castings, is a stable form of humus with some nutrient value. At this time, 10 pounds costs about $8 plus postage (see Appendix). At such a price I'm not suggesting wide spreading of the material; however, as we'll see later, you can use it with seedlings, and it will go a long way under those conditions.

Leaf Compost

The last fertilizer and soil amendment I'll suggest, compost, is the most economical. You can easily make it yourself, and it will be quite effective to use if you follow the hints that I'll give you. These hints are tried and true, since I spent several years conducting professional research studies with compost. If you're already an organic gardener, you probably know that garden compost contains approximately 1.5 to 3.5 percent nitrogen and roughly 1 to 2 percent phosphorus and potassium, as well as small amounts of trace elements. Compost, once called artificial manure, is roughly equivalent to manure in terms of its nutrients, but it sure smells better. Of course, compost is a wonderful soil conditioner. It improves water retention, aeration, and nutrient storage and release in soils.

Let's start with the easiest approach to making your own compost. You can make an excellent compost with an easily available waste at a convenient time, when garden chores are winding down for the year. The waste is those fall leaves that you never quite know what to do with. If you bag them, you feel guilty. If you make them into compost, you help both the environment and your garden. A fall leaf pile without any added nitrogen will produce compost sometime late the following summer. You can speed up the process by adding nitrogen, which will give you leaf compost by late spring to early summer. The one exception to this statement is if your leaves are largely oak or pine. These two types of leaves take twice as long to form compost. You can mix oak leaves or pine needles with other kinds of leaves, but don't use them heavily. You will also need 20 pounds of blood meal for your leaf compost pile. Even if you have less, still use it, because the process will be faster than using less blood meal than using none.

Now you are ready to start forming your compost pile. First decide where you are going to place it. Pick a sunny, level, well-drained spot. If shade is all you have, go for it. Some people like to construct a retainer bin from wood or cinder blocks, while others like to use chicken wire fence on poles. You don't need these "leaf holders," though. Since you must keep the leaves moist, you shouldn't have to worry about their blowing away.

Now start raking leaves. If you have a big yard and a long way to go, rake the leaves into an old bed sheet. Pulling the four sheet corners into your hand, drag it to where you plan to construct your compost pile. As you place your leaves into a pile, keep certain points in mind. The leaves should be moist; if these are dry, you must wet them down as you make the pile. I like to make my leaf pile a day or so after a rain, because I save a step and don't have to drag out the garden hose.

The best and most effective shape and size for your compost pile is a 7-foot-square base that tapers to a 5-foot-square top. The ideal height is 5 feet. Don't aim for perfection, because approximations will work just as well. If you are using blood meal, sprinkle some on the leaves at 1-foot intervals. With 20 pounds of blood meal, I sprinkle about 4 pounds every foot in height. If you have a lot of leaves, you don't have to make a second pile. You can just make a longer pile, but keep the width and height the same.

Forget all those other compost recipes that you've seen or heard about. All you need is the leaves, moisture, and possibly blood meal or some other nitrogen-rich equivalent (see Table 1). You do not have to add soil or buy the so-called compost starters. Supposedly these two additives enrich your compost with the right microorganisms so that your compost pile gets a quick start. In reality, the microorganisms you need are already there on the fallen, damp leaves; so don't waste your money on compost starters.

A concern you may have is whether or not to add limestone. I suggest that you don't do it because the pH of your compost will be fine without adding limestone. The finished product will have a pH of near neutral to slightly alkaline, the correct pH for most flowers and vegetables. Of course, if your leaf mixture is heavy in oak leaves and pine needles, the pH will be slightly acidic. If you do add limestone, you will create conditions that favor the production of ammonia. The ammonia will release into the air, taking your precious nitrogen with it. You will end up with nitrogen-deficient compost and a smelly compost pile. Don't waste your nutrients like this; avoid adding limestone to the composting process.

Essentially once you make your leaf pile, you have finished your work. With an hour of work, you get rid of your leaves and have a rich compost as a reward. Do check the pile once in a while to see that it remains moist, because drying can disrupt the composting process. There's generally adequate precipitation in fall and winter so I have never needed to wet down my leaf piles after the initial wetting. You don't have to turn the pile

TABLE 1. USEFUL COMPOST MATERIALS

Material	Source Of	Nitrogen %	Phosphoric Acid %	Potash %
Bark	C	L	L	L
Blood meal	N	10-14	1-5	—
Bone meal	N	2	2-3	—
Coffee grounds	N	2	L	L
Cottonseed meal	N	6	2-3	1-2
Eggshells	—	1	L	L
Fish scrap	N	2-8	1-6	L
Food wastes	C/N	2-3	L	L
Fruit wastes	C/N	1-2	L	L
Garden plants/ weeds	C/N	L-2	L	L
Grass clippings	N	1-2	L	L
Hair	N	12-16	L	L
Hay	C	1-2	L	L
Hoof/horn meal	N	10-15	1-2	L
Leather meal	N	10-12	L	L
Leaves	C/N	L-1	L	L
Manure	C/N	1-5	1-2	1-2
Meat scraps	N	5-7	L	L
Paper	C	L	L	L
Salt-marsh hay	C	1	L	L
Sawdust	C	L	L	L
Seaweed (washed)	C/N	1-2	L	3-4
Wood ashes (unleached)	—	L	1-2	4-10
Wood chips	C	L	L	L

Note: In column 2, C stands for carbon and N for nitrogen. A material listed as a source of C/N contains a good ratio of carbon and nitrogen. It will easily compost alone, or can be counted as a source of either nitrogen or carbon in a mixed compost pile. In columns 3-5, L indicates a low content—less than 1% of the given nutrient.

either. Turning it may speed up the composting process, but it's hard work. Allow a nitrogen source like blood meal to do your speed-up work.

Perhaps one caution relating to composts is in order. Your pile will warm up in a few weeks. Within a month or two it will heat up considerably. The temperature of the pile goes over 140°F and often reaches 158°F— temperatures that will scald your hand. Do *not* poke your hand down into the pile. The outside may feel cool, but the inside may be scalding hot. I have broken open what appeared to be a frozen pile on the outside only to find hot, moist steam escaping from the inside. All you really have to do is sit back and let the microscopic compost critters do their job.

How do you tell when the compost is ready to use on your garden? As I stated previously, if you used blood meal or some other nitrogen source, the compost will be ready sometime in the late spring or early summer. You can check its readiness by digging out some of the compost with a spading fork. The material should look dark and crumbly. The compost temperature should be about the same as the air temperature. If the compost feels warm to the touch, it needs a little time to complete its cool-down period. I'm sure, though, that it will feel either cool or about the same warmth as nearby soil. If it does, your compost is ready to use.

Carbon/Nitrogen Balanced Compost

If you want more compost than your leaf pile produces and have additional time to commit, you can increase production with a garden compost pile. The key to success is to use organic materials in a mixture that gives you balanced amounts of carbon, nitrogen, phosphorus, and potassium. This nutrient balance makes the difference between a true compost and what I call a trash heap.

The microorganisms that make compost require a certain proportion of carbon to nitrogen if they are to do their job efficiently. The waste materials that we use as the carbon and nitrogen sources also contain sufficient amounts of phosphorus and potassium. We can divide the waste products we need into two categories: carbonaceous wastes, which are

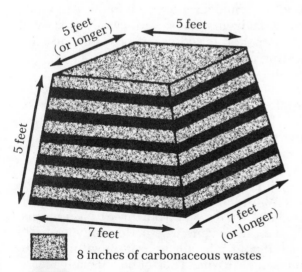

4-1 Garden compost piles work well, if you have the right ratio of carbonaceous to nitrogenous wastes.

 8 inches of carbonaceous wastes

4 inches of nitrogenous wastes

rich in carbon, and nitrogenous wastes, which are rich in nitrogen. As a rule of thumb, carbonaceous wastes are lightweight, dry, and tan to dark brown in color. Nitrogenous wastes are usually heavy, wet, and green or dark brown in color. ·

But how do you provide these wastes to your compost in the best proportion? You build your pile with alternating 8-inch layers of carbonaceous wastes and 4-inch layers of nitrogenous wastes. The pile size and shape should be just like the one described for leaves. (Look at Figure 4-1 if you are in doubt.) The right carbon-to-nitrogen ratio is easy to achieve. To find out which compost materials are carbonaceous or nitrogenous and which ones are good sources of phosphorus and potassium, look back at Table 1 (on page 88).

The nice part about using this method is that you can build your pile as ingredients become available. If you have all your materials present at once and have a good eye for proportions, you can just mix everything together without using layers.

Again, as when you make leaf compost, I recommend you don't use soil, limestone, or commercial additives with your compost. Work with moist materials, and keep your pile moist at all times. Anytime the material feels drier than a damp, wrung-out sponge, you must add water.

You may be wondering whether or not to shred the compost materials. Shredding the compost materials will definitely speed up the composting process. With a bit of shredding you could have compost in three months. You can shred the compost material by making several passes over small piles with your rotary power mower. Not shredding will probably add a few months' time onto the composting process.

You may also be wondering if turning the compost pile is helpful to the process. Turning aerates the pile and speeds up the composting process; but as I mentioned earlier, it's hard work. If you do decide to turn the compost, turn it six weeks after you build the compost pile and then again four weeks later, both times using a spading fork.

Again, as with leaf compost, there will be a heating phase followed by a cooling off period. Once the compost has cooled down, it's safe to use in your garden. The cooling period will usually vary from three to six months, depending upon the materials you utilized and whether or not you shredded and/or turned the compost. If your pile fails to heat up within two to four weeks of building it, something is wrong. Lack of heat usually means there's not enough nitrogen in the pile. To correct it, add a nitrogen source such as blood meal or green grass clippings to the pile.

If you notice an ammonialike odor emanating from the compost pile, your problem is excess nitrogen. You can either add some more carbonaceous wastes or ignore the smell, which will stop. Next time you make compost don't use as many nitrogen sources, because the ammonia odor is actually nitrogen wasted into the air. You may also have a rotten egg odor. This stink comes from lack of air in the compost pile, which can result from prolonged, heavy rains filling the air spaces in the pile. Turning the pile should correct the problem. You can also wait until the pile dries out a bit, and the smell will disappear.

Here are a few more troubleshooting suggestions for your compost pile. Don't add any meat scraps to your pile; if you must add some, bury them deeply so animals can't smell them. If you carelessly place meat scraps near the pile, don't be surprised if you find dogs, cats, raccoons, opossoms, mice, or even rats on the scene.

Do you have a cat? If so, I urge you *not* to add the used contents of your cat's litter tray to either your garden or compost pile. Cat wastes may harbor the microorganism that causes toxoplasmosis, a disease that attacks the central nervous system. While unpleasant for adults, this disease is really bad news for infants. Although it is rare, it's wise not to encourage the microorganisms. And under no circumstances should a pregnant woman handle the litter tray or areas contaminated by solid wastes from cats.

I would be equally cautious about sewage sludge. Two dangers concern me. First, many sewage sludges contain heavy metals, such as lead or cadmium, which result from industrial discharges. Heavy metals are especially hazardous if they enter the food chain and if you eat them with your garden vegetables. The only way to check sludges for these metals is with sophisticated analytical tests done in laboratories. The test results can be evaluated to determine whether or not the heavy metal content poses a hazard. Ignorance in this case is not bliss, but danger. Second, some sludges, if improperly treated, can harbor pathogens that infect humans; again it's not wise to take any chances with their existence in your compost.

One last thought concerns the use of diseased plant material in the compost pile. If you compost correctly, you will destroy disease-causing organisms. Essentially, you must expose all the compost to temperatures over 131°F for roughly three weeks. This means it's important to attain good heating through using the correct pile size, proper balance of carbon- and nitrogen-containing materials, sufficient moisture, and enough air. You must frequently mix all outside materials inward to expose all materials to the proper temperature. Remember, the outer edges of a compost pile are cooler than the middle. A far simpler solution to the problem of destroying disease-causing organisms exists: Don't put diseased plant remains in the compost pile.

Special Helpers

As you recall, I mentioned a few starter solutions and seedling helpers in Chapter 2. These fertilizers are easy to prepare from the previously discussed materials. Do take a few minutes to make them, because the results are well worth the effort. Your transplants and seedlings will take off rapidly and leave untreated plants behind in the dust.

Rapid Starter Solution

First let's consider the rapid starter solution. This water-soluble, organic fertilizer is a combination of fish emulsion and seaweed extract. It's the same formula I suggested earlier for foliar feeding. The hormones (mostly auxins) in the seaweed extract may promote rapid rooting of the newly placed transplant. At the same time, the nitrogen, phosphorus, potassium, and trace elements contributed from both the seaweed and the fish emulsion nourish the transplant quickly, giving it a head start. With seeds, the reputed antibiotic properties of the seaweed keep soilborne disease at bay, thus greatly improving the percentage of successful germination. The hormones may even help to speed up the germination process; then the combined nutrients quickly accelerate your seedlings into the passing lane for growth.

Here's a hint for those of you who have separate bottles of fish emulsion and seaweed extract on hand. You can make your own combination by mixing both together to make a half-and-half solution. For example, you can mix ½ cup (4 ounces) of each together to produce 8 ounces of a product containing 3 percent nitrogen, 2 percent phosphorus, and 2 percent potassium. For purposes of dilution, here's what to do. If I use the commercially available combined fish emulsion and seaweed extract, I follow the label directions. If you mix your own formula, I suggest a dilution rate of 3 tablespoons of the mix to 1 gallon of water. This dilution rate is excellent for transplants, seeds, seedlings, and even foliar feeding.

Organic Oasis Mixture

Remember the organic oases used earlier around transplants? These oases provide a rich nutrient bank and aeration chimney for the transplant roots. The organic matter helps aerate the soil and improve drainage while keeping the nutrients trapped until the plant roots arrive. The preparation of the oasis mixture is relatively easy; I simply mix some organic nutrients with my compost. Into each standard pail of compost, I add, first of all,

2 tablespoons of either blood meal, leather meal, or hoof/horn meal for nitrogen. If these materials (see Appendix) are not available, I suggest you use manure or coffee grounds and double the amount. Next I add 2 tablespoons of steamed bone meal for phosphorus and a similar amount of unleached wood ashes for potash. If the ashes are wet, they have lost some potash, so double the amount. Mix all the ingredients thoroughly into the compost and use the enriched compost to make organic oases for your transplants.

Seedling Helper

The outdoor seedling helper is similar to the organic oasis mixture. The difference is that the seedling helper goes underneath seeds in furrows, while the organic oases go alongside transplants. Also, because seedlings are young and have small root systems, they do not benefit as much from nutrients as do robust transplants. Indeed, too many nutrients may harm the seedlings. Therefore, I prepare the seedling helper by cutting the organic oasis material in half with either garden soil, potting soil, or even sand. Incidentally, you can use the worm castings described earlier in this chapter in place of the seedling helper. An 8-quart bag of worm castings should be enough for an average garden.

Soil Helper

The last special mixture I will mention is optional and not really a fertilizer or soil conditioner. It is really a soil helper, and you will find it useful if your soil is not in good condition. For instance, if the soil covering your seeds becomes concrete hard after a rain, you definitely need the soil helper's help. To make it simply mix some of your garden's soil or sand with vermiculite in a 1-1 ratio and cover your seeds with it. Of course, the long-term answer to the problem of concrete-hard soil is to improve your soil, which we'll talk about next.

Step-by-Step Soil Improvement

Now that you have the basics for feeding your no-dig garden, you must learn how to put these basics to work to create a well-nourished no-dig garden. Let me be your guide as we improve your no-dig garden step by step.

The first thing we need is that soil test report you now have, assuming you followed my advice in the previous chapter. If you didn't, you still have a chance to obtain one, but don't delay. The soil analysis report is going to be your road map, your guide to a better soil. What does the report say about pH? Ideally, we want a pH value near 6.5 for a vegetable or flower garden; and depending on your geographic location and garden history, you will either be close or way off. If you have an established garden and have adjusted the pH in the past, you should be reasonably close and need only minor corrections. A new garden east of the Mississippi River will probably be somewhat acidic, that is, below pH 6.2. (Remember, a pH of 7.0 is neutral.) Those of you in the Northeast will probably find a new garden has a pH of about 5.5. Gardeners in the Southwest will probably find an alkaline soil with a pH over 7.0.

Whatever the pH, your report will offer the necessary remedy for your situation. If your soil is too acidic, the correction will be to add so many pounds of ground limestone (preferably dolomitic form) per so many square feet. Don't add more; in this case, more is not better, it's worse. Alkaline soils will require correction with powdered sulfur.

If your no-dig garden is new, first mow it; then follow up the mowing with either a one-time tilling or covering the mowed vegetation with either black plastic or an organic mulch. If you use the rotary tiller method, sprinkle the limestone (or sulphur) over the tilled soil and water it in. If you are going to mulch instead, broadcast the limestone and water it into the mowed vegetation. Don't apply the mulch just yet, because you may need to add some fertilizer first. If so, wait at least a few days after watering in the limestone, then add the necessary fertilizer (as explained below). Now you can put the mulch over the mowed vegetation. Make sure you read about the easy way to apply black plastic in the next chapter, if it is your choice of mulch.

If you have an established garden with no mulch, just broadcast the limestone and water it in. If you have an all-year-round organic mulch, sprinkle the limestone over the surface of the mulch and thoroughly water the limestone into the soil until little or no white shows. Is a leftover black plastic mulch still in place from last year? You'll have to remove it to apply and water the limestone.

Nutrient Levels

Next look over the soil report's levels of the various nutrients, such as nitrogen, phosphorus, potassium, and calcium, that your soil contains. Some nutrient levels may be low. If so, the report will suggest the addition of some fertilizer to correct the deficiency. If calcium and/or magnesium are low, you took care of the problem when you added dolomitic limestone to correct the pH. Chances are your trace element concentrations are fine; but if they are not, the report will indicate the correct trace elements and how much to add.

Generally the report will call for the addition of some chemical fertil-izer such as 5-10-5 or 10-10-10. More progressive agricultural soil laborato-ries may suggest organic alternatives, if you indicated you were an organic gardener. If they don't you still have alternatives to consider. You can buy a bag of assorted rock dusts and various other organic materials all mixed and ready to use. Fertrell is one manufacturer of these organic fertilizers, and you may find them at your garden center or from sources listed in the Appendix.

Don't allow the label detailing nutrients to mislead you. The blends appear low, because current laws allow for listing only the quickly available, soluble nutrients. The label does not list the slowly released amounts, so these organic fertilizers are actually much higher in total nutrients than the label suggests. These fertilizers will feed your garden long after rain washes away the chemical fertilizers.

If your report calls for 10-10-10 (N-P-K ratio) chemical fertilizer, you should consider using an organic blend with an analysis of 2-1-2. As I said, the nutrient label looks low at 2-1-2, but the total of the quickly and slowly released nutrients makes this fertilizer equivalent to a chemical 12-12-12. Perhaps the soil report calls for 5-10-5; then you might want an organic fertilizer with a rating of 1-1-1. This formulation is roughly equivalent to 5-10-10. If your soil is very low in nutrients according to the soil report (most listed as L for low), you might want to consider an organic formula rated at 4-2-4. There are also organic fertilizer mixes available which supply higher concentraions of N, P, or K.

You can broadcast these fertilizers over your soil, organic mulch, or mowed vegetation a few days after you add the limestone, or you can wait longer if you wish. You can also scratch the fertilizer into the soil with a light raking or water it through the mulch. If possible, add the fertilizers one week prior to planting your garden so that your plants do not lose out on the quickly available part of your organic fertilizer. If you fertilized over mowed vegetation, don't delay on installing the black plastic mulch; other-wise you'll be feeding the mowed vegetation instead of your crops.

How much fertilizer should you add? Go by the rates suggested by your soil report. For example, if your report calls for 10 pounds of chemical 10-10-10 per 1,000 feet, add the same amount of the organic fertilizer that is equivalent to chemical 10-10-10. Do the same for 5-10-10, but use your organic substitute. For really poor soils, use the 4-2-4 fertilizer at 20 pounds per 1,000 square feet, or 2 pounds for every 100 square feet. Should you not have a soil report but wish to fertilize anyway, I suggest you use an organic blend with a rating of 1-1-1 or 2-1-2 at a rate of 10 pounds for every

1,000 square feet. For purposes of convenient measuring, you can figure that each pint of fertilizer weighs roughly 1 pound.

If you want to use rock dusts and various organic meals in an unmixed form, feel free to do so. For example, if your soil is nitrogen deficient, you can correct this problem by using leather meal (10-10-0), blood meal (15-3-0), or cottonseed meal (6-2-1). My suggestion is to use leather meal, because it has a good balance of both quickly and slowly available nitrogen. You can apply it at rates up to 8 pounds (roughly 8 pints) per 1,000 square feet. I suggest you use blood meal or cottonseed meal at rates of about two-thirds those suggested for leather meal. The Appendix lists sources for these products.

Also, you can correct phosphorus deficiencies with rock phosphate, colloidal phosphate, or bone meal. My suggestion is to use either rock or colloidal phosphate, because bone meal releases phosphate too slowly. You can safely apply rock or colloidal phosphate at rates of 10 pounds for every 1,000 square feet.

Sources of potassium for the garden include greensand and granite meal. Moderate application rates are about 100 pounds per 1,000 square feet. Or you can apply about 25 pounds of wood ashes that have never been wet for each 1,000 square feet of garden.

A word of caution is in order. Do not routinely apply any of the recommended fertilizers each year. If you do, you'll probably end up with nutrient imbalances. You should get a soil test each year and use the report's suggestions for a fertilizing guideline. In reality, the no-dig gardening method and the use of seaweed and fish extracts for foliar feeding during your garden season will help maintain soil fertility. You may only need to add other fertilizers every two or three years. A few minutes invested in an annual soil sample can save you a lot of fertilizer bucks and reward you with the best-ever garden.

Organic Matter Content

Up to now I haven't said anything about organic matter. Your soil report may or may not indicate a problem with organic matter content. If you are starting a new garden in a sodded area or if you are an organic gardener using good practices, you probably have enough organic matter in your soil. Enough organic matter now means you'll have enough later on, too. Remember, as I explained in Chapter 1, no-dig methods conserve organic matter. Essentially, the remains of the plants' root systems plus the addition of small amounts of organic matter with the bulb planter or furrower will maintain good levels of organic matter.

But suppose the soil test indicates a need for organic matter. How do we quickly get to the point where our garden requires only low maintenance? We can achieve this by one of two methods. The first method involves a one-time tilling of organic matter, while the second is a no-dig application of gradually decreasing amounts of organic matter over a few years. The choice is yours, but let's look at the two methods to help you make your decision. Remember, once you reach a decent level, you can very easily maintain organic matter with our no-dig procedures.

First, if you decide to improve the soil in a hurry, the best bet is to rent a rotary tiller or hire someone who owns one to till the organic matter, using either manure, compost, or leaves. If you use fresh manure, you should till it under at least four weeks prior to planting or during the fall. If you use fresh, moist horse or cow manure, apply anywhere from 25 to roughly 50 pounds per 100 square feet. Equivalent units include ½ to 1 cubic yard per 1,000 square feet or about 1 to 2 bushels for each 100 square feet. If you use poultry, rabbit, or hog manure, cut the rates in half. If you use manure to raise your organic matter levels, don't forget that it contains nitrogen, phosphorus, and potassium; therefore, you'll need less fertilizer, possibly as little as one-third or less the normal amount. To be sure of your needs, have a soil test done after manuring, preferably close to planting time.

You can also apply compost in place of manure. Using finished compost, apply it between 1 to 3 inches deep on your soil. Like manure, you should till it under at least four weeks prior to planting activities or in the fall.

A last alternative for providing organic matter is to use leaves in the fall. This plan does not allow for any other time frame because the supply is on hand only in the fall and the leaves will need a while to decompose in the soil. While leaves decompose, they use nitrogen. Plants grown while leaves are decomposing lose out in the nitrogen race and become nitrogen deficient. In addition, some chemicals produced during leaf decomposition don't seem to agree with plants. I suggest you use 2 to 3 inches of leaves sprinkled with some nitrogen-containing fertilizer at the rate of 3 to 5 pounds (3 to 5 pints) for every 100 square feet. Next rototill the leaves into the soil using your rented tiller or hired tiller operator. Make sure you get a soil test in the spring prior to planting your garden; you must know and correct the nutrient status of your soil after leaf decomposition, if needed.

The second approach to achieving and maintaining organic levels involves the no-dig addition of organic matter only in the vicinity of the

4-2 *For a soil low in organic matter, make four holes with the bulb planter as shown, on a 12-inch square. Fill them with organic matter. This procedure is only for the rapid build-up of organic matter. Don't confuse it with the organic oases around transplants. Organic oases differ in that their intent is to maintain organic matter, once the proper level is established. They are usually used one to a transplant, contain organic matter* mixed *with nutrients, and are placed 4 inches away from the transplant.*

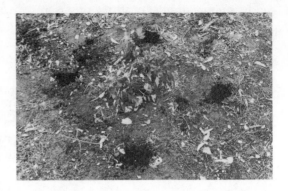

plants. This approach gives you efficient returns on your organic matter investment and helps to reduce amounts of needed material and lessen work. In fact, the no-dig garden procedure will eventually produce an even distribution of organic matter that you can maintain quite easily. But for now, let's worry about the immediate shortfall of organic matter.

My choice of organic matter for a quick build-up with no-dig methods is either garden or leaf compost, aged and well-rotted manure, or commercial dehydrated manure. If you don't have or can't purchase any of these materials, you can substitute peat moss. I do not suggest fresh manure or leaves, since these materials will be applied at planting time. Fresh manure or leaves are not compatible with seedlings and transplants.

The plan is very simple. For transplants make four holes with the bulb planter at the corners of an imaginary 12-inch square that has the transplant at its center (Figure 4-2). Fill each of these holes with one of the suggested organic amendments. If you use the peat moss, sprinkle a few teaspoons of limestone over it to correct for acidity. Essentially, you are creating four organic oases for each transplant.

For seeds, make a furrow between every two rows, or a couple in each band or bed, using the furrower (Figure 4-3) at a depth of around 3 or 4 inches. Now fill the furrow with one of the organic materials. Again, if you use peat moss, cover it with a light dusting of limestone. You can leave the soil ridges or rake the soil over the organic material. If you live in a somewhat dry area, leave the ridges; they will help capture water in the bottom of the furrow. If too much rain is your problem, rake the area level. Essentially, you have created fertile furrows or organic matter strips for your row, band, or bed crops.

4-3 Surround your seed furrows (center) with furrows or no-dig holes of organic matter, if you need to build up organic matter in a hurry.

How long do you proceed with this treatment? It depends on your soil type and the deficiency of the beginning amount of organic matter. The only way to know for sure if you have corrected the problem is to check your next year's soil report. If the report calls for more organic matter, repeat the procedure. If it doesn't, commence with the minimal mainte-nance procedure for organic matter, which I will cover later in the chapter. Incidentally, leave the root systems of all plants in the soil, except those of root crops. The root systems left in the soil will contribute additional organic matter to the soil. Based on my experience, the build-up of organic matter will most likely take only a few years. Remember, no-dig gardening conserves organic matter and does not burn up organic matter as does the conventional digging of soil.

No-Dig Soil Maintenance

Now let's turn to methods of no-dig maintenance of nutrients and organic matter during the garden season. What we have accomplished so far is to give our seedlings and transplants a great start in the garden race.

Like any runner, your plants will need some water and nutrients along the way, if the fast pace is to last.

Foliar Feeding

My mainstay for nutrient supply is foliar feeding with the combined fish emulsion and seaweed extract described earlier (Figure 4-4). If the mixture is a commercial one, follow the directions for dilution on the bottle. Should your mixture be the homemade combination of fish emulsion and seaweed extract described earlier, dilute at the rate of 3 tablespoons to 1 gallon.

To get the most from your foliar feeding, you must get as much of your nutrient supply into the leaves as possible, which depends largely on your spraying technique. Obviously, if the spray does not stay on the leaves, it's not likely to get into the plant; therefore, you need a product to help the watery solution stick to the leaves without harming the leaves. I solve the problem by adding four to five drops of liquid soap to each gallon of fish and seaweed solution. You can use mild liquids intended for washing either dishes or clothes.

Several other factors also determine how much spray enters the plant. Generally, the smaller the spray droplets, the better. Remember, many of the droplets will enter through pores (stomata) in the leaf, which are quite small; therefore, the best sprayers for applying foliar feeds are those with adjustable nozzles. Make sure you adjust the nozzle for the finest mistlike or foglike spray. Also make sure you spray both the top and bottom of the leaves because both sides of a leaf have stomata. In fact, the bottom often has more stomata than the top. By spraying both leaf sides, you assure a larger number of entry points for the spray.

4-4 The easiest way to foliar feed your garden is with a hand-pressurized sprayer.

Spraying time is also important. Stomata start opening with the first light in the morning, the best time to spray, and gradually close in the afternoon. They also close rapidly when the plant is wilting, when it is very hot, and when it is windy. Of course, on windy days, much of what you spray on the plant will blow off target anyway, so you would be wasting the spray in terms of foliar nutrition. Also, never knowingly spray prior to rain. The spray must remain on the plant for at least several hours if the feeding is to be effective.

The spraying schedule is yet another important consideration. You don't want to overfeed the plant and be wasteful. On the other hand, a nutrient starvation diet isn't good for the plant either. I usually start my first foliar feeding of transplants two weeks after setting them out. By then the plant has used up the rapid starter solution. With seedlings, I usually wait to foliar feed until three weeks after germination, because by then the nutrients added with the seeds are running low. From that point on throughout the gardening season, I repeat my foliar feeding every three weeks. This schedule need not be exact. If three weeks arrives along with rain, postpone the feeding until the next day. Should it rain within twelve hours after a leaf feeding, repeat the spraying because the rain will have reduced its effectiveness. If you're worrying because you'll be on vacation during the next due feeding, don't. You can either have someone else spray the plants or let it go and do it when you return.

Before I move on to the next topic, I'd like to mention a few things that I have experienced in regard to foliar feeding. When you spray, make sure you spray to the point of foliage runoff. Once the leaves start to drip, stop spraying. I find the best results occur when I observe this pattern of spraying. Don't worry about the drops; they will soak into the soil and will help to improve the soil and nourish the plant through the root system.

Another of my observations concerns insect control. Before I began spraying with the seaweed and fish product, I had trouble with spider mites on my transplants grown in greenhouses; however, I found little trouble in my garden when I started spraying with the seaweed and fish product. While the evidence is circumstantial, I like to think the seaweed and fish extract not only feeds the plant but helps in pest control as well.

I also mentioned earlier that evidence exists that seaweed extracts give plants some degree of frost protection. I noticed that when the first fall frost hit, many plants seemed to survive much better after I had started spraying than in prespray years. I happened to mention this observation to a gardening friend who also uses seaweed extracts, and he had noticed the same result. There just might be truth to the claim, then, that spraying with seaweed extracts provides frost protection.

Supplemental Fertilizer Treatments

Is this seaweed extract and fish emulsion treatment my entire fertilization approach during the gardening season? Not quite; I do use a bit of extra fertilizer along the way. About once a month I side-dress my vegetables and flowers with a little solid fertilizer. You can use one of the all-purpose organic fertilizers I mentioned earlier (several are listed in the Appendix). Of course, you can also use any of the homemade organic solid fertilizers I covered earlier in this chapter.

I usually start the first treatment about two weeks after the initial foliar feeding. I sprinkle a light dusting either around individual, large plants or alongside rows with smaller plants (Figure 4-5). For example, I'll sprinkle a circle around tomatoes or eggplants that runs just under the point where the foliage ends (the drip line). I'll run a band alongside a row of bean plants or onions. Remember, these bands or circles need only be a dusting and about 1 or 2 inches wide. I then gently water the plant to aid the entry of the fertilizer into the soil.

How do we do this feeding when a mulch covers the garden? If you have a loose organic mulch instead of plain soil, you can still make your circles or bands. Then use your watering can or a light spray from the hose to soak or wash the fertilizer through the mulch so it contacts the soil. If you are using black plastic or paper mulch, with your dibble poke two or three holes around each plant or one hole every 12 inches along the row. Make the holes about 2 inches deep, and fill them with fertilizer. Now gently water these areas to help wash the fertilizer into the soil.

Milk Bottle Dispenser for a Special Boost

There are a few steps you might enjoy trying if you're looking for that super-productive, special plant, such as the pumpkin that will win a contest or the tomato plants for which you have little room and from which you expect the most. If so, try my hints for these special plants. If you are using transplants for tomatoes, peppers, eggplants, squash, melons, or pumpkins, prepare a slightly deeper no-dig hole with the bulb planter. Now sprinkle in a couple of tablespoons of a mixed-nutrient organic fertilizer. Cover it over with about 1 inch of soil, or even better, with compost. Now treat your transplant as described in Chapter 2. Remember to use the organic rapid starter solution before putting the transplant in the hole.

Next, take an empty, rinsed, 1-gallon plastic milk bottle and carefully punch several holes from top to bottom on each side with an ice pick, screwdriver, or other pointed object. Now cut out the bottom, and leave the cap on to prevent quick downward drainage and to afford slow, sideward drainage. Dig a hole large enough to accept the milk bottle near your special plant or plants. If you have only one plant, place it within 12 to 18

A

B

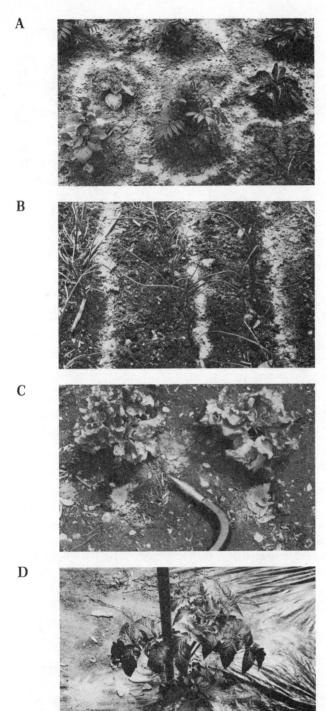

C

D

4-5 *You can sidedress an intensively planted garden with a circular pattern (A) or fertilize rows with a straight-line approach (B). You can also fill with organic fertilizer a dibble hole made next to the plant directly in soil (C), or punched through black plastic mulch (D).*

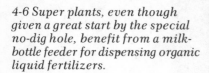

4-6 Super plants, even though given a great start by the special no-dig hole, benefit from a milk-bottle feeder for dispensing organic liquid fertilizers.

inches of the plant. If you have a group of plants, such as three or four tomatoes, squash, melons, or pumpkins, situate the hole in the middle of the group. Place your bottle, cut bottom up, into the hole so that the top edge is level with the soil line. Push soil around the sides to fill in any gaps. Now you have an in-soil liquid fertilizer dispenser!

About every three weeks, fill the dispenser with your favorite liquid organic fertilizer (Figure 4-6). I prefer the diluted seaweed and fish extract, but you can use manure, compost "tea," or any other water-soluble fertilizer. The fertilizer solution will slowly seep out of the side holes of the bottle and diffuse into the soil and, hence, the root zone of your prize plant. Your reward will be the best-ever, most productive plants. If you're looking for size over productivity, remove most of the young pumpkins so as to channel nutrients into one or two.

Maintaining the Levels of Organic Matter

Now we'll take a look at maintaining levels of organic matter in your no-dig garden. Of course, I am assuming your soil already has a reasonable amount of organic matter either from the virtue of your being an organic gardener or from your starting a new garden in a sodded area. As you may recall, losses of organic matter are much more rapid in dug or tilled soil than in no-dig soils. Digging favors the bringing of organic matter to the surface where oxygen-loving surface microorganisms hungrily consume it. No-dig methods keep it protected down below, where the surface dwellers can't get at it. This feature makes maintenance quite easy, since we're not losing much organic matter.

Let's start first with the tranpslants. Your home-grown or commercial transplants are usually grown in growing media quite rich in organic matter. If you purchase transplants, be sure they are in organic-rich media and not in normal soil. Each time you put in a no-dig transplant, you will create an organic-rich island in your soil. By placing transplants in slightly different locations each year, you will gradually increase and spread the organic matter throughout your growing area. When your garden transplants die at the end of the season, do not pull them up, but simply cut the plants off at soil level. The roots left behind will help to increase the organic matter in the soil zone surrounding your original organic-rich no-dig hole. In a few years organic matter will spread throughout your garden soil. Of course you will recycle the removed tops of your finished plants into your compost pile.

A similar situation exists for plants raised directly from seeds outdoors. As you may recall, each furrow received a bottom filling of seedling helper, which you prepared from compost. You might also have used commercial worm castings, as indicated earlier. Being very rich in organic matter, these materials help raise your level of soil organic matter, just as with the transplants. By slightly shifting rows each year, you will spread organic matter. Again, leave the root systems of any finished plants raised directly from seed, except root crops, in the soil. Recycle the tops in the compost pile. Between transplants and seedlings, you'll have an organic-rich soil in no time!

Organic Oases

One other step for maintaining organic levels in your garden remains. Use the bulb planter to make the, by now, familiar organic oases. This step was actually part of the planting method we covered in Chapter 3 and was mentioned more recently in this chapter for accelerated introduction of organic matter. However, one very big difference exists now. This time we will be maintaining, not increasing, the level of organic matter in the soil. Place just one no-dig hole (not four) by each transplant, about 4 inches away. You will be making holes at 12-inch intervals about 4 inches to the right or left of each row. Fill each hole, not with straight organic matter as described for rapid build-up, but instead with the nutrient-fortified compost recommended as the organic oasis mixture in the section Special Helpers.

There you have it. The maintenance of organic matter is really so simple that it's part of the no-dig planting process. You get the easy planting with no-dig methods and the simultaneous maintenance of organic matter, whether you mulch or not. If you are using loose, organic mulch, just push it aside for the maintenance steps. Plastic or paper mulch poses no problem either, since the bulb planter cuts right through it.

Mulches remind me that we should get to the heart of the no-weed concept next. Let's consider the alternatives to weeding, especially those that don't tire our muscles or make our backs ache.

Chapter 5
Mulching to Save Weeding and Watering

The decision of whether or not to mulch is one that you must consider carefully. Although some disadvantages may arise with mulches, the no-weed return you get is quite inviting. The decision of whether or not to mulch really boils down to determining if the joy of not weeding outweighs the disadvantages of mulching. If less work is your primary motivating factor, mulches are the answer.

If you have been involved in gardening for a long time, you probably associate the late Ruth Stout with the popularization of the all-year-round mulching system. Certainly her approach—covering the garden with a deep layer of straw all year long—will give you a no-weed garden. But there are other ways to use mulches that can bring you no-weed status as well. There is even an alternative to mulches that will give you an *almost* weed-free garden. Let's consider your choices.

The Advantages and Disadvantages of Mulch

First, let's examine the case for and against mulches in the garden courtroom. I'm sure none of you will dispute the smothering effect mulches have upon weeds. It's simply amazing how a few inches of organic mulch or a few thousandths of an inch of plastic or paper mulch beat those weeds. Equally important in my mind is the ability of mulches to conserve soil moisture by acting as a barrier against the evaporation of water by sun and

106

wind. The need for water is less; therefore, the need for work and time associated with watering activity is less as well. In some areas, the limited availability of water may provide even more incentive for mulching than does weed control.

Mulches also have a moderating effect upon soil temperatures. During the hot days of July and August, soil temperatures rise dramatically as the sun beats down on the garden. At night the temperature of the soil plunges. This seesaw of temperature extremes is not beneficial to your garden. Sure, plants will continue to grow; but many will not do their best. A mulch acts as an insulating barrier, slowing both daytime heating and nighttime cooling. Consequently, the soil temperature remains more nearly constant, thus favoring good plant growth.

If you are concerned about aesthetics or dislike rotten vegetables, mulches will please you with another advantage. A mulch in the flower garden prevents mud from splashing onto the flowers during rain or watering. Your flowers are always clean and beautiful. In the same way, mulches keep your vegetables clean and dry and prevent their contact with soil. Chances of ending up with a moldy tomato, mildewed squash, or rotten melon are quite low.

An organic mulch or plastic/paper mulch offers several advantages as you can see. But the organic mulch offers yet another benefit. Decomposition of the organic mulch releases various nutrients, which rain or applied water slowly washes into the soil. The decaying organic matter at the soil surface also helps gradually to improve the soil structure and the entry or infiltration of water into the soil. Thus, you won't lose much soil to water runoff or wind.

Counteracting the Disadvantages of Mulching

If these advantages of mulching sound great, they are. Still, in all fairness, there are some possible disadvantages to mulching. However, keep in mind that you can work around any of these problems. First, mulches retain soil moisture, a decided advantage during most of the garden season. But there is one time when too much soil moisture can be a problem. During germination too much moisture, especially where organic mulches are in place, can encourage the attack of seedlings by damping-off disease. The solution here is really quite simple. You can delay the application of an organic mulch until the seedlings have become well established. At this point the seedlings will have outgrown their susceptibility to damping-off. Delayed mulching with organic materials can also solve temperature problems that early mulching causes, as we'll see later. If you want to maintain a permanent organic mulch (à la Ruth Stout), then just push the mulch aside around newly planted seeds and young seedlings.

A second way to solve the excess moisture problem is to use black plastic mulch. While it conserves moisture, its nonorganic nature tends not to encourage damping-off. As you will recall, in Chapter 3 we discussed methods for direct planting of seeds or transplants through plastic. The technique for planting seeds left a small, plastic-free zone on either side of the seedlings. Such a zone reduces moisture levels around the seedlings, thus preventing problems in regard to excessive moisture with seeds or seedlings.

Another disadvantage to using mulches is that while they moderate temperature extremes in the summer (or winter), they can slow soil warming in the spring. The problem is especially noticeable during cold, wet springs and with heavy clay soils. Both of these conditions result in cool soil temperatures. The mulch, since it's an insulator, tends to slow the rate at which the soil is warmed by the sun and rising air temperatures. Even the rapid warming that usually occurs in sandy soils can be slowed by a mulch cover.

So how do we resolve the problem of soil warmth? The old rule of "don't apply a mulch until the tomatoes blossom" does have some basis in fact. When tomatoes blossom, soil temperatures have exceeded 55°F. Seeds of some warm-season crops, such as beans or squash, require soil temperatures over 55°F in order to germinate properly. Other warm-season crops, like tomatoes or eggplants, won't set flowers at lower temperatures. You can be sure it's safe to mulch the garden when the tomatoes are in bloom. If the mulch causes the soil to warm more slowly, at this point, it will not be harmful. So, delaying the application of mulch will solve the soil-warming problem. If you have a permanent organic mulch on your garden, you can scrape it aside in areas where you will be planting early seeds or transplants to create localized warm spots where they will do the most good for your seedlings or transplants. To keep down weeds, you can apply your mulch early every place except in the immediate area you will be planting.

There's another way to solve the soil-warming problem besides delaying use of organic mulches. Organic mulches retard the warming of spring soil, but plastic mulches do not. In fact, plastic mulches, depending on their color, actually increase soil temperatures to varying degrees. Black plastic mulches in particular absorb heat and help raise soil temperatures a few degrees. You can easily see this effect with melon plants grown side by side on soil versus black plastic. The melons mulched with black plastic yield earlier because of quicker soil warming.

Clear plastic mulch acts like a greenhouse and also raises soil temperatures several degrees or more. Using clear plastic as a mulch, you can pick sweet corn two to three weeks earlier than normal. One problem you might have with clear plastics, though, is that they pass light. The greenhouse effect that warms the soil also encourages a fine crop of weeds. Still, there are ways to utilize clear plastic to get the benefits but not the weeds. We'll cover these techniques in Chapter 7.

Some people think the application of mulches is troublesome. I think that probably the main objection arises with mulches that are thin, such as plastic or paper. These mulches *can* be difficult to apply but need not be. Later on I'll show you an easy way to apply plastic mulches that will be secure against the blowing wind.

One particular problem with mulches in the Northeast has been a recent string of cool, wet springs. Mulches coupled with cool, wet spring weather can spell bad news for germinating seeds and tender young transplants. Still, solutions are possible. You can wait out the weather and apply your mulch when warmer, drier weather arrives. If you have an all-year-round organic mulch, push it away from seeds, seedlings, and transplants until they have become well established.

If you are using an all-season black plastic mulch, don't worry about the coolness. The black plastic mulch helps to increase soil temperature by a few degrees. Instead you can worry about having too much rain, because the mulch slows evaporation. You may end up with a very soggy, wet soil that is low in air, a condition that favors rotting of seedling and transplant roots. To resolve this problem, you must take a few simple steps that will allow the plastic mulch to repel, not retain, water. Instead of immediately punching holes in the plastic to allow water to penetrate to plant roots, delay the punching of holes until the warmer, drier weather appears. This will make the plastic waterproof and will keep the soil drier.

You can take a second step to alleviate excess moisture at the planting sites. If you put in a transplant with the bulb planter, use part of the removed soil plug to create a small, sloping hill around the transplant. This slope helps to reduce drainage into the soil because it channels the water onto the plastic. Later, you can punch holes in the plastic to allow plenty of water to enter for the plants.

Follow the same procedure with seed rows that you cut through the plastic. After you slit the plastic and make your furrow with the furrower, leave the soil in place to hold down the edges of the plastic, as described in Chapter 3. Then build up the seedling row with extra soil or seedling helper to make it higher. Now you will have to recut your furrow, but cut it just deeply enough for the right seed depth. The position of the seeds should be about 1 or 2 inches above the nearby plastic surface. Essentially you will have a mini-raised bed adapted to row size. You will get great drainage, thus alleviating the problem of excessive spring rains.

How to Lay Down Organic Mulches

Mulches are inexpensive and are probably one of the best garden investments you can make. I'm sure I need to say little about the familiar organic mulches, since many of you probably already use them. I'll just go over the basics and save most of my words to talk about the easy way to apply plastic and paper mulches. Remember to apply organic mulches 2 to 4 inches deep.

Many choices exist for those who use organic mulches. Availability, cost, and personal preference will undoubtedly influence your choice. Bark mulches, for example, can be costly unless you live near a tree service company or have a friend in the business. They do have a tendency to rob soil nitrogen from crops because of their high carbon-to-nitrogen ratio (see the section on compost in Chapter 4 for an explanation of ratio). Remember to apply nitrogen fertilizer before you put down your bark mulch. If you have composted the bark mulch, you won't need to use fertilizer, because the carbon-to-nitrogen ratio will change for the better during composting. Keep the bark mulch from direct contact with plants to avoid disease problems. And keep the bark mulch away from nearby wooden structures, too, because termites in the bark might munch their way on to bigger and better things.

Another organic mulch, peat moss, is expensive and, unlike bark, it's hard to find a cheap supply under any conditions. I personally dislike peat moss as a mulch because it requires a lot of water and time to get wet. Another disadvantage to peat moss is that it dries out during droughts. Once it's dry, it becomes hard and difficult to wet, and rain will run off it. It's best to keep peat moss as an organic amendment for growing mixtures and soils where you plan to plant acid-loving shrubs.

Another group of organic mulches that is desirable but not always available includes buckwheat hulls, cocoa shells, ground corncobs, ground tobacco stems, licorice roots, peanut shells, spent hops, and crushed sugarcane. Buckwheat hulls can cake and prevent water getting to the soil, so keep them to a 2-inch depth. Watch how you water, since forceful watering will scatter buckwheat hulls. Cocoa shells have some fertilizer value, but keep them to 2 inches in depth. Their potash content is high, so deeper layers of cocoa shells might harm sensitive plants. Ground corncobs, unless you object to their light color, are relatively problem free. Don't use ground tobacco stems to mulch tomatoes, peppers, eggplants, dahlias, or any other plants susceptible to tobacco mosaic virus. Tobacco stem mulches may carry this virus. Licorice roots resist blowing and floating, making them ideal candidates for sloping gardens. Several qualities of peanut shells, such as their significant nitrogen content, ease of application, durability, and attractive appearance, make the shells an excellent mulch. Spent hops have some nutrient value and resist blowing. If you use spent hops, make sure they are aged; if they are not, they may heat up, have an unpleasant odor, and even damage your plants.

Some mulches, in particular sawdust and wood chips, are relatively common and inexpensive, but have some decided drawbacks. Unless you have composted them (and few people do), these woody materials have a very high carbon-to-nitrogen ratio. The high ratio means that these woody materials will steal soil nitrogen away from your plants as they decompose. Therefore, you have to put down some nitrogen fertilizer before you put on the mulch, if you want to avoid depleting your soil. This need for fertilizer translates into extra cost and work. I think sawdust and wood chips are more trouble than they're worth.

Now on to the last category, the organic mulches that I used to use: compost, grass clippings, leaves, straw or hay, and salt-marsh hay.

Compost makes an excellent mulch, especially if your soil is low in organic matter. It's one of the few mulches that also acts as a slow-release fertilizer. Water from your hose or from rain leaches out nutrients that microbial activity has converted to soluble forms. By the end of the growing season, the lower part of the compost mulch has become part of the upper soil profile. In a few years, you can have an organic-rich soil without any work.

The problem I faced was that my compost supply was never enough for all the uses I had in mind. You might say that I couldn't get enough of a good thing. I now reserve my compost for making the special fertilizer blends for seedlings and transplants, as I described in the previous chapter. Using it in this way also improves the organic conditions around the plants. The plus is that you need far less compost to take care of the area around or under plants than you need for a mulch covering a much larger area. Still, if you make lots of compost, you might consider using the excess as a mulch.

If you don't recycle your grass clippings to your lawn with a mulching mower, you can use the clippings as a garden mulch. Just don't apply your layer of grass clippings all at once. Do it gradually, because a thick layer of green clippings will heat up and form a dense mat as decay sets in. The mat will restrict the flow of air and water to the soil. Apply the clippings in thin layers and allow each layer to dry and turn brown before you add the next layer. One bonus to using grass clippings is that they contain nitrogen, which will eventually leach into your soil, thus slowly fertilizing your plants.

You can also use leaves as a mulch, as long as you're aware of a couple of problems that exist. First, leaves are available mostly in the fall. Such timing is great for winter mulches or the leaf compost pile but is bad for a summer mulch. To get around this problem, you can pile the leaves until next year; but if you're going to go through that trouble, why not prepare a leaf compost pile as I described in Chapter 4? The other problem is that leaves can mat into a soggy mess. To overcome the matting problem, you can mix the leaves with fluffy materials, such as hay or straw, or you can shred the leaves. Leaves do release some nutrients during decomposition as a mulch; but I still prefer using them to make leaf compost.

Straw, hay, and salt-marsh hay all make reasonable mulches. You can sometimes buy spoiled hay at a modest price. The going rate for unspoiled hay or salt-marsh hay argues against their use as mulches; however, if you find a bargain, these mulches are great for vegetables and the year-round mulching system popularized by Ruth Stout. As flower garden mulches, though, both kinds of hay are unattractive. Also, these mulches often carry large numbers of weed seeds. If you remove these mulches or turn them under, look out: You'll probably find that you have a luxurious crop of mixed weeds. Slugs seem to love these mulches, too.

Now I think you are ready for my mulching system that gives you a no-weed garden. As they once said in the movie *The Graduate*, "The future is in plastics."

The No-Weed Mulching System

My solution to weeds is the use of a semipermanent to permanent mulch. In one sense my system may remind you of Ruth Stout's approach; however, a big difference between my way and her way concerns the choice of mulching materials. I recommend using black plastic rather than organic mulch. If you object to black plastic as unnatural, I do have another option for you. A horticultural brown, heavy paper mulch is now available in rolls like black plastic. A second difference between Ruth Stout's method and my own is that my mulch can be either permanent or removable; Ruth Stout's mulch is permanent. A last point is the ease with which you can adapt black plastic to no-dig methods.

Tools and Materials

One tool is a must for the easy installation of black plastic mulch: the already familiar furrower. The second tool, the garden straightline, is optional. Can you make a straight line by eye? If not, you'll need the garden straightline. With these tools you can easily cover your garden with plastic or paper mulch in less than one morning or afternoon. Only a few hours of work will save several times as many hours of weeding and watering. You will be able to secure the plastic mulch tightly with my method. I know, since my mulches have survived heavy winds and even a tropical storm.

Make sure you have your mulch on hand before you begin. Black polyethylene plastic mulches come in folded sheets or rolls and are available in different thicknesses and several widths. Go for the roll, because rolled plastic is much easier to apply with my method and is the most economical buy. I recommend the 4-foot-wide roll. It's wide enough to cover a lot of ground and it cuts down on the number of widths you need to apply. The 4-foot widths are not awkward to work with and they are compatible with the newest cloches, slitted row covers, and polyester fiber sheets. We'll discuss the great relationship that black plastic has with cloches later. Peat paper mulches also come in rolls, except I have found only 3-foot widths to date.

What thickness of plastic is best for a mulch? The answer depends on how long you want to reuse the plastic mulch. I personally like the 1.5-mil thickness (0.0015 inch). When purchased in a 1,000-foot roll, it's the most economical to use. I have also reused it a second growing season. A 1,000-by-4-foot roll of 1.5-mil black plastic costs about $40.

A recent innovation is a 1.25-mil-thick embossed black plastic. This thickness appears to be as strong as my 1.5-mil plastic, but it's less expensive. I have not had this newer plastic long enough to test it for reuse. A 2,000-by-4-foot roll of this embossed plastic costs roughly $60. This size has enough square footage to redo a 1,000-square-foot garden annually for eight years.

The annual cost of weed control and water conservation on a 1,000-square-foot garden comes to $7.50 and $10 for the thinner and thicker plastics, respectively. What a bargain! For pennies a day, you can be free of the backbreaking labor of weeding, save money on water, and have a lot more free time for yourself. You can share a roll with a gardening friend to cut costs. Rolls in 50-foot lengths are available, should you prefer smaller amounts. While more costly, even these smaller rolls are a bargain!

How to Lay Down Plastic Mulches

Now let me tell you about my easy, quick, yet secure way to apply plastic mulch. First take your furrower and make one furrow roughly 3 inches deep to whatever length your plastic mulch requires. For the purpose of example, we'll assume we are working with a 4-foot-wide roll of plastic. I suggest you use the straightline helper described in Chapter 1 to

A

5-1 The first step in laying plastic mulch is to prepare one of the long side trenches with the furrower and straightline (A). Next make one of the shorter trenches at right angles. Complete the remaining trenches. Don't forget to put down the limestone, if you need it (B).

B

assure that the furrow is straight (Figure 5-1). Next, make a second furrow at a right angle to either end of the first furrow. Don't make the furrow 4 feet wide; instead make it about 40 inches wide, so that you can cover a 4-inch overhang on each side when you refill the furrow trench. Next, make the long furrow for the other side of the plastic mulch. Then complete the last short side. You now have a rectangular furrow outline ready to receive the plastic mulch.

Unroll a short bit of the roll of plastic and place about 4 inches in the short furrow. Cover the plastic over with the soil on the outward ridge of the furrow (Figure 5-2). Now use your foot to press the soil down, thus locking in the short edge of the plastic mulch. Unroll the entire length of the plastic, and cut across the width at the other end. Don't forget to leave about 4 inches extra for burial. Work your way around the furrow line, pushing soil over the plastic edge with your hand. Using your other hand, pull gently to put a little tension on the plastic as you fill over the edges. If you leave the plastic too loose, blowing wind will make the plastic flap. Firm the soil around the edges of the plastic with your foot. You now have a securely installed sheet of black plastic. You can apply a paper mulch in the same manner (Figure 5-3).

A

B

5-2 Place the leading edge of the roll of black plastic in one of the short end trenches (A). Use your foot or hoe to kick in the soil so that the trench is filled and the edge of the plastic is covered. Firmly press the soil with your foot to lock in the plastic. Unroll the plastic and continue to fill and press at the sides until all sides are done (B).

One timesaving trick is to use your foot to mark off the 40-inch width of the bed. My shoe is roughly 11 inches long, so I know the correct width is just about equal to three and three-quarters times my shoe. To measure the width I just pace off with my shoes end-to-end and insert the straightline peg at the appropriate place.

Using this simple technique, you can mulch a good-sized garden in less than one morning or afternoon. Just make sure you don't do it on a windy day. The small amount of time you spend mulching is really a great investment when you consider the time and effort you will save throughout the season on weeding and watering. Yields will be a little earlier, because of the warming effect of the black plastic, and they'll be a little greater, too, because of less competition from weeds.

I'd like to offer a few helpful observations at this time. In some spots you will probably have to deal with the edge of the lawn. Here the furrower

5-3 *A paper peat mulch is shown on the left and black plastic on the right.*

doesn't work as well. You throw the soil on the grass and have trouble recovering it. If you move the furrower inward to avoid the problem, you leave an area for grass invasion. I do, however, have an answer to the problem. Sink a square-bladed shovel or lawn edger about 4 inches into the soil. Pull the shovel or edger toward yourself, making a cut that slants outward (Figure 5-4). Continue cutting the slit to the correct length. Tuck the plastic edge into the slit. Now press the soil down and inward on an angle with your foot from the slanted side of the slit. The pressure will close the slit, sealing the plastic firmly into the soil. Incidentally, you can use this technique of applying black plastic mulch in place of the furrow method, if you like it better. An alternative to making furrows or slits in the soil is to pin the black plastic to the soil with U-pins cut from wire coat hangers.

How close together you can place the black plastic with these techniques depends on what you want. With the furrower method, the shortest spacing between separate sheets is about 1 foot. Spacing that is any closer will not lock the sheets in place as securely. With the shovel-slit method, you can butt sheets to within a few inches of each other. I like to leave about 12 to 15 inches between sheets. These uncovered areas make great pathways and help me to stay off the plastic, thus preventing soil compaction. Remember, the plastic sheets are roughly 4 feet across, a width that makes them highly adaptable to either band or bed planting. The uncovered areas between sheets afford you a nice, comfortable reach to the middle of the planting area. If these uncovered areas tend to become weedy, just mulch them with some hay or grass clippings or any organic mulch of your choice. Scrap wood boards can also be used to provide both weed control and a durable, narrow pathway.

I'll bet you have a lot of questions concerning the application of black plastic mulch. Let me try to answer them. First, you way be wondering

A

B

5-4 With grassy areas or for another installation method, use a square-edge shovel to make a slit instead of a furrow trench (A). Use your heel to close the slit after the plastic is pushed in with a flat, thin piece of wood. The completed mulch will smother the turf and leave rich organic matter in its place. A short-term installation method is to pin the plastic to the soil with U-pins made from coat hangers (B). Two U-pins can be made by cutting the coat hanger in half and cutting off the hook.

when to apply the mulch. If you are applying plastic mulch for the first time, the earlier you apply it, the better. Remember, black plastic mulch has a slight heating effect, so you won't have to worry about slowing down soil warming if the mulch is laid early. The early application gets the jump on weeds and also fits more comfortably into your gardening schedule. It's difficult to plant and mulch at the same time. If you are late with your mulch and the weeds beat you to the garden, mow them down with a lawn mower if they are more than 2 or 3 inches high. Then just lay your mulch over the stubble. I usually apply my mulch sometime after I've planted my peas but before I plant onions and potatoes. Weeds have usually sprouted by then, but they are small and easy to cover. If you are replacing some black plastic mulch from a previous year, your main concern should be to replace it before the time you'll be ready to set your plants or seeds through it.

A reminder is in order here. If your soil requires pH adjustment with either limestone or sulfur, put the limestone or sulfur down before you apply your plastic mulch. If your soil is badly in need of nutrients, you can apply your organic fertilizers about one week after the pH adjustment and then lay your black plastic. Otherwise don't worry about fertilizing before mulching. You can apply fertilizer directly in the no-dig hole or furrow, or by using foliar spray, as I discussed in Chapter 4. You can also add organic matter to your soil after the mulch is down. This procedure, too, was covered in the preceding chapter.

What to Mulch with Black Plastic

Another concern you may have is what you can mulch with black plastic. My experience is that you can mulch just about anything. A few exceptions in my garden include peas, carrots, onions, and corn. I do use black plastic mulch with the majority of my vegetables and flowers. It also works extremely well with strawberries. Paper mulch works equally well. Frankly, my experience with plastic mulch has been excellent. Don't hesitate to try out plastic mulches, even with crops that the experts say don't work with mulches. For example, mulches and peppers supposedly do not mix well, but I planted my best pepper crop to date through black plastic. I think the early warming of the soil by the plastic got my peppers off and running well.

Keep another factor in mind. Although we'll cover it later in Chapter 7, it deserves a brief and certainly appropriate mention here. Black plastic has a moderate warming effect upon soil temperature. A cloche also warms the soil but it especially raises the air temperature around plants. When you combine a cloche over black plastic, you essentially create a time change in the protected area, that is, you advance your cloched area roughly two or three weeks into the future. You improve frost protection and provide an earlier harvest by using the cloche/black plastic combination rather than a cloche alone.

How Long to Use Black Plastic

Before I leave the subject of black plastic mulch, let's discuss one last point. How long do you leave the plastic mulch in your garden? That's a good question with several possible answers. One answer is to leave the mulch in place until it deteriorates. How long that turns out to be depends on the mulch's thickness and weather conditions. In my garden, the time works out to be about two years, after which I have to replace the plastic.

Another answer is to move the plastic annually at the end of the gardening season. If you opt for this approach, don't remove the plastic at the end of the gardening season. Instead, let it sit through the winter, and remove it early the following spring as you replace it. This precaution prevents any ungerminated weed seeds from sprouting in the fall or early spring. I've seen chickweed pop up after I removed a mulch, spreading quickly in the fall and growing like wildfire in the early spring. Purslane also takes off in the early spring. Of course you can just cover over the weeds with the plastic, but life is a little easier without having them underfoot. It will surprise you how a plastic-covered chickweed 2 feet from your no-dig hole will suddenly peek out through the hole a few weeks later.

The last option concerning when to remove the plastic involves using the black plastic for a few years and then not using it ever again. I discovered this option as a consequence of crop rotation. Each year I rotate my vegetables to keep diseases at bay. Since I grew a few vegetables without using plastic mulch, every few years I exposed small parts of my garden. These exposed sections remained weed free. My first reaction was to attribute the complete effect to solarization. But after thinking about it, I realized this was not likely. Solarization occurs when soil is covered with clear plastic, which functions like a solar collector or greenhouse. The soil temperature under clear plastic rises much higher than soil temperature under black plastic. You do get soil heating of $10°$ to $15°F$ with black plastic, which is enough to kill more sensitive weed seeds over several weeks. But many of the tougher seeds survive.

After some more thought, I found the rest of the answer. It's in the combination of no-dig soil practices and the black plastic. Let me explain. You may recall from Chapter 1 that one advantage of using no-dig techniques is that you grow far fewer weeds as compared to a garden that's dug the conventional way. When soil is dug, deeply buried weed seeds are brought to the surface. These new soldiers replace the weeds that you fought so vigorously against the preceding year. With no-dig handling of the soil, you have only those weed seeds near the surface with which to contend. If you wipe out those surface pests, you win the war, because there will be no replacements. At this point the black plastic mulch takes over.

When I first used the black plastic in my no-dig garden, I recalled that a large number of weeds had germinated early in the spring. The weed seedlings were quite small, though, and I just covered them over with the plastic mulch. The black plastic quickly killed the weeds, and deeper weed

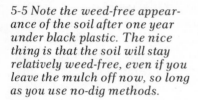

5-5 Note the weed-free appearance of the soil after one year under black plastic. The nice thing is that the soil will stay relatively weed-free, even if you leave the mulch off now, so long as you use no-dig methods.

seed reinforcements could not replace them because I was using no-dig practices. When I uncovered the soil (Figure 5-5), it was free of weeds and it stayed relatively weed-free during the growing season. The only weeds to appear after I removed the mulch were those that had a late spring germination time. These few weeds had not yet germinated when I applied the plastic, so they survived in the dormant stage. A few swipes with the action hoe wiped out the last survivors.

The conclusion is that you can go from a seriously weedy garden to a weed-free garden through the temporary use of black plastic mulch. The only other requirement is to use no-dig methods to keep the deeper weed seeds underground where they can't cause you any harm. Therefore, you may opt to stop using black plastic mulch after a year or two, if weed control was your only interest. Before you stop, though, you might want to reread the earlier part of this chapter. Other advantages of mulches, such as water conservation, might offer enough reasons for continuing the use of plastic or other mulches.

No-Weed Gardening without Mulch

I suppose a few of you readers are saying that you can get from a weedy to a no-weed garden without using a mulch as long as you use no-dig practices. Well, you are correct; but you will have to weed your garden for one growing season. The surface weed seeds will germinate in the early spring; and because the mulch won't be there to smother them, you will have to wipe them out yourself. Show no mercy, as any survivors that go to seed will haunt you next year. Keep the nearby area weed free through mowing so that no wind-blown seeds get into your garden. If you are thorough, you will have no weeds the next year, because the no-dig approach to gardening will prevent the exposure of deeply buried weed seeds the following year. If you use this approach, though, you will have more work than with a mulch.

If you want to garden without mulching there are three key points that, if followed, will make your one-year weed battle easier. The key points are to use the most efficient weed remover, to adopt a ruthless weeding schedule (for weeds, not yourself), and to cultivate the soil to the right depth.

Efficient Weed Removal

The best weeder, as I explained in Chapter 1, is the action or oscillating hoe. Its flow-through design, swivel action, and double-sided cutting edge make it easy to cut weeds just below the soil surface on both the push and pull strokes. For early weeding close to crops, I find the Easi-Weeder (Figure 5-6) an ideal complement to the action hoe. Its small, sharp, U-shaped blade makes short work of young weeds without hurting the roots of the nearby vegetables or flowers. While these tools are great and easy to use, you can, with proper scheduling, cut the need for them to the bare minimum. The old adage, "The early bird gets the worm," could be paraphrased to say "The early weeder wins the race." Weeds are off and running early in the garden season. They may look small next to your peas or lettuce, but their root systems are large and are already stealing nutrients so that your crop yield will be less. Knock off those early weed seedlings on those cool spring days. The action hoe will make short work of them and save you a lot of work later.

A second trick for controlling weeds is to weed around seeds or transplants about four or five days after the initial sowing or planting. Although you may not see any weed seedlings, the weed seeds have germinated, because of the soil activity and watering associated with planting crops. Even no-dig transplanting holes and furrows disturb the soil a little. And, of course, soil disturbance is far worse with conventional digging. A quick swipe with your action hoe about 1 or 2 inches below the soil surface nips those weeds right in the bud, so to speak. Recently germinated weeds

5-6 The Easi-Weeder is great for intensive plantings and for getting in close.

are very susceptible to the breakage and drying activity that cultivation with a hoe causes.

Weeding Schedule

Your next step to making your one-year weed battle easier is to settle into a regular weeding schedule. Spend ten or fifteen minutes once a week knocking off any weeds that have the audacity in invade your garden. If you plan on taking more than two weeks of summer vacation, hire a substitute weeder. Better yet, if you take extended summer variations away from home, you should mulch your garden.

Don't ever let any weed go to seed. Some of those prolific weeds can set seed, if conditions are good, within six weeks of sprouting. Remember in Chapter 1 when we discussed the huge numbers of seeds an individual weed plant could set? If you miss a few, you could find your entire garden reseeded with obnoxious bums like purslane. This seed-setting profligacy accounts for the observation by Mark Kane, in the June 1982 issue of *Organic Gardening*, that removing 90 percent of the weeds from a garden plot reduced the subsequent yield of weed seeds by only 10 percent. The survivors had less competition and their already prolific seed production exploded by several factors.

This seed factor accounts for the next bit of advice. Weed your garden until frost, even if the crops have stopped bearing. Weeds won't stop setting seeds early; they go on until the freeze. If you stop weeding, you will have undone all your work for the next year. The surviving weeds will sow their seeds of destruction, which even no-dig methods won't stop, because these new seeds will be on the soil surface. If you weed late in the season, you'll also knock out any weeds that winter over as small plants. Remember, the weed war is grim. Show no quarter and leave no survivors.

Cultivation Depth

The third key point in making your weed battle easier involves the cultivation depth. You want to rid your garden of all those weeds, but you don't want to bring deeper seeds upward where they can germinate. How deep is this zone of weed seed activation? My own experience says that you shouldn't cultivate deeper than 2 inches under any circumstances. I get good results when I cultivate anywhere from 1 to 2 inches deep with my action hoe. This depth of cultivation wipes out the weeds from near-surface seeds but doesn't bring up the more deeply buried ones. Interestingly, gardener Peter Young experimented with depth of cultivation and weed control, and he arrived at the same conclusion, which he reported in the May 1983 issue of *Organic Gardening*.

If you keep these three key points in mind, you can wipe out your weeds in one season; but you must be diligent or you will have wasted all of your time and effort. The early weeding will knock out the majority of the weeds, and the later weeding will be quick and easy.

As an aside, I'd also like to mention that bed, broad row, or band planting will also cut weed work. Wherever you practice intensive gardening, the closer spacing of crops produces shade underneath them and increased competition for soil nutrients. This combined one-two punch knocks the wind right out of the weeds, making their start-up much harder.

The only downfall to the no-weed gardening approach without the use of mulch concerns perennial weeds. If weeds such as quack grass or thistle have overrun your garden, you won't be able to get away without using mulch. In a case like this, discretion is the better part of valor; go for the mulch and save yourself a lot of trouble.

Solarization

Before we leave the subject of weeds, let's look at one last idea for weed control, a process known as solarization. Essentially, this technique uses the sun and the greenhouse effect to bake weed seeds and disease organisms to death. If you have severe disease problems caused by soil organisms, you might want to give serious consideration to this technique. Solarization causes soil pasteurization, resulting in the destruction of not only weed seeds but also fungi, nematodes, and insect eggs. The one disadvantage to solarization is that you need six weeks of dependable sunshine and relatively warm temperatures outdoors for it to be effective. Unfortunately this occurs right in the middle of your garden season. Also, you can't plant the area you want to solarize. If you solarize your entire garden at once, the only crops you'll harvest that year will be the quick-maturing ones.

An alternative to solarizing your whole garden is to do part of your garden, say about one-half each year. This two-year method will leave half the area free for crops, and you can plant the solarized area to short-term crops later. If you have a lot of space, you might solarize a new area for a garden while planting your present garden.

If you decide to solarize, you will need sturdy, clear plastic. A thickness of 1 mil is acceptable if you intend to solarize one area and then discard the plastic. If you want to reuse the plastic a second year for your other half of the garden, you will need a thickness of at least 3 mils. Your best bet is to buy the large sheets of clear polyethylene plastic sold as paint dropcloths.

I suggest that you start the solarization process about the time you would normally set out tomato plants or plant other warm-season crops such as corn or squash. At that time sunshine levels are reasonable for providing solarization. You must apply clear plastic sheets to a relatively clean and wet garden soil. Give the area an action hoe treatment and water it well, unless the soil is wet from a recent rain. Apply the plastic with the same techniques discussed earlier for applying black plastic mulch. Don't use black plastic, though, because it doesn't allow the sun's rays to pass through it and heat the soil, as does the clear plastic.

If you are solarizing a new garden area, you will have to change your procedure somewhat. Such an area will be either grassy or quite weedy, so it is best to apply black plastic first to kill the unwanted vegetation. Three or four weeks of keeping the area covered with black plastic should do the trick. When you remove the black plastic, wet the soil and then install the clear plastic sheet.

The clear plastic traps solar energy and heats the soil. The temperature at the soil surface heats up to roughly 140°F, essentially a respectable compost pile temperature. Soil temperature can approach 100°F. The heated, wet soil will produce a lot of condensation on the clear plastic, a sign that the solarization process is working well. These high temperatures over six weeks will pasteurize the soil.

After six weeks have gone by, you can take off the plastic. If you don't plan on planting any crops in the solarized area, you can leave the plastic in place for a few weeks more. The six-week time frame assumes that you have relatively sunny conditions. If there are several days of rain or heavy cloudiness, the soil will need a few more weeks of treatment. While the solarization process will destroy most of the weed seeds, a few species may germinate and grow under the plastic. If any of these tough survivors make it through solarization, give them the boot with your action hoe before you plant anything.

Watering Systems

Watering the garden is a very personal thing with gardeners. Most gardeners seem to respond to watering in one of two ways (with some variation, of course). One type of gardener enjoys watering his pride and joy. You will see him or her standing there with a hose that has the nozzle finely tuned to mimic a gentle spring rain. This gardener sees watering time as an opportunity to commune with the garden and enjoy the solitude. The watering event is often a chance to relax at the end of a busy day, usually shortly after the dinner hour. This gardener does not begrudge the time needed to water the garden. At the other extreme we see the gardener who is ever so busy. He or she has little time to spare and wants to get the watering done quickly. He needs to do many other things in the garden and elsewhere, and he welcomes anything he can do to save time.

I shall not judge which is the better position, because each position has its virtues. In point of fact, I am both gardeners. Which one you see depends on how I feel and what I have to do that particular day when I water the garden.

Can we find better ways for both kinds of gardeners to water? We certainly can. Do you want to cut the time involved in watering your garden? Is water scarce in your area or perhaps even rationed? Would you like to use less water and still do the job right? If the answer to any of these questions is yes, I have some helpful suggestions for you.

First, don't forget the lesson we learned from mulches. All mulches slow the evaporation of water from the surface of the soil. How much water you save depends on the type of mulch you use, prevailing weather conditions, and soil qualities. I can only comment on what I have observed in my own garden. When I switched from an unmulched garden and conventional tillage to a no-dig, no-weed garden mulched with black plastic, my watering needs seemed to be cut in half.

Beyond the manual hose approach are two ways to automate gardening watering chores. One of these is drip irrigation. Perhaps you wish to keep things simple or feel such systems too costly for your moderate-size garden. If so, you might be interested in an inexpensive compromise method. We'll look at that approach first and come back to the drip system.

The compromise approach worked well for me over several years. I used it when I was too busy for the hose, but not yet convinced of the need for a drip system. In this method, you still use your hose, but you attach a sprinkler on the end. I prefer the adjustable, oscillating kinds over the revolving ones, since the water pattern on the former is easier to adjust to the typical garden shape. You turn on the water and leave until the garden is well watered (the first time you'll need to stay and see how long it takes). If you're forgetful, you could use the simple inexpensive mechanical timer described later for the drip systems.

You can start out at the beginning of the garden season at ground level, so to speak, and place the sprinkler right on the ground. As the garden grows, you will need to add height for the sprinkler water to reach all the plants. If the sprinkler is lower than the plants, the nearby plants will intercept the water, preventing it from going to plants further removed.

The best answer is a step ladder. When your garden gets too large for ground level watering, just put the sprinkler on top of the step ladder for real "overhead" watering.

Eventually I decided to install an automatic watering system in my garden. You don't have to put in an automatic watering system to have a no-dig garden. It's a luxury, but one that can make your life a lot easier. I'm sure you have seen or heard much about trickle or drip irrigation. This technique slowly and sparingly supplies water directly to the root zones of plants. Originally this form of irrigation was developed for agricultural use in arid regions. Farmers who used the system realized water savings of 15 to 30 percent over conventional irrigation and noted savings in energy usage as well. The last few years have seen the appearance of drip irrigation kits in the home garden market.

At first I was resistant to using the irrigation system. I felt that it might be too complicated, not adaptable, and an unneeded expense. Besides, my hose worked just fine. Slowly I relented. I decided to try this new garden technology when the Burpee people released a complete kit suitable for an 800-square-foot garden. They also had a kit for a 400-square-foot area. The large kit cost $30, and the components were of high-tech polymers. These components could weather extreme heat and cold, and you could leave them in place all year long. I figured the kit would last several years, making my annual cost about the price of a movie. It wasn't a bad deal. The clincher was the claim for water right on target with little waste. If I figured in a modest savings on water, all arguments on cost went out the window.

Then I thought of how complicated assembly might be. Of course the advertisement said something about its being simple. I read on with some suspicion. Supposedly you could easily put the parts together and you didn't need any special skills or tools. You only needed an hour or so to install the system. I kept hearing my inner voice saying, "You can do it. Think of no more winding and unwinding of long hoses, no more unnoticed hoses accidentally choking a plant as they move, and no more lugging of sprinklers."

Then I considered the system's adaptability to different crops. Drip systems are fine for larger, widely spaced crops like tomatoes and squash, but I didn't think drip lines and zillions of water emitters would work out too well for closely spaced crops planted in bands or beds, such as onions, peas, carrots, or lettuce. Burpee had the answer. You could use emitters and sprinklers in any pattern you wanted. They even had a parts list so you could change patterns or enlarge the system to meet future needs.

My resistance was crumbling rapidly. The lure of an inexpensive mechanical water timer that you could set and forget just about did it. The final lure of promises that the system prevents water runoff and erosion helped me decide. I knew this fact was true from my reading on drip systems. I finally went for it.

It was the best thing I ever did, and I am totally satisfied with my system. Burpee doesn't have the only kit on the market; others might be just as good or even better. You can find a list of suppliers of garden drip irrigation systems in the Appendix. Check out prices, adaptability, and the opinions of other users, then make your own choice.

I thought I might miss those peaceful moments with the hose, but I don't. Instead I have peace of mind on the hectic days when I have to water my garden. When I do have extra time, I pull out my lawn chair. I set it near the garden and relax with a drink of coffee, tea, or even wine sometimes. I can still commune with my garden, just like I used to when I stood holding the hose.

Now let me walk you through the automatic drip and sprinkler system. Once you learn the hows and whys of the system's functions, you'll be able to make a better choice. I'll start with the business end, the point where water comes out.

Sprinklers and Drippers

Sprinklers come in different patterns: full circle, half circle, and quarter circle. Better sprinklers also allow for adjustment of the water reach, or radius of the spray. My system permits a radius adjustment from 0 to 10 feet. At their maximum flow rate (full radius), my sprinklers put out 24 gallons of water per hour. By combining the various sprinkler patterns and adjusting the radius of each, you can get uniform coverage of just about any shape or area of garden. I find sprinklers that integrate into drip systems ideal for raised or unraised beds, wide rows, bands, or any form of intensive planting.

Drippers are good for watering an area about 1 foot in diameter (Figure 5-7). Each dripper emits about 1 gallon of water per hour. Twenty-four drippers consume 24 gallons of water and cover an area of roughly 20 square feet. This figure is for actual watering area. The total amount of garden space covered could be larger; for example, one dripper at each of 24 tomato plants spaced 2 feet apart would supply water to a total area of 140 square feet.

At first glance this figure might lead you to believe the sprinkler is more economical. A full-circle sprinkler with a 10-foot radius and a full output of 24 gallons per hour would cover 314 square feet. This coverage is a bit more than twice the area covered by the dripper in the previous

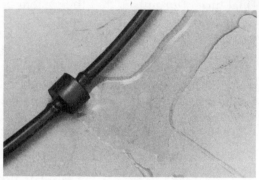

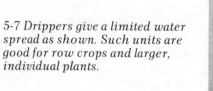

5-7 Drippers give a limited water spread as shown. Such units are good for row crops and larger, individual plants.

example. However, the sprinkler doesn't apply the water exactly where the plants need it. Drippers, on the other hand, apply water right at the root zone with essentially no waste. Sprinklers apply water everywhere. Some water goes to the root zone, but much goes on the foliage or on soil beyond the root zone. Beyond this waste are the losses that occur from wind and evaporation. When you figure in these water losses allowed by sprinklers, you get more efficient water use with drippers than with sprinklers.

So why do I bother to talk about these mini-spinklers that are compatible with drip systems? I like them for several reasons and mix them in with drippers. Each has its best use, in my mind. Drippers are fine for large plants at generous spacing; however, for smaller plants at closer spacings in wide rows, bands, or beds, you have more dripper installation work. You install many drippers versus one sprinkler. Secondly, you lose some flexibility with drippers. You carefully lay out the pattern of drippers for plants the first year. This pattern is somewhat fixed, but your garden isn't. When you rotate plants the next year to minimize diseases, you will create a new pattern. Now you must adapt the new planting arrangement to the existing dripper pattern or redo the dripper layout. This is not so with a sprinkler! You can rearrange plant patterns in a sprinkler-coverage area to your heart's content.

I made my choices with those facts in mind. I use sprinklers for closely spaced crops, especially intensive plantings of carrots, lettuce, onions, peas, peppers, and strawberries. I use drippers with larger, more generously spaced crops, such as melons, raspberries, squash, or tomatoes. I also use drippers with crops that can easily develop fungal diseases from water on foliage, such as beans.

Tubing and Hoses for Watering Systems

Now that we have completed the business end of the watering system, let's work backward to the water source. First, we need something to elevate the sprinklers. If they are too low and plants nearby are high, the spray distribution will be incomplete because of something engineers call impact interference. Plastic stakes that snap into the sprinkler heads are available to resolve the elevation problem. You can use joiners to combine two or more stakes if you need additional height on the sprinkler. Short spikes are also available to elevate drippers or the thin tubing leading into either sprinklers or drippers.

Sprinklers and drippers attach to thin plastic tubing, usually having an inner diameter of about 0.175 inch. Sprinklers generally have a fitting that threads into the tubing; drippers, on the other hand, usually have a flared fitting or barb over which the tubing is force-fitted. Drippers are of two types: flow-through and end-of-line. Flow-through drippers have a fitting at each end so that you can install them along a run of tubing wherever you wish. End-of-line drippers have only one fitting, and you place them at the end of the tubing run.

If you follow the thin tubing, you will find it joins with a larger hose having an internal diameter of 0.49 inch. We usually refer to the larger plastic tubing as a feeder hose. This hose connects directly into your water supply. The thin tubing connects into the feeder hose with an adapter. One end of the adapter is generally threaded, and the other end is flared or barbed. The threaded end twists into the thin tubing, and the flared or barbed end is force-fitted into a hole in the feeder hose that you have punched into the hose with a hole puncher. I have seen two forms of hole punchers. One looks like a pair of pliers. You squeeze the handles together and a cutter forms a hole in the feeder hose. The second type looks like an oversized clothespin with a knob on it. You put the feeder hose in this plastic clothespin. With one hand you hold the clothespin closed; with the other hand you turn the plastic knob. A cutter attached to the knob perforates the feeder hose.

5-8 *On one end of the feed hose is a flushing end cap. This cap can be unscrewed to flush the feed tube of accumulated debris.*

If you follow the feeder hose, you find that one end terminates, usually with a flushing end cap (Figure 5-8). You can force-fit the flushing end cap onto the end of the feeder hose. By unscrewing the cap and running water, you can flush out the feeder hose. Flush the feeder hose several times during the growing season, because foreign matter will accumulate inside the hose, possibly leading to clogging of sprinkler heads and drippers.

At the other end of the feeder hose is a force-fitted faucet/hose adapter. You can screw this adapter directly to a faucet or a garden hose. I prefer the latter, since my faucet is not close to the garden. A feeder hose in a permanent resting place across my lawn would interfere with the running feet of my children and the easy movement of my lawn mower. I can connect the hose as the need arises, keeping the lawn free of interference. The faucet/hose adapter has either a plastic or metal cone-shaped mesh filter. This filter helps trap foreign material in your water supply and protects the small openings on sprinklers and drippers. Check it a few times during the season. When the mesh clogs, clean it out with an old toothbrush.

Watering System Accessories

These items that I just mentioned are the basics of a garden drip/sprinkler watering system. You can buy several accessories for the system that can make life even easier. Timers that connect between the faucet and your watering system are available. The simplest type of timer is mechanical, like a wind-up alarm clock. You can set it at half-hour intervals for up to two hours. At roughly $12, it's not a bad deal. You can get along without one, as long as you have a memory that reminds you to turn off the water at a reasonable time.

On the other extreme in modern technology is a programmable, battery-operated timer. You can set this kind of timer to come on at changeable intervals and days. If you plan on taking an extended vacation, you may want to invest in this timer. It costs around $60.

Another accessory you may want to buy is a pressure-regulator valve. This valve fits between your faucet and watering system and maintains a constant pressure in your water system. Variations in your water pressure will then have no effect on your flow rates. While low pressures can reduce and even stop water flow at the farthest points, I'm not sure whether pressures could go high enough to damage the sprinklers and drippers. At $4 or $5, it seems to be a reasonable investment.

Several other minor accessories can be useful as well. Suppose you wish to relocate a sprinkler or a line with installed drippers; for example, you arranged your garden somewhat differently than the year before or perhaps you harvested one group of vegetables earlier and you wish to move the watering device to a fall crop. This change leaves you with a hole in the feeder hose. No problem; just block it with a plastic maintenance plug.

Suppose you need to change the shape of your layout to accommodate a new garden section, or perhaps your garden is not square or rectangular in shape. Several items can solve these problems. If you need more straight-run feeder hose, a straight coupler allows you to join two or more feeder hoses. If you have a new garden section or an irregularly shaped garden, you may want to buy T-couplers and T-connectors for the feeder hoses and tubing, respectively.

What if you want to run two watering systems from one faucet? Suppose you have an L-shaped garden and wish to have two separate watering systems. You can attach a Siamese valve at the faucet. This accessory has two hose acceptors with a shut-off valve for each side. Distributors that can accommodate several watering systems are also available. These attach to your faucet and provide the means to have separate systems for landscape borders, flower beds, vegetable gardens, fruit trees, or even container plants.

An added convenience is that you can also buy some drip components preassembled. I have seen drip lines in various lengths with installed drippers, usually at 2-foot intervals. You can connect these lines to each other by removing the end-of-line dripper and joining the second drip line to the first via the last flow-through dripper. You can also insert a T-connector for shape changes.

I'd like to say a few last words about these watering systems. You can install these systems on the soil's or mulch's surface or even under the mulch. I like to install the system where I can see it so that if a leak or break appears, I can quickly repair it.

Second, I suggest you run your feeder hoses along garden edges and pathways, because it will be easier for you to make pattern changes and add mulch this way. You can easily remove or reposition thin tubing with sprinklers or drippers temporarily. It is more difficult to move feeder hoses around.

How long and how often should you run your watering system? First, if you experience any week-long period in your unmulched garden without at least an inch of rain, turn on your watering system. To determine the amount of rain you have had, use a rain gauge or a tin can or rely upon the data from your local weather service office. A visual clue to the need for watering is the drying of the first 1 to 2 inches of garden soil. If you have an organic mulch, move it aside to check the surface dryness. With black plastic mulch, peek in at one of your no-dig holes as you stretch the plastic aside a little. Mulched gardens can easily go two to three weeks longer without water than unmulched gardens.

The length of time to run your watering system depends a lot upon soil texture. My experience suggests that the average garden soil needs somewhere between 1 to 2 inches of water. You want to wet the soil to a depth of several inches, but the soil may be wet from 3 inches down; therefore, you need less water than with a soil dry down to 5 inches. My suggestion is to apply 1 inch of water during periods of moderate dryness. You can place an empty tuna can in the sprinkler area and under a dripper. Note the amount of time it takes to collect 1 inch of water in the can and use it as your standard. During very dry or drought periods, double the application time so that you apply 2 inches of water to the garden.

I'd like to make one final note. If for some reason a pressure drop occurred in your house's water lines, water in your garden's water system can enter your house's water lines. The thought of drinking such contamination scares me because bacteria, algae or fungi; chemicals from the plastic components; or perhaps even fertilizers may be present in these lines. A simple antisiphon valve, available from hardware stores and many drip system suppliers, will prevent this problem. These are a few bucks well spent.

Chapter 6
Beating Bugs and Diseases

Organic methods of insect control are a good alternative to chemical methods, but some pests and diseases, such as squash vine borer, root maggots, cucumber beetles, pepper and eggplant maggots, cucumber wilt, and flea beetles, may elude control by organic approaches. Because of my desire for safe vegetables and a clean environment for my family, I used organic methods for pest control. I took some produce losses and accepted them as the price I had to pay for safe pest control; however, I didn't like the losses and resolved to beat the pests that were causing me problems.

One day a few years ago, I came across the answer to safe pest control while reading a magazine article on the use of polyester as a cloche. The actual product was Dupont's spun-bonded polyester, which bore the trademark Reemay. Drs. Wells and Loy at the University of New Hampshire developed the use of the polyester material as a cloche for commercial vegetable growers.

I found the use of polyester as a cloche fascinating. Its light weight meant that it didn't need supports to hold it above the plants. You just draped it over the plants loosely, and the growing plant adjusted the height. The porous nature of the polyester cloche allowed rain to penetrate it and also permitted air circulation, so I didn't have to provide ventilation, either. Bill and I decided to try this amazing cloche. We found extended harvests, improved yields, and pest protection. In this chapter I'd like to take a closer look at this interesting material as it relates to pest protection.

Polyester Pest Protection

By now you are probably curious about this polyester material, so examine it in the photographs in this chapter. Some of you might say that it looks familiar. Fabric stores sell a very similar product as interfacing for the tailoring of clothes. You can find bolts of interfacing in various widths, and you could probably use it in the garden; however, interfacing is heavier than the spun-bonded polyester intended for garden use.

You can buy Reemay in a 67-inch width (see the Appendix for a list of suppliers). It is white, porous, and very light in weight. The width of Reemay is ideal for making cloches over garden beds and wide rows. About 85 percent of the entering light penetrates the Reemay; therefore, plants can grow under the material. In fact, I found that plants grew under the covering better than I had expected. It appeared to me that the reflection of light under the Reemay allowed for its very efficient use, making the 85 percent light received almost as effective as normal sun with uncovered crops. Although the pores in Reemay allow light, air, and water to enter, they are too small for insect entry; therefore, you have a carefree, safe form of plant protection with Reemay.

Reemay costs about $9 per 50-foot roll. This cost works out to about $.18 a running foot for plant protection, not to mention the cloche benefits it supplies as well. If you find that you like Reemay, you can buy a 250-foot roll for $40, or roughly $.16 a running foot.

How you install Reemay depends upon its intended use. Remember, you can use it for insect and disease protection, as a cloche, or both.

Installing a Polyester Cloche

Let's consider the use of Reemay as a cloche for insect and disease protection. For example, suppose you want to get melons or eggplants off to a quick start but want to protect them from flea beetles (insects that eat hundreds of holes in plant leaves and carry bacterial and viral diseases that eventually kill the plant). In a situation such as this, I suggest using black plastic mulch and a polyester cloche. Install your black plastic, using either the furrower or a square-edged shovel to prepare the trench for the plastic. After you place the black plastic in the furrow or widened slit, don't cover the furrow or close the slit. Instead, slide about 4 inches of Reemay right over the plastic; then close up the area with soil and foot pressure. You can also pin the plastic and polyester together to the soil with U-pins made from coat hangers (Figure 6-1). This step gives you an almost 4-foot-wide,

A

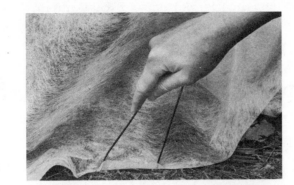

B

6-1 The polyester barrier and black plastic together can be pinned into the soil by wire coat hanger U-pins (A). This combined cloche and bug protector can give plants a head start, while keeping bugs away (B).

weed-free base covered by roughly 5 feet of Reemay. The polyester will expand upward as the growing plants take up the slack. When the plants become too tall to grow straight under the cloche, or the temperatures inside the cloche become too warm for plant comfort, remove the polyester. Fold it up and store it, because you will be able to reuse it later.

Although my example involved transplants, you can also cover seeds with Reemay. Using the polyester cloche over bare soil, you can successfully grow crops such as lettuce and peas with earlier-than-normal, direct seeding. While the seeds are germinating, the polyester protects them against insect damage.

You can also use the polyester over seeds to get what I call a thermal, protective seed blanket that lets you get earlier seed germination while protecting the seeds from birds, squirrels, and other critters. To install the blanket, prepare the furrow or slit as for black plastic; then put the polyester in the furrow or slit, cover it with soil, and press the slit closed with your foot. Just leave a little slack, because you will only need to allow sufficient room for seedling growth for a few weeks. The 67-inch-wide polyester can cover roughly a 4-foot width of garden.

You can, however, extend the width to almost 5 feet if you make your seed furrows deeper than normal. After you plant your seeds at the fur-

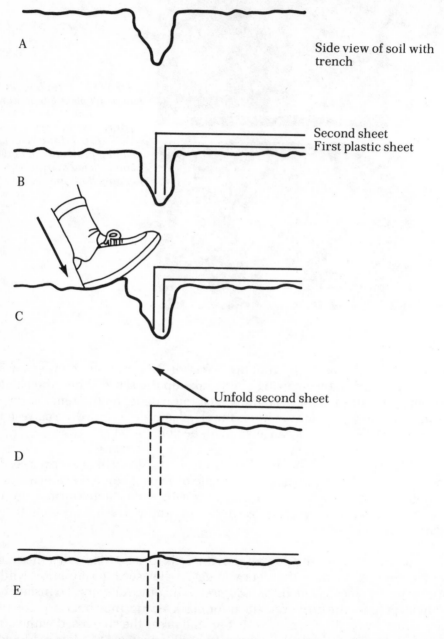

6-2 *Larger areas can be blanketed by joining the edges of two polyester sheets in a soil trench (A). Put the two edges in, fold one sheet over the other (B), foot-seal the trench (C), and unfold the second sheet (D, E).*

6-3 A polyester bug protector can be stapled or tacked easily onto the frame of a mini-hill.

row's bottom, only partially fill the furrow with soil. For example, with corn, make a 6-inch-deep furrow and cover the seeds with the usual 1 inch of soil. This approach leaves 5 inches of furrow headroom before the corn plant encounters the taut polyester blanket overhead. You can gain even more headroom by anchoring the polyester with coat-hanger U-pins instead of trenches.

Suppose you want to blanket a larger area than the width of the polyester allows. Prepare the usual slits or furrows for one polyester width, but join two widths of polyester material at the same opening (Figure 6-2). Then prepare the furrow or slit to finish the installation of the second sheet. Can we adapt this polyester protection to our wood-sided mini-hills (see Chapter 3), where we want an early but protected start for melons or squash? Yes, we can. One approach is just to tack or staple the polyester edges to the top of the wood frame (Figure 6-3), being sure to leave enough slack to allow some plant growth. You can also seal the polyester's edges with soil at the outer edges between the wood and soil in the mini-hill.

Late-Season Plant Protection

Suppose you want to use the polyester material for insect or disease protection with existing plants later in the season. For example, you might want to protect summer squash from the squash vine borer, broccoli and cabbage from the cabbage looper or imported cabbageworm, or cucumbers from the cucumber beetle and the miserable cucumber wilt disease. Or perhaps you're tired of birds or squirrels getting your ripe strawberries before you do. Maybe, like me, you gave up growing radishes, carrots, or rutabagas because of heavy root maggot damage. If so, take heart, for the polyester barrier solves all of these later-season problems.

You can tackle these insect problems, or any other bug attack, with one simple step: Cover the plants with Reemay before the pests appear. Of course you must first learn what the potential pests look like, so that you know them when they arrive to eat your crops. It would be wise to purchase a good book with color pictures for insect identification, such as *Rodale's Color Handbook of Garden Insects.* Or you can ask your gardening neighbors what pests bother them, or call your local agricultural experiment station or extension service to find out what insects are prevalent in your area (phone numbers are listed under state government in the telephone directory). You can also get a rough idea of when these pests are apt to appear from the state services or from helpful books like *The Encyclopedia of Natural Insect and Disease Control* (Rodale Press, 1984) or *The Gardener's Bug Book* (Doubleday), written by Cynthia Westcott and revised in 1973.

At the first sign of the pest, or even better just before, cover the plants with polyester. You can cover plants in several ways, depending on whether the plants are growing in rows, bands, or beds. First, inspect the plants to make sure no insects are present. If you find insects, get rid of them with the organic remedies recommended later in this chapter. These insects, if covered over, would lead a sheltered life with good meals. If you protect your plants against specific pests before or close to when they appear, you will find few or no pests when you make your plant inspection.

Next drape the polyester over the plants you want to cover, whether they are in rows, beds, or bands. To secure the Reemay, pin it into the soil with U-shaped wire. You can use any sturdy wire that you can bend into a U- or V-shape. Another possiblity is to cut a coat hanger with a wire cutter. Make sure the wire pin is long enough to securely lock into the soil. A pin 5 to 6 inches long is usually fine. As you pin the polyester down (Figure 6-4), make sure you leave enough slack for the plant to grow during the protection period. You can place the pins at 2- to 3-foot intervals. The reason I suggest using pins to secure the Reemay rather than using the trench method is because we are dealing with established plants and don't want to risk causing root damage by digging trenches.

Another way to protect large, individual plants, such as summer squash, eggplant, or tomato, is to make a polyester bag. Drape the polyester over each plant, and gather the edges of the Reemay at the base of the plant. Secure the edges together with either string or a wire twist tie. Don't tie the string too tightly, as you don't want to damage the stem. Essentially, you have made a polyester bug bag for each plant (Figure 6-5).

Perhaps you are wondering whether or not you can use polyester bags for individual vegetables. The polyester bug cover works well with a row or band of summer squash and the polyester bug bag helps protect individual summer squash plants, but what's a gardener to do to protect plants such as vining winter squash or melon? I have the solution, if you'll bear with me. Upon examining a damaged squash, I noticed that the squash vine borer,

6-4 Later in the season you can protect a group of existing plants from insects by pinning the polyester barrier over plants, as I did with these staked eggplants, which were protected from flea beetles and eggplant maggots.

an insect that attacks squash, penetrated squash only about 1 or 2 inches. I could easily cut out the borer and use the squash, but I couldn't store it in the cellar for later use. The limited damage gave me the idea that if I protected the young squash and the stem where it attached to the vine, I would be able to harvest undamaged fruit. My idea worked.

To protect plants such as the vining winter squash, place the polyester around individual winter squashes that are susceptible to the squash vine borers. With either string or a twist tie, secure each bag at the stem and where the stub joins the vine when the squash first appears. make the bag large enough to accommodate either the final size of the ripe squash or the size at which you notice the squash vine borer stops laying eggs. You can use this method for any vegetable (Figure 6-6) or fruit, if you don't mind the job of making many polyester bags. If you grow cucumbers and other vining plants vertically, trained on a fence or trellis, you can protect them with a polyester envelope. Drape the polyester over the plants from bottom to top and back down to the bottom. Then staple the edges shut on each side.

6-5 Larger plants can be put into their own individual polyester bags.

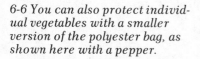

6-6 You can also protect individual vegetables with a smaller version of the polyester bag, as shown here with a pepper.

Using the various forms of polyester protection that I discussed, you can protect seedlings, transplants, or established plants from most insects and several diseases. Although polyester barriers offer protection from any insect above the ground, they can't protect plants from a few soil dwellers like the cutworm, because the insects lay their eggs too early for you to stop them with Reemay. However, you can stop root maggots, because flying insects lay root maggot eggs during the garden season. You can also prevent insect-transmitted diseases such as cucumber wilt or various aphid- or leafhopper-carried viruses with a polyester barrier. Chapters 8 and 9 give specific recommendations for controlling pests on crops.

When to Apply and Remove Polyester Barriers

Are these barriers a temporary or all-season-long measure? The answer is mostly temporary, that is, only while the pest is active. Your experience or the information you get from books and state agriculture offices will give you a rough idea of how long you should protect your crops with Reemay. If you notice that the pest has disappeared for a few days, you can remove the covers. Chapters 8 and 9 provide the covering time lengths for the individual crops, for the pests I know.

Long-term use of polyester barriers can interfere with pollination in some plants. Remember, these barriers keep all insects, including honeybees, away from the plants. Any crop requiring pollination by honeybees, therefore, will not set fruit if the barrier is present at flowering time. The picture is not as bleak as it may appear, though. First, we don't harvest all of our crops for fruit. Some crops are leaf crops, such as cabbage, lettuce, and spinach. Some crops are root crops, such as beets, carrots, onions, radishes, and turnips. Still other crops are flower crops, such as broccoli and cauliflower. The lack of pollen transported by honeybees to the plants' flowers therefore poses no threat to these crops.

Does the problem, then, occur with all fruit-bearing crops? Not really. Some fruit-bearing crops pollinate themselves and don't need insects to perform the job for them. Crops such as tomatoes and peppers set fruit with the help of the wind, which carries the needed pollen. As a matter of fact, it is possible to use polyester protection for peppers even during the time of flowering, because the wind will flow through the polyester and move pollen around.

The problem actually occurs only with bee-pollinated plants. You can't completely cover such plants with a polyester barrier at flowering time, because you will interfere with bees traveling to the plant's flowers. If polyester barriers are present, you must remove them. Although not being able to keep the barriers on the plants at flowering time seems to be a serious problem, it really is not.

Some pests cause trouble only before or after flowering time; for instance, flea beetles heavily attack eggplants right before flowering and adult eggplant maggots lay eggs on the young, developing fruit. If you cover the plant with polyester before and after the initial burst of flowering, you will eliminate the pest problem. Unfortunately, you may also lose some of the later-setting fruit; but you can avoid this problem as well.

To get all the eggplants possible, you can pollinate the flowers yourself. Touch a flower with a soft, camel hair paint brush; then remove the brush and inspect it for a kind of yellow dust, or pollen grains. If pollen is present, twirl the brush around the flower, repeating the process with each flower on the plant.

If you don't wish to pollinate the flowers yourself, put a polyester bug bag around each fruit as it appears rather than over the whole plant. This is the same procedure I described earlier for protecting winter squash and melons.

Yet another problem exists with bee-pollinated plants that have serious pest problems during fruit set; for instance, the summer squash depends totally on bees for pollination, but one of its greatest enemies, the squash vine borer, is very active during blossom time. Besides performing the pollination between male and female flower (the flower with the tiny squash at its base) yourself, there are two other ways you can deal with this problem.

In my garden, the squash vine borer appears in the late days of June and lays eggs in July. If I plant summer squash directly from seeds, heavy flowering occurs at the same time that the borers arrive. However, if I start squash as transplants, the heavy blossom time occurs before the squash vine borer appears; therefore, I don't need the polyester barrier right away. When the pests do appear, I put the barrier over the plant. At that point I already have a heavy fruit set. During July I lose a few weeks of fruit set while the barrier is up, but I don't lose the whole month. After a few weeks of frustration, the adult egg layer seems to get the hint and leaves for someone else's squash patch. At this point I take off the cover and fruit set continues. While I lose a few weeks, I don't lose half the season, as I did in years past with unprotected plants.

If you don't use transplants but want to directly seed the garden instead, cover the plants as soon as the pests appear. They will leave in a few weeks.

Essentially the polyester barrier and pollination can be compatible. Most plants pose no conflict either because their crops don't involve fruit, they don't need bees for pollination, or the pests that affect them aren't present during flowering time. You can easily resolve the problems with the few plants where pests, flowers, and bees all coincide. I will point out these special problems and solutions in the sections on the individual vegetables in Chapter 8.

Homemade Insect Traps

Sometimes we can turn the insects' desire for food into a trap. Your garden can become a deadly trap for certain insects and yet not be a hazard to you, your family, or beneficial insects. We can accomplish this simply by making the trap attractive to the pest insect.

Your vegetables and flowers, because of the color of their foliage, attract certain insects. Their eyes key in on the reflected colors of the leaf, essentially yellow mixed with green. If you use this fact about insects to your advantage, you can make a sure-fire trap for them by simply adding a sticky substance to a material of the proper color.

In years past, I made my own sticky, yellow traps by painting posterboard yellow and then applying a sticky substance to it. I eventually tired of painting, so I decided to buy yellow posterboard instead. My labor went down, but the price of materials went up.

Finally, my no-dig partner, Bill, came up with an ingenious solution for recycling the yellow posterboard for reuse. The secret to his recycling method involves using plastic freezer bags. Any size of clear plastic bag is acceptable, but I prefer to use the thin, inexpensive type that is about 11 by 14 inches in size. You can even use the plastic bags in which shirts come. Cut your yellow cardboard so that you can slide it inside the bag. Then coat the plastic bag with a sticky material. I use Tanglefoot, a commercial product that is very popular for trapping gypsy moth caterpillars as they climb trees looking for food. Another good product to use is Stikem, although I have also used substances such as heavy motor oil and petroleum jelly in the past. When your sticky substance becomes covered with bugs, simply slide off the plastic bag and discard it. Put on a new bag and coating, and you're back in business, using the same piece of cardboard. If you prefer not to bother with the plastic bags and sticky coating, you can buy ready-made sticky cards (see Appendix).

Installing Homemade Insect Traps

There are several methods you can use to install your insect traps in the garden. You can staple them onto stakes that you push into the ground, or you can hang them by strings. If you are using the former method, staple the yellow cardboard to the wood stake; then slide the plastic bag over the staked cardboard from the top. If you have a lot of trouble with wind, you can staple shut the open end of the bag. For the wood stakes I use thin wood strips, such as the discarded wood strip from the bottom of old windowshades, or wood paint stirrers. The thin wood allows me simply to staple the yellow cardboard right to the wood stake.

Another alternative for installing insect traps is to slide the yellow cardboard into the plastic bag with the open end of the bag on top; then staple string to the top of the bag. You can also staple the bag closed, but don't staple the bag to the cardboard because this will make recycling difficult. Tie the trap to a stake, such as a tomato plant stake, and you've got a suspended insect trap. Where vine crops are being grown on a fence or trellis, you can tie the traps to the netting, trellis, or fence that you are using as the garden's supports. You can also tie the traps to a string suspended between two poles, forming a sort of clothesline for bug traps.

When to Install Traps

At this point you may be wondering when to place your traps in your garden. The solution is quite simple. Watch your plants very closely and carefully for any signs of insects. As soon as you see any, install the traps. You will want to head off any and all pests before their numbers get too high, because high numbers of pests mean more traps will be needed and more damage will be done to your crops before you can get the pests under control. In particular, watch your tomato and squash plants for whiteflies and your peas, cabbage, and broccoli for aphids. These insects are the early arrivals—they most commonly appear on the early crops I just mentioned. Be especially sure that you check the undersides of the plant leaves for insects as well. After a period of time you will also want to watch the tips of roses and the undersides of squash leaves for aphids. These sites seem to be the first attack zone of aphids if they haven't arrived with the earlier crops. Be sure you make your plant inspections frequently and early, because the sooner you get your insect traps in place, the sooner you will do away with you garden pests.

How Many Traps to Use

You may now be wondering how far apart to place these sticky cards and how many you need for your garden. There is no simple answer, because the number of cards you need really depends on how bad the whitefly infestation is and how big your card is. With an 11-by-14 inch card, use one card for about every 10 square feet you want to protect from whiteflies and aphids. A larger or smaller card will increase or decrease, respectively, the protected area. Keep track of the card in terms of the number of whiteflies you find stuck to it. If the card becomes saturated with whiteflies in less than one week go to two cards per 10 square feet. Should one card go for a week or longer, great. If cards last two weeks or longer, cut down the number of sticky cards when you replace them.

The Quickie Method

Bill and I have one last suggestion. Should you wish, you can trap whiteflies quite rapidly, a point that might come in handy if you didn't notice the whiteflies until a large number were present. The secret to our technique lies in disturbance. Generally whiteflies fly off a plant infrequently; however, if you disturb the plant, you get a cloud of "flying dandruff." Our idea is to cause whitefly flight from one side of the plant while having the sticky traps located on the other side.

To get rid of the whiteflies, Bill and I place two sharpened stakes at each end of a group of plants, whether rows, bands, or bed. Next we run a taut cord between the two stakes, like a clothesline, and tie one sticky card every 3 feet along the line. Then one of us gets on the opposite side of the plants and directs a fine spray of water at the undersides of the leaves (Figure 6-7). To achieve a fine spray you can use a fogging nozzle, an adjustable nozzle adjusted down to a fine spray, preferably on a curved hose extension. If you don't have the extension, don't worry; spraying the tops of leaves gets the whiteflies moving but just takes a little longer. In short order you capture the cloud of whiteflies on your sticky traps and you've solved your problem. We recommend using our technique twice a week.

Acceptable Sprays for Pest Protection

While the polyester barrier and sticky cards will solve most of your pest problems, you may wish to use an occasional insect spray. Perhaps you have only a few pests and don't wish to bother with either the polyester barrier or sticky card. Maybe a pest has gotten completely out of hand and you want rapid control. What you need is a safe but reliable spray.

6-7 Yellow cards "hung on the line" trap whiteflies as they try to leave these squash plants in a hurry when the water spray disturbs the leaves.

Soap Spray

One spray that Bill and I like is a soap spray. Soap sprays are gentle on beneficial insects, bees, and birds. Based upon personal results in my garden, I like Safer Agro-Chem's Insecticidal Soap, which controls aphids, earwigs, fungus gnats, leafhoppers, mealybugs, scales, spider mites, thrips, and whiteflies. This spray also has approval for use on vegetables and fruits, such as beans, broccoli, Brussels sprouts, cabbages, cucumbers, eggplants, melons, peas, peppers, pumpkins, squash, and tomatoes. You can use it right up to the day of harvest. The soap spray is also useful on flowers, shrubs, ornamental trees, and fruit or nut trees. You can even use it on house plants indoors and in the greenhouse.

Pyrethrin

Another favorite spray of mine is pyrethrum preparations. The extract of pyrethrum flowers is termed pyrethrin. If the spray label lists pyrethroids, allethrin, phenothrin, permethrin, or kadethrin, these are synthetic chemical versions of pyrethrin. Look for the real thing instead. The label also often lists piperonyl butoxide, a natural derivative that greatly improves the effectiveness of the pyrethrin. The Appendix lists sources for pyrethrum.

Pyrethrin controls a number of insects, such as aphids, cabbage looper, Colorado potato beetle, cucumber beetle, flea beetle, leafhoppers, Mexican bean beetle, and whitefly. Pyrethrin is safe, and you can use it up to and including the day of harvest. You can use pyrethrin sprays on most edible crops and ornamentals.

Rotenone

Rotenone is another natural organic insecticide that I find valuable. You can use rotenone on a large number of edible plants and ornamentals up to one day before harvest. Rotenone eliminates aphids, cabbage looper, cabbage worm, carrot rust fly, Colorado potato beetle, cucumber beetle, flea beetle, leafhopper, Japanese beetle, mealybugs, melonworm, Mexican bean beetle, pickleworm, spider mites, squash bugs, tomato hornworm, thrips, and whitefly. You can find the sources for rotenone in the Appendix. You can also buy a combination product containing both pyrethrum and rotenone.

While these organic insecticides are not harmful to the environment, you should still be respectful of them. Do only as the label says in terms of dilution, spray schedules, harvest time, disposal, and any other precautions. Don't breathe the spray; and don't spray when it is windy, over 80°F (can harm plants), or going to rain in 24 hours or less. Always wash your hands well when through with spraying and rinsing your sprayer. If you spill any spray on your clothes, remove the clothes, wash the area of contact, and wash the clothes.

Seaweed Extract

Whether you know it or not, you are probably already using a spray against bugs. If you are using seaweed extract for foliar fertilization, you are indeed using an acceptable insecticide, also. Some evidence suggests that seaweed extracts, when used as foliar sprays, reduce the numbers of red spider mites and aphids, because the trace elements in seaweed extract seem to interfere with the breeding process of these pests. My garden does seem less troubled by these pests now that I use the seaweed extract.

Incidentally, you can combine the seaweed extract and fish emulsion solution with the diluted soap spray to feed your plants and control insects at the same time. Just prepare the two in their usual dilution and then combine them. Another plus is that the soap acts as a wetting agent, which improves both the sticking and entering of the seaweed/fish extract into the leaves. In point of fact, Safer's sells a combined soap/fertilizer spray that you can use on house plants.

The Bottom Line

Now let's look at the bottom line for pest control in your garden. Your first line of defense should be to use the polyester insect barrier and the sticky, yellow traps. Most times these methods will solve your bug problem. If you aren't able to control some pests or you suddenly discover a serious infestation of a pest, you can escalate the battle against insects by using the safest effective spray, the soap spray. To save time I usually combine it with one of my sprayings using seaweed/fish extracts. The last resort is to use either pyrethrin or rotenone, or combine the two. Even going to level three, the botanical pesticides, is preferable to resorting to the use of chemical insecticides around your garden.

More Ways to Outwit Pests

The key to success is to take advantage of every worthwhile opportunity. This view is true in business, but it also holds up in the garden. If you take advantage of many of the materials and techniques I have mentioned in previous chapters, you will help to alleviate some pest and disease problems. Let's expand on this idea a bit further.

Styrofoam Coffee Cups for Insect Protection

Do the fat, curled, dismal-colored grubs that attack your transplants, called cutworms, bother you? If so, take advantage of the way we suggested for growing transplants in modified Styrofoam coffee cups to alleviate your problem. Instead of removing the transplant and discarding the cup, use it as a cutworm collar. Simply break away the bottom of the cup with your hand; then sink the bottomless cup into the no-dig hole, allowing 1 to 2 inches of the cup to protrude above the soil level (Figure 6-8). By doing this, you will lock out the cutworm while still allowing the roots to grow through the slits in the sides and out the bottom of the cup.

6-8 Cutworm collars are easy to make from our Styrofoam cups; just remove the bottom of each cup.

You can also use the Styrofoam coffee cup against pests by holding transplants over in the cups until they develop better. I have observed that the 12-ounce coffee cups have tremendous holding-over capacity. A few times I had some extra tomato and pepper plants left over. Rather than discard them, I supplied them with water and fertilizer. To my surprise the plants grew large and actually yielded a few tomatoes and peppers while still in the cups. Sometimes if you allow the transplants to mature a bit more, their resistance to some pests seems better. In other cases, you may miss an insect problem entirely by putting out the transplant a few weeks later than usual. Basically, the extra hold-over ability of the coffee cups lets you either develop a more mature transplant or hold one longer than is possible with conventional containers, probably due to the larger cup size and the special slit design that produces extra-good roots. Such a root system seems to hold up the transplant for those few extra weeks.

I have also noticed that more mature transplants act tougher; that is, they hold their own against certain insects. In my experience this observation seems true with eggplants or tomatoes against flea beetles and with most transplants against aphids. In addition, although squash and cucumber will eventually die from the ravages of squash vine borer and the cucumber beetle, more mature transplants seem to hold out longer. This observation of greater resistance of older transplants against insects even seems to hold true with cutworms, slugs, and several other pests that operate at transplant time.

You can produce a more mature, tougher transplant with the coffee cups in one of two ways. For one, you can simply hold the transplant beyond normal planting time for two weeks. If you live in an area that has unsettled weather at your normal transplanting time, you might prefer this approach, because it gives you some leeway on weather. The other way to produce tougher transplants is to start your transplants two weeks earlier than normal in the cups. The extra advantage here is that an advanced transplant will give you an earlier harvest as compared to the conventional transplant. Either way, don't worry; our cup system can handle the extra two weeks and still give you a great root system raring to go!

Our Styrofoam cups can work to your advantage in another way beyond the cutworm situation mentioned earlier. Suppose you have the following situation. Perhaps your garden soil stays abnormally wet in the spring because there's a lot of clay, a high water table, or an excessively rainy spring. Maybe you experience either poor germination or a high rate of seedling death from soil diseases or insects. With our cups you can bypass this problem time. Start all your seeds indoors, using our cups. When you place the transplants in the garden later, the garden soil should be drier; and the transplants, being tougher than seeds or tiny seedlings, will pull through for you.

Cloches for Insect Protection

Cloches also give you advantages that are similar to those of the coffee cup and can build additional protection into your garden. Suppose you put out transplants under cloches. First you get barrier protection against insects, especially with the polyester cloche (see next chapter); and when you remove the cloche, you get another kind of protection that I noticed with cantaloupes.

For growing these melons, I insist upon using black plastic and a cloche. One year I had a few extra melon plants, so for comparison I planted two sets. I placed both sets in black plastic but covered only one set with a cloche. When it came time to remove the cloche, I was shocked to see that the running vines under the cloche were twice the length of the unprotected ones! Soon after I had removed the cloche, some cucumber beetles appeared with a taste for cantaloupe leaves. These insects ignored the longer and probably tougher vines and went straight for the smaller vines right in the next row. So why not use a cloche for both early harvest and fewer bug problems?

Fighting Diseases

Diseases can sometimes be troublesome, but you can often keep them in check with some organic practices. For instance, certain diseases seem to be less of a problem when you feed your plants with seaweed extract. I have noticed few disease problems in my garden since I started using seaweed extract. Other gardeners and academic researchers have reported similar results, according to W. A. Stephenson, in *Seaweed in Agriculture and Horticulture* (see Chapter 4). This benefit appears to result from increased plant vigor caused by the use of seaweed nutrients. What can you lose, since you are guaranteed fertilizer value at the least and maybe insect and disease protection as an extra?

Some of the insect-fighting tactics I described earlier also solve disease problems. I'm referring in particular to the use of polyester either as a cloche or insect barrier. Certain insects carry diseases that they transmit to the plant when they feed. By keeping out insects with polyester, you also keep out certain diseases. This method is most effective against the cucumber wilt carried by cucumber beetles and a number of viral diseases carried by aphids and leafhoppers.

Organic Matter, Resistant Plants, and Rotations for Disease Protection

Insofar as all garden diseases are concerned, your best defense is organic matter, resistant plants, and rotations. The last two practices also offer considerable defense against insects. First, let's look at organic matter.

Considerable evidence suggests that organic matter reduces the incidence of several soil diseases, including root rots of beans, beets, and peas; lettuce rot; peanut rot; and potato scab. In addition, organic matter increases the numbers of several soil microorganisms known to fight the pathogens that cause root rot, fusarium wilt, and verticillium wilt. Organic matter also reduces nematodes in the soil. It would seem that organic matter works to your advantage in promoting soil and plant health; so make sure you keep up the organic matter levels in your soil with our no-dig methods discussed in Chapters 3 and 4.

Resistant plants are front-line soldiers in the battle against diseases and insects. Seed catalogs and seed racks are full of cultivars advertising their resistance to this or that disease. If you have a specific disease problem, use these tougher plants to your advantage. A list of such helpers is not possible here, but you can find disease resistant varieties of asparagus, beans, cabbage, cauliflower, celery, corn, cucumbers, eggplants, lettuce, melons, onions, parsley, peas, peppers, potatoes, radishes, shallots, spinach, squash, sweet potatoes, and tomatoes. In addition, you can find resistance in a number of fruits and flowers. So why not stack the deck against diseases by making the right choice of plants when you have a problem?

Don't forget rotations! If you put your plants on a merry-go-round, you'll get the brass ring. The problem with keeping plants in the same place is that disease-causing microorganisms build up huge populations if they have a food source (your plants) present year after year. By moving your crops around, you keep the disease-causing microorganism populations low because of starvation. While one crop may be food for a disease, another crop will be unacceptable; hence, the microorganisms will starve. Another help is that new plants may create a habitat for different organisms that are antagonistic to the original troublemakers. Rotations discourage a lot of soilborne diseases, such as verticillium and fusarium wilts, to name a few. So play musical chairs with your crops, and keep those pests guessing!

Solarization for Disease Protection

For serious disease problems, you might want to consider the last resort: solarization. I covered the method for this form of soil pasteurization in Chapter 5 as a weed control measure; however, solarization is also effective at eliminating several soilborne diseases, including fusarium and rhizoctonia in onions and potatoes; sclerotium in peanuts; and verticillium in eggplants, potatoes, and tomatoes. Solarization undoubtedly wipes out a number of microbes that cause other rots and wilts yet doesn't harm the beneficial soil organisms involved in nutrient utilization and plant growth. As a bonus, nematodes and weed seeds get the boot! So why not consider this form of "soil cooking" if you have serious problems?

Fences to Keep Out Big Pests

Sometimes the mention of certain garden fixtures fails to excite the gardener, unless a problem or application forces a need. The fence is one such fixture. As a beginning gardener, my first thought of fences was a mental image of the range wars in the Old West as remembered from movies. Our history books mention that cattle barons became upset about farmers and sheep herders fencing their land and blocking the cattle trails. The farmers used fences to keep the cattle from tramping through their fields and destroying their crops.

The primary use of fences is to keep animals out of gardens, a small-scale, modern-day version of the "range wars." The worst garden raiders include deer, rabbits, skunks, squirrels, chipmunks, raccoons, dogs, cats, woodchucks, and opossums. Unhappily, we add humans to this list as well. Your garden location determines which of these animals are troublesome.

Fences also provide a way to overcome space limitations in the garden. Fences can support certain climbing crops, including pole snap and lima beans, peas, cucumbers, small melons, squash, and even some pumpkins. You even tie tomato plants to fences. Instead of spreading horizontally, such crops encompass vertical space, freeing up gardening space for other crops.

Both of these attributes of fences appealed to me early as a gardener. Over the years I have tried many types of fences in pursuit of the perfect one. My goal was to find the ideal, all-purpose fence suitable for both protection from small animals and support of climbing crops. Did I succeed? Well, yes and no. I'm still looking but not nearly as much as in years past.

The question of whether or not you can have a double-purpose fence needs answering. The answer is maybe, depending on circumstances peculiar to your own garden. Fences used to surround and protect crops that appeal to animals, such as corn and salad crops, may also support climbing crops that animals don't molest. The location of the fence, the kinds of animals present, and the other available food sources determine how effective the fence will be. The only sure way to know if the fence works is to try it, or as the scientist would say, experiment.

Choosing a Fence

To determine what kind of fence you need, you first have to determine what kinds of animals find your garden attractive. For example, deer can be troublesome in rural areas, because they can damage vegetables and shrubbery. To deter them you need a high fence. Little pests like rabbits and woodchucks can dig under fences, so to keep them out you need a fence that goes underground. Woodchucks are double trouble because they can climb; for them you'll need some sort of anticlimbing device on top of the fence, as well as an underground extension. Other notorious climbers include squirrels, raccoons, and opossums. You can easily discourage dogs and cats by using fences; but human garden vandals are the most challenging lot. They may respond to education or the passage of time but certainly not to fences, unless the fences are barbed wire or electric.

Next, you must examine your garden's location. From my own experience, I feel some location factors reduce the garden's need for protection. For example, city gardens are not usually troubled by animal pests, but the odds that animals will invade the garden increase in the suburbs, and increase still more in country gardens. However, exceptions do exist. I presently have a city garden at my home on the corner of two heavily traveled streets. I have a lot of vegetation on my lot, which is also a short distance from a park. I have frequent garden visitors, including skunks, raccoons, opossums, and squirrels; but I can still grow climbing crops on my fence, because these animals seems to have other food preferences. However, if their alternative natural food supplies decreased, I could have trouble.

Another choice faced by the gardener is whether the fence is to be permanent or temporary. Both cases have their pros and cons, as I learned over the years. The joy of permanence is that you do the job once and don't have to repeat it. The problem is a lack of flexibility and aesthetics. For example, if you use permanent fencing, it becomes difficult to change the size or shape of your garden. Also, you may not want to look out your window in winter to see a stark, forbidding fence looming out of a snow drift. On the other hand, the annual erection and removal of temporary fences involve a lot of labor and frustration, besides the fact that you may not have the storage space for your fences. Although I, personally, have felt unhappy with both choices, I still settled on the more permanent approach, because it made my life easier.

Permanent Fencing

With that in mind, I will tell you about fences I have known and loved, beginning with the major assault category. If deer and climbing or digging beasts have troubled you, you face a formidable challenge. The fence must be tall, difficult to climb over or dig under, and yet not cost a fortune or be overly difficult to assemble yourself. Talk about challenges! Yet, I think you can well meet the task, except, perhaps, for a few tired muscles. You must consider this fence, because of the construction tasks, a permanent installation. One hopes it will not be an eyesore near one of your important views. First, sink 8-foot-long 2 by 4s to a depth of 2 feet at 8- to 10-foot intervals. You must use a post hole digger for this task, but you can rent one rather than buy one. The posts will last longer if you use pressure-treated lumber and set them in concrete. Next make a 1-foot-deep slit or trench from post to post, such that the fencing can slip down into it. A square-point nursery spade is ideal; you can push it in with your foot and then rock it forward and back to create a narrow slit. Happily, the standard blade of these tools is 12 inches in length.

Place 1-inch chicken wire mesh, 4 feet high, in the slit. Attach the upper 3 feet to the posts with wire brads hammered by hand, or use a heavy-duty staple gun. You can use 2-inch mesh for the next wire course, because small ground animals are unlikely to get this high and the larger mesh is more economical. Make this course 5 feet high, leaving 2 feet unattached to the poles. Then attach one of the remaining feet to a 1-foot piece of 2 by 4, which you attach at right angles to the post and face outward. This leaves the remaining wire unattached. If a climbing animal should get this far, its weight will cause the unattached wire to droop, making it difficult to get around. One final thought comes to mind: Remember to keep an open area around the fence. Animals are less likely to approach the garden if they must cross open space.

The fence is no better than its weakest point: the gate. You must construct the gate with an eye toward crafty animals who will soon find their way to the entrance. The gate can be as simple as a wood frame composed of 2 by 4 lumber and covered in chicken wire. You should make the clearance between the ground and the gate bottom as tight as possible. Bury the chicken wire in the ground as you did for the rest of the fence; but, of course, don't attach it to the gate bottom. Make the top of the gate with the same angled and loose construction as the rest of the fence. One word of caution is in order. Because of the protrusion at the top, it is best to hinge the gate so that it opens inward.

The old adage about good fences making good neighbors applies here. This fence should make good neighbors of your local animal pests and be strong enough to support any climbing crop. The only fence that might be more effective for protection is an electric fence but it might shock you in more than one way when you see its price. One reasonably priced electric fence does exist (see Appendix). For $170 you can protect about one-fourth of an acre with battery power. If your problem is two-legged vandals, though, no fence will offer complete security.

The basic nonelectric fence we just covered is quite versatile because you can adapt it to deflect lesser animal threats. If deer and climbing animals pose no problem, you can do without the top overhang, use 1-inch mesh throughout, and even decrease the height to 3 or 4 feet. However, the height should remain at 6 feet if you plan to use the fence for double duty, that is, for animal protection and support of climbing crops. If you have no problem with four-legged garden gourmets, you could just place this fence at two parts of your garden perimeter if you wish to support plants with it. This should be at the east-to-west line at the northern end of your garden and at the north-to-south line at the western end. This configuration will minimize shading of your lower-growing garden crops.

One disadvantage with our nonelectric fence is that the chicken wire tends to deteriorate with time. In about three to six years, depending on climatic conditions, it will rust and eventually break. You can resolve this problem either by replacing the old chicken wire with new chicken wire or by using a higher quality fence wire. You can stretch the replacement time by removing, rolling, and storing the wire at the end of each garden year. To do this requires an attachment technique that lacks the permanence of staples or brads. The ideal attachment choice seems to be cup hooks that have a simple latch clip that you can open and close by finger pressure. If you remove the chicken wire every year, you might expect your fence to last twice as long.

When Not to Use Fences

My last point concerns when not to use a fence. When my children were young, I had a garden partially fenced for climbing vegetables. One Monday I arrived home from work after a weekend of transplanting tomatoes, peppers, and eggplants. Evidently my older boy, then a toddler, had learned a garden lesson when he watched me that weekend. He had gone out on Monday, pulled out my plants, and placed some of them in new holes before he tired of his chore. I knew by my wife's look and words, "Promise me you won't get mad," that something was wrong. After my anxiety attack, I set about repairing the damage and decided a total enclosure was in order; however, after some thought, I came up with a new plan.

Essentially, I created a buffer zone that acted as a psychological fence. I gave my child a small strip of garden at the end, complete with seeds and plants, which we both put in place. It turned out to be excellent insurance against accidental intrusion. My second son and then my daughter each, in turn, received a strip of soil. Some years later, these strips are still in use. This past year I thought the oldest would not want his strip garden, because of his other interests that compete with gardens. He surprised me; he did want it. I suspect I have invested in the future gardeners of America, because I knew when not to use a fence!

Chapter 7
Faster, Longer, Bigger Harvests

Less work is great. Getting more vegetables with less work is even better. Up to now in this book we have concerned ourselves with discussing ways to cut the amount of garden work. In this chapter, though, I'm going to change direction a bit by showing you how to get the most out of your no-dig no-weed garden. What we'll do is stretch the garden season at its beginning and end while getting more out of the middle, an idea any businessman would call increased productivity.

Cloches for Early Gardening

Mention early gardening to gardeners and you always get into a discussion on cloches. These protective devices are supposedly fantastic for getting early gardening starts, but I always used to wonder if the results that cloches produced were worth the trouble. I don't know about you, but I hate to spend my money and labor on something that fails to deliver all that it promises. In the past, cloches had disappointed me on numerous occasions; however, I finally found some cloches that I can now recommend with great enthusiasm.

Let's first look at the secret to success that underlies the cloche, black plastic. Why do we need black plastic underneath the cloche? The answer to this question involves the fact that plants have two basic parts, each in a different environment: the shoot and the root. The plant's shoot is above the ground and spends its time enveloped in the surrounding air. Shoot development heavily depends upon the temperature of this surrounding air. The root dwells in the soil, which heats up differently than does air. Root temperatures also have an effect on plant growth. Cloches trap the sun's heat and raise the air temperature around the plant; however, they can't raise the soil temperature to as great an extent as air temperature. A straight cloche, therefore, produces uneven heating. By itself, it actually mixes the signals it gives to the plant's parts for growth. The cloche provides a warmer air temperature that advances the shoot two weeks into its growth pattern, but it does not provide the same warming benefits to the soil temperature to advance the root's growth pattern. Although the cloche does allow some growth improvement and frost protection for the plant, it does not provide the full potential for these benefits that using it in combination with black plastic provides.

Now the need for black plastic becomes clear. The black plastic in place under the cloche allows the sun to heat both the air and the soil. The sun heats the air and the black plastic, which in turn conducts some heat into the soil; therefore, the plant has warm roots and shoots. Although the black plastic affords much better plant growth, its benefits don't stop there. The warm soil that results from using the plastic radiates heat at night, offering more frost protection than is possible with using the cloche alone.

Exactly what can we expect from a cloche combined with black plastic? Clearly the dynamic duo of black plastic and cloches produces enough warmth to allow earlier planting. My experience indicates that you can plant your garden two weeks earlier than normal. I have even stretched three weeks of earlier planting out of a cloche/black plastic combination; however, in some years I had light but fatal frost damage occur within the three-week stretch. I've never had this problem when starting my plants only two weeks earlier, though.

The two-week head start figures apply for warm-season crops like tomatoes, peppers, beans, melons, corn, or eggplants. With cool-season crops such as peas, lettuce, broccoli, spinach, and carrots, you can easily get a three-week and even four-week head start. Most gardeners think of needing a head start for warm-season crops. The desire for Fourth of July corn or tomatoes is high in my area. In some areas farther north, using a cloche with black plastic makes the difference between having and not having melons. The earlier harvest of cool-season crops, however, is also possible with the use of cloches and black plastic. Don't neglect this possibility. The idea of enjoying peas or broccoli from your garden three weeks earlier than usual is quite attractive.

At this point I'd like to be even more specific about the benefits of using a cloche/black plastic combination. First let me tell you what I have observed with soil temperature. The use of black plastic with a cloche has produced a soil temperature 6 to 12 degrees higher than that of nearby, unprotected garden soil. The temperature variation depends on the time of day and whether the day is very cloudy or sunny. Air temperature increases have varied from 5 to 40 degrees. Again, air temperature variations relate to the same factors as do soil temperature variations.

By reading the above facts, I'm sure you can see how April outside becomes May inside the toasty cloche. But what about frost protection specifics? Suppose you go for the early start and get tripped up by an unexpected late frost? My experience indicates that you can escape frost damage if temperatures don't go below 28°F. The odds of this occurring are quite low during the early part of the garden season, even if you plant two weeks before the average date of your last killing spring frost.

The combined black plastic and cloche also offer earlier crop yields; but surprisingly, the yields occur even sooner than the earlier-than-normal planting head start affords the plants. This happy turn of events stems from the accumulation of heat units. The cloche and black plastic trap more heat units than do unprotected garden areas. In fact, over a period of four to six weeks, the cloche system traps at least twice as many heat units as do the uncovered areas. The important thing to remember here is that heat units directly affect plant development; therefore, the cloche system not only gives the plants a head start but also increases their growth relative to uncovered plants. The result is the earliest-ever harvest.

Types of Cloches

By now I'm sure you're eager to know what cloches I like. Based on my experience, slitted, clear plastic row covers and Reemay spunbonded polyester are the best cloches. The polyester cloche is made of the same material we discussed for insect protection in the previous chapter. The row covers are clear polyethylene with precut ventilation slits. You can find sources for both types of cloches in the Appendix.

First, let's look at the polyester cloche. The polyester cloche does not require supports or ventilation because the material is lightweight and porous. As a matter of fact, the weight is light enough that even onions can hold the cloche up as they grow. The natural ventilation provided by the polyester cloche removes the necessity of constantly opening and closing the cloche to ventilate the plants. The porous nature of the cloche prevents excessive heat build-up for periods up to six weeks. Additional polyester cloche properties include the ability to allow good rain and light penetra-

7-1 The ventilating slits in this polyethylene cloche are forced open by rising hot air.

tion (85 percent light transmission) and the ability to serve as a very effective insect barrier.

The methods for polyester cloche installation are the same as those described for insect protection in the previous chapter. You can either prepare a trench with the furrower or a slit with the square-edged spade, and lock in both the black plastic and polyester edges. Perhaps the easiest installation method is to pin both the black plastic and polyester together to the soil in one simple step, using the U-shaped pins made from coat hangers, as covered in the previous chapter. The 67-inch width of the cloche allows for easy installation over raised beds, mini-hills, and multiple rows or bands.

When installing the polyester cloche, remember to do one side of the cloche first, whether using a trench, slit, or pins. Next pin the other side of the black plastic to the soil as a temporary measure. Using a few U-pins to hold the black plastic steady, plant your seeds or transplants before you completely install the cloche. Plant seeds through the plastic with either the dibble or bulb planter, and plant transplants with the bulb planter (see

Chapter 3). Once you have completed the planting, you can complete the installation of the remaining cloche sides whichever way you prefer. Because the wind can move *through* the polyester cloches, U-pins sufficiently keep them in place in windy areas and provide the easiest installation.

The slitted polyethylene cloche demands somewhat different treatment. The slits (Figure 7-1) do allow for ventilation and rain entry; however, I have noted that the slits also allow some insects to sneak in, namely the cucumber beetle. The weight of this type of cloche also requires the use of wire hoops for support. Light entry through the slitted polyethylene seems as good as with the polyester.

At this point you might be wondering why I bother with the slitted plastic in view of the need for hoop support and some insect problems. In terms of crop earliness and higher yields, the slitted plastic has a slight edge over the polyester, possibly because the polyethylene's venting system retains more night heat. The slitted pieces in the plastic rise upward as the warm air under the cloche rises and pushes against them. This upward flex allows the hot air to escape. At night these pieces of plastic drop back into place once the hot air pressure disappears. During the cool night, then, these slitted pieces essentially close down the vents and keep the warmth inside the cloche. The polyester, on the other hand, loses heat in both the night and day because its pores are always open.

The installation of the slitted polyethylene cloche is about the same as for the polyester. You can use slits, trenches, or U-pins to secure the cloche, although the pins make the process easy. The hoops also offer extra hold-down power for the black plastic. Lay out the black plastic and pin it down with the wire hoops at 5-foot intervals. Next plant either seeds or transplants through the plastic as already described. Finally, use the U-pins to secure the plastic cloche and the plastic mulch directly to the soil (Figure 7-2). Figure 7-2 also shows a typical slitted cloche in my garden.

Cloche Crops

You may be wondering what kinds of plants I have grown with these cloches, so let's start by talking about melons. In the years B.C. (Before Cloches), I was unable to grow good muskmelons and watermelons in my garden. The Connecticut climate and melons were about as compatible as oil and water. But now I have the sweetest melons this side of Dixie. First I start melons in our special Styrofoam cups and use the bulb planter to plant them through the black plastic, over which I put the cloche. When the melons bloom, I take off the cloche, and the melons arrive. Both kinds of cloches produce great melons, but the plants under slitted plastic yield ripe melons about one week earlier than those under polyester.

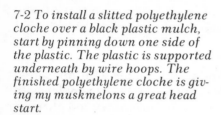

7-2 *To install a slitted polyethylene cloche over a black plastic mulch, start by pinning down one side of the plastic. The plastic is supported underneath by wire hoops. The finished polyethylene cloche is giving my muskmelons a great head start.*

Other warm-season crops that I have gotten off to good starts with these cloches include corn, cucumbers, eggplants, peppers, and tomatoes. All produce well and early under cloches. A big treat in my area is to have Fourth of July, garden-fresh corn and tomatoes. Although few conventional gardeners around Connecticut can pull off such a trick, no-dig gardeners can routinely produce such results with our transplant cups and black plastic with cloches. (I'll give you the details on how to do it under the individual vegetable entries in Chapter 8.)

As previously mentioned, warm-season crops are not the only ones that can take advantage of the cloche. You can also get a head start and early harvests with cool-season crops grown under cloches. I have had excellent results with broccoli, lettuce, and peas. The main point to remember with these and other cool-season crops is: Don't leave the cloche on too long, because the later warmth can cut or even retard yields. Remove the cloches when temperatures remain near 50°F for a few nights. For cool-season crops, I prefer the polyester cloche, because it has less heat retention than does the slitted plastic.

Cloches for Late Gardening

Up to now we have talked about early starts, or stretching the garden season at the beginning. You can also use cloches to stretch your garden season at the end. Let's see, we can add two weeks at the start for warm-season crops and three weeks for cool-loving crops. Can we do the same at the end? Yes! Essentially we can stretch the entire garden season by six weeks. In my area this means going from 195 to 237 days. In other terms, this means you could take a Vermont garden and turn it into a Connecticut garden for only a few bucks.

In the fall, cloches address the same two needs they address in the spring: frost protection and extended warmth. At this end of the garden season, I use only the polyester cloche, because plants are usually too large for the slitted plastic cloche forms. Simply drape the polyester over the plant or plants, beds, rows, or whatever you wish to protect, and pin the polyester to the soil with coat hanger U-pins.

Usually I find that my area gets hit with a frost around Halloween; then we enjoy two or three weeks of mild weather, which we refer to as "Indian summer." The weather that finishes warm-season plants follows the Indian summer lull. If I cover my tomatoes, peppers, and eggplants with polyester, I can ride out the first frost and coast into Indian summer. The polyester cloche protects the plants from the first frost but also provides the warmth that makes the tomatoes and other relatives ripen. The process of ripening is clearly much better under the cloche in comparison to nearby uncovered plants protected from frost only with newspaper.

The cloche of polyester also lets you stretch cool-season crops past several frosts, a protection I find just great for those remaining broccoli, carrot, lettuce, and turnip plants. When protected by polyester, such crops seem to turn out so sweet after being hit by a few frosts.

With care you can reuse the slitted plastic or polyester cloches a second time; but I don't recommend using them more than twice, because unnoticed deterioration sets into the cloche, reducing the amount of light that can pass through the plastic or polyester. This light loss reduces the heat units and also the plant growth, and you lose the very advantage you hoped to gain with the cloche.

After their spring use, I lay the cloches out to dry in the sun; then I carefully fold the material and store it in the cellar. I recycle both the plastic and polyester a second time during the fall for the late stretch. If you use cloches only in the spring, you can reuse them for the following spring. These cloches are relatively inexpensive, especially in view of what you get; so buy new ones after you have used the cloches twice.

A

7-3 *Inexpensive cloches are available, such as a homemade milk-bottle cloche (A), an inexpensive hot cap (B), or a wire-reinforced polyethylene tunnel (C). These cloches do not give as much frost protection as cloches made of polyester or slitted polyethylene, so use them to get early starts with hardier crops, such as lettuce.*

Before leaving the subject of cloches, let me mention the "poor man's cloche." As its name implies, the cost is just right. You can get one of these cloches by rinsing out a 1-gallon plastic milk bottle. Make sure you save the cap. Carefully cut out the bottom with scissors, a single-edged razor blade, or better yet, a razor knife. Now you have a portable cloche for individual plants. I suggest that you place a rock on top of the cloche to prevent the wind from blowing it over (Figure 7-3). Leave the cap on at night, on cloudy days, or in cool weather. On hot days you can vent the cloche by removing the cap. Poor man's cloches are sufficient if you have only a few plants and wish a modest head start or light frost protection.

Efficient Gardening Techniques

By now you know that no-dig no-weed methods save you from a lot of work. In addition, you need less fertilizer, water, and organic matter. Up to this point my theme has been getting the same for less; but now I'm going to switch gears to get the most from the least. What I'm talking about here is harvesting more crops without increasing the size of your garden or the amount of work, fertilizer, water, or organic matter that you put into your garden. Anyone can reach this goal by taking advantage of four garden

B

C

techniques: intensive planting, vertical gardening, interplanting, and succession planting. The trick is to understand these practices so that you use them correctly and in a manner that benefits you.

Intensive Planting

Let's start with intensive planting. This approach increases plant density to the maximum so that you get the greatest possible harvest. The one caution here is that you can increase the planting density only so far before you run afoul of the law of diminishing returns. After adding a certain number of plants to a given area, you introduce the elements of shade and competition. Some plants shade others, thus reducing photosynthesis and yields. Competition for nutrients and water increases beyond the carrying capacity of the soil. At that point you put the system into reverse; you get less from more.

As long as you are aware of the limitation, you can get more from your garden than you think; for example, the row concept of gardening is an inefficient use of space. The large spacing recommended between rows has little to do with the space needs of plants. The intent is to allow for mechanical cultivation between rows, that is, to leave you enough space for moving equipment between rows. But we don't have to worry about cultivation for a couple of reasons. First, if you are using our no-weed concept and our suggested mulch, there are no weeds. No weeds between rows means no need for rows. Even if you are not using mulches, you will eventually have a no-weed garden by using our no-dig method. The other reason you don't have cultivation worries is that closely spaced plants will produce a soil cover that shades out weeds, thus reducing the few problems even further.

So why bother using rows or a lot of paths for getting around? All they do is cause soil compaction. We cut down on paths and eliminate rows, replacing them with blocks, beds, or bands. Blocks are essentially squares, ideally sized about 4 feet on each side. Paths surround each block, thus giving you a checkerboard look. One very popular block approach divides the block into sixteen 1-foot squares.

Each crop's space needs determine the number of plants in a block; for example a 1-foot square is suitable for one plant of broccoli, cabbage, cauliflower, corn, eggplant, or pepper. On the other hand, you can fit sixteen beets or carrots or nine bush beans in a square. A bush summer squash would need nine squares of a block. If this block method is starting to sound familiar, it is. Some of you might recognize it from Mel Bartholomew's book *Square Foot Gardening* (Rodale Press). If you want to use this block method, you will probably enjoy reading his book.

Let's move on to beds and bands, which differ from blocks in shape. The two planting patterns are rectangular rather than square. The distinction between the bed and band is in the width of the rectangle, with the bed being the wider of the two. The bed should be 4 feet wide and whatever length you choose. This width is just about right for an arm's reach to the center of the bed. Anything wider can cause you inconvenience. The band, on the other hand, is narrower than 4 feet. By the way, if you use the suggested 4-foot-wide black plastic mulch, you have a ready-made bed (see Chapter 5). If you use less than the full width of the plastic, you can have a band complete with encircling pathway.

Prolific smaller crops might be more suitable to planting in a band and larger crops to a bed; for instance, I would plant beets, carrots, onions, or radishes in a band, but corn, squash, or tomatoes in a bed. You can plant some crops, such as the bush bean, in either a band or bed, depending on your food needs and preference.

A. Less efficient   B. More efficient

7-4 Conventional single rows with equally spaced plants (A) give you fewer plants in an area than does a staggered planting pattern with plants equidistant in all directions (B).

Let's look at the possible spacing for some crops, starting with tomatoes. If you go by conventional spacing, tomatoes are garden hogs. Yet most of us don't think a garden is complete without tomatoes. I've seen suggested spacings between rows of 2 to 4 feet, but my own experience is that a spacing of 18 inches between staked tomato plants gives great yields. Incidentally, a major university recently publicized a finding that high-density plantings of staked tomatoes give the best yield at 18-inch spacings, a confirmation of my own ideas.

The discussion of spacing brings me to an interesting point. Is there more than one way to space, and if so, does it matter how you space? The answer to both questions is yes. If you use the conventional spacing approach, the usual pattern is to line up the plants side by side. The row concept dies hard, even with beds and bands. Instead you should stagger the plantings so that the plants are side by side only with every other row, as Figure 7-4 illustrates. Using this pattern, you actually squeeze a few extra plants in the area and get more uniform shading and use of nutrients and water. In plain English, you use space and soil more efficiently.

The 18-inch spacing rule also holds for the relatives of the tomato — eggplants and peppers. It also works for broccoli, cabbage, cauliflower, and large cultivars of sweet corn. Smaller cultivars of corn can get by with 12 inches of space between plants. This tight packing of corn makes it possible to grow corn in small gardens and assures pollination; thus all the ears form well.

Vertical Gardening

While intensive planting can give a mighty boost to the yields for any size garden, there are three other practices that can make you an efficient but underworked gardener: vertical gardening, interplanting, and succession planting. Let's talk about vertical gardening first. Vertical gardening is a natural for certain plants that, even at their closest allowed spacing, are space-hungry crops. If your garden is small, you might give up on growing the vining and climbing vegetables; but don't. Using vertical gardening, you can tame these space-hungry crops to become little space users.

Suppose you had a dozen cucumber plants. If you planted these on the ground at intensive garden spacing, you would place one plant every 12 inches. Since the vines run about 6 to 8 feet in length, the mature plants would need roughly 100 square feet of space. Instead, if you put the cucumber plants in a vertical garden, you will lose only about 14 square feet of ground space. You cut down space needs to only 14 percent of the original. No wonder vertical gardening has a popular following!

The only important vertical gardening need is upright support that is strong enough to bear the weight of the mature crop. Place your supports in an east-to-west line at the northern end of your garden so that the shadow cast by the support will not shade out your lower-growing crops. While less desirable, you can run the supports north to south on the western side of your garden. Here you lose only the late afternoon sun.

Over the years I have tried all kinds of crop supports. Figure 7-5 shows my current supports for my vertical garden. I originally chose chicken wire mesh because it was strong and I never had to worry about the weight of any climbing crop. The drawback to using chicken wire was the storage

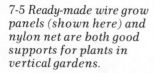

7-5 Ready-made wire grow panels (shown here) and nylon net are both good supports for plants in vertical gardens.

and reuse. Costs were high enough that I wanted to reuse the wire for at least three years, which led to the problem of whether I should install it permanently or temporarily. First I put it up permanently, since the idea of taking it down and storing it wasn't attractive. I figured it would last three years if left up all year round, but of course it didn't. Rust appeared in no time, and by the end of the second garden season, the rust weakened the wire to the point where I couldn't trust its strength the following year.

The next year I opted for temporary installation of the chicken wire but wasn't sure how to install it so that it would be strong enough for the crop but easy enough to take down. I solved the problem by using spring-latch cup hooks. These cup hooks have a metal strip under tension, which keeps cups from falling off them. You push the strip downward with the cup handle or chicken wire, and it snaps closed once the wire or handle is under it. To release it, you press the strip down with your finger and slide the wire out of it. I attached the screw-type cup hooks to wood posts. Although the wire went up easily and came down easily in the fall, I didn't know where to store it. Also the wire never seemed to roll up neatly like the original roll; instead it appeared to enlarge by a factor of two or three. I had to cram it into the corner of my tool shed. I finally got tired of using chicken wire.

I have also tried nylon netting, which works well using the same cup hooks mentioned above. Nylon netting is relatively easy to store because you can fold it into a nice, neat package. The cost of nylon netting is moderate, and it lasts for several years.

To support the nylon net, I usually buy cheap grades of 8-foot-long 2 by 4s. I use a post hole digger to set the posts 2 feet deep. You can also pack the posts in concrete if you want very well-set posts. If you so desire, you can paint the wood with a wood preservative. Cuprinol has special wood preservative formulations that are compatible with soil and garden plants; but do not use their regular formulation for this purpose. Ask for Cuprinol No. 10, No. 14, or No. 20.

For lightweight crops, such as cucumbers, peas, and beans, I place the supports at 8-foot intervals. For heavy climbers, such as melons, small pumpkins, and squash, I place the supports at 6-foot intervals. In terms of support, I have found it helpful to weave a wire through the netting top and attach the wire to the wood support posts. This keeps the net from sagging in the middle. You will also need slings or support sacks for the melons, pumpkins, or squash. Discarded nylons or panty hose make wonderful slings when you place them underneath the fruit and tie the tops at the crosspiece of the net. Remember, you can attach the net with cup hooks for easy removal or with wire brads for permanent installations.

The netting post support method places your netting 6 feet above ground. You may get some plant hangover at the top but nothing serious. The net usually comes in a 5-foot height and rarely in a 6-foot height. Start the net 1 foot above the soil. You may have to tie some plants, such as cucumbers, to the net bottom; but others, such as peas or beans, jump the 1-foot gap by themselves.

The main annoyance I found with nylon netting was its tendency to tangle; however, tangles may soon become a thing of the past. This year I noticed that Burpee advertised an improved nylon netting that wouldn't tangle, so naturally I decided to try it. My initial impression was good. I haven't passed the acid test yet. As I recycle it for the next few years, I will be watching it closely for tangles. If this netting lives up to its promise, I may become a complete nylon net vertical gardener.

Another new support system that I have been using over the past few garden seasons is the grow panel. Grow panels provide good support strength, ease of assembly and disassembly, and a sturdiness that promises a long life. I have been using my grow panels for three seasons, and they still look great. They are 4 by 2 feet, with the heavy-duty wire forming 6-inch squares. You can tie the panels with twine or twist ties to two strong stakes and place them side by side to any desired length. Adjoining panels can share one stake. My cucumbers, beans, and other climbers adapt admirably to them. If you can't find grow panels, you can use the wire reinforcement mesh used in concrete work as an adequate substitute. Building supply stores usually carry the wire mesh. So far I've been happy with my grow panels because they are easy to store and install. As a matter of fact, I prefer using grow panels to nylon net for short vines, although nylon net wins for long vines.

To support grow panels, use sturdy wood stakes such as those you might use for tomatoes or dahlias. These stakes will offer sufficient support because the panels are only 2 feet wide. Since many of the panels are only 4 feet high, I start them 1 foot above the ground and tie them to the stakes with heavy twine or wire twist ties. The 5-foot height is fine for cucumbers, small melons, and beans. If you don't want to start the panels 1 foot above the ground, you can fill in the last foot by stringing twine between the support stakes.

Before I leave the subject of vertical gardening, I'd like to mention one more item: the pea fence. This new product is 8 feet long and 3⅓ feet high. It folds into seven 14-inch sections. Usually this fence has long metal extensions on the bottom so you can stick it into the soil, and it doesn't need any additional support. Its height limits it to use with the shorter pea plants, such as some cultivars of sugar peas or the newer snap peas like 'Sweet Snap' or 'Sugar Daddy'. Although a pile of brush serves the same purpose, the pea fence is really not a bad little item to buy.

Interplanting

Another gardening practice that can produce a better garden is interplanting, a technique that puts two compatible crops in an area normally devoted to one. In this way you space more efficiently, but you also get a varied harvest over a longer time.

Generally, you pair the crops for one of two reasons. First, you can place a crop that matures quickly with one that takes its time; therefore, by the time you harvest the early crop, the later one is about ready to take over the available space. Another choice is to pair two crops not on the basis of harvest time but on the consideration of different growth habits.

Let's look at some examples of interplanting. My favorite is the summer squash and lettuce combination, a combination that meets both require-

7-6 *Squash and lettuce make good interplanting partners. This photo shows squash planted to the left and right of the central row of lettuce. Early in the season there's plenty of room for both, as seen here. By the time the squash needs more space to grow, the lettuce is ready to harvest.*

ments mentioned above. First the lettuce goes out as early transplants two to four weeks before the summer squash, because it is less tender; therefore, the lettuce reaches maturity before the squash. Second, the plants differ in their growth habits (Figure 7-6). Squash tends to rise as an inverted triangle from its base, giving you a compressed or squashed (pardon the pun) ice cream cone-shaped foliage mass. This shape leaves a lot of wasted understory space. But lettuce is low and compact, so it fits nicely in between young squash plants.

I usually plant a double bed of summer squash. First I install two side-by-side sheets of the 4-foot-wide black plastic, leaving a 1-foot gap between the sheets. I then plant lettuce transplants into the soil row at 6-inch spacing for leaf lettuce, 9-inch for romaine types, and 12-inch for head lettuce. Later on I put summer squash transplants into the black plastic with the bulb planter. I place one row down the center of each sheet at 3-foot intervals. I harvest the leaf lettuce first and pick the romaine and head lettuce as the squash leaves close overhead. The covering squash leaves shade the lettuce below, thus letting it grow just a little longer into the hot days of summer. Now that's what I call interplanting at its best!

Other examples of good partners exist. You can mix onions with either carrots or leaf lettuce. Onions, being skinny and tall, leave the lower space for the leaf lettuce or carrots to spread out. You can also slip lettuce between cabbage or bush bean plants. Leaf lettuce matures quickly; after you pick the lettuce, the beans or cabbage fill in the space. For the same reason, you can tuck lettuce around broccoli or cauliflower.

Radishes also make a versatile planting partner. Since they mature ever so quickly, you can mix them with several plants that mature later; for example, you can mix radishes with lettuce, beets, tomatoes, peppers, eggplants, or carrots. During sowing, you can mix the radishes with carrot seeds. Carrot seeds germinate very slowly, and the fast-start radish seedlings provide an excellent visual marker for the row; hence, you can weed early without worrying about the location of the carrots.

The Indians of New England provided what was probably the oldest example of American interplanting. When the colonists arrived, the Indians taught them the trick of mixing pumpkins and corn. Both growth habits and maturity differ, so these partners mix very well. Pumpkins and winter squash are rampant growers; therefore, if you want to grow a few but have little space, mix them with your corn. The Indians also taught the colonists to place dead fish at the planting site. We now know that fish meal is an excellent source of plant nutrients. History books make little mention of the Indians' contribution to gardening, but it is clear that they were the first Americans to practice both interplanting and organic gardening.

Early potatoes and winter squash are a good example of plants with differing harvest times. Just plant the two side by side. After you harvest the early potatoes, the space-hogging winter squash will quickly fill in the space. The same possibility exists with peas and winter squash. You can also marry early tomatoes with fall cabbage. As the tomatoes slow down and you remove the tomato plants, the cabbage takes over. You can also mix bush beans with either tomatoes, peppers, or eggplants. The beans come in quickly, and the others finish the race later. You can also mix spinach with these same plants, since spinach finishes more quickly.

Succession Planting

We have one more gardening practice to cover: succession planting. Here the use of space is efficient, but the main thrust is for continuous and longer harvests. You can accomplish succession planting in three ways. For some crops you can get a continuous harvest by the simultaneous planting of early, midseason, and late cultivars. You can also get the same effect by using only one cultivar but planting batchs at two- or three-week intervals (Figure 7-7), for continuous harvests of the same crop. We can also get continuous, longer harvests with mixed crops by following the harvest of early-season crops with a succession crop placed either as seeds or transplants.

Corn and tomatoes are good examples of crops where early and late cultivars exist; for example, you might sow both 'Early Xtra Sweet' and 'Silver Queen' corn at the same time. You can pick the early corn starting in about 71 days and the latter in about 92 days. This trick will spread your corn harvest over a period of roughly four weeks instead of only a few. Perhaps you prefer just one of the newer corn cultivars that are sweeter and hold their sugar longer. No problem, just make multiple sowings of the corn at two-week intervals, and you'll have a continuous corn harvest.

7-7 *A succession planting of broccoli is shown in the foreground. The youngest plants are on the left and the oldest on the right.*

With tomatoes I usually plant an early, late, and really late variety. The early choice can be a small tomato like 'Gardener's Delight', 'Pixie', 'Sweet 100 Hybrid', or 'Bitsy VF'. Perhaps you prefer a standard-size, early tomato such as 'Burpee's Big Early', 'Early Girl', or 'Park's Extra Early VFNT'. For the later tomato I choose something big like 'Park's Whopper', 'Burpee's Big Boy Hybrid', 'Burpee's Supersteak Hybrid VFN', or 'Burpee's Big Girl'. For the really late tomato, there is only one choice: 'Burpee's Long Keeper'. I pick these tomatoes late, usually just before the frost. Some are red, but most are green. I store these tomatoes in my cellar and enjoy them to the end of January. How can that be, you ask? Plant breeders fooled around with the ripening gene so that these tomatoes stall when they become ripe and don't rush into the rotten stage. How do they taste? I would say somewhere between a fresh garden tomato and the golf balls they call tomatoes in the supermarket. Of course, when you have finished all of your other garden tomatoes, their taste rates high! In this winter storage tomato interests you, you can find out more about it under Tomatoes in the next chapter.

The tomato succession I have just discussed is one of my favorites. With it I have garden tomatoes for seven months, from July through January. That's not bad for an area with a growing season of about 195 days! Of course, most plant successions can't match the longevity of the tomato group. Perhaps the genetic engineers will someday make improved longevity possible for other crops.

Let's look at some other successions. You should sow some crops as early as possible for two reasons. One is early harvest. Nothing beats early sweet snap peas as the season's first fresh vegetable. The second reason is that early harvests leave free space that you can fill with a succession crop. Early spring sowings are possible for broccoli, Brussels sprouts, cabbage, lettuce, onions, peas, rutabaga, and spinach. You can sow carrots, chard, Chinese cabbage, collards, cress, endive, garlic, kale, mustard, parsnips, radishes, shallots, and turnips a little later but much earlier than warm-season crops. All of these crops, the very hardy and hardy vegetables, are potential candidates for a succession plan. All you need to know is the number of growing days left in the season after you harvest the early crops. This number helps to determine which crops can mature in the remainder of your garden season. For example, radishes finish producing in 25 to 30 days, leaving a lot of free time and empty space. You can follow the radishes with snap beans and follow the beans with rutabagas. Even if the rutabagas get tagged by a frost or two, don't worry; rutabagas are hardy and the frost just sweetens them. That's what I call a triple-play succession.

Not all successions can be triples, though. Some are only doubles; but even doubles help you win the continuous, longer harvest game. For instance, you can follow radishes with carrots, celery, snap beans, lettuce, or onions planted as sets. You can harvest early potatoes and still get in a planting of corn. How about sneaking in some beets, late cabbages, or carrots after your peas? Perhaps you still have time after your corn finishes to get in a fall crop of spinach, rutabagas, or turnips. You only have a little time left? Maybe you can fit in something quick like leaf lettuce or radishes.

Successions are quite numerous. You make the choice; but keep some points in mind. When you replace some vegetable, try not to pick a successor that's closely related; the second crop, if closely related, could be susceptible to the same insects and diseases as the first one. Also, keep track of your remaining days. If you have 40 days to the killing frost, don't plant snap beans, which need 50 or more days to grow and are frost-tender. You could try a crop that needs 50 days but can tolerate a few light frosts; for example, chard, cress, kale, lettuce, or mustard could fit the situation. You must also watch out for temperature preferences for coolness or heat. Lettuce, peas, radishes, or spinach do not make good midsummer fillers but would work out late in the summer.

At this time I'd like to remind you of the transplant nursery in Chapter 2 (Figure 2-14) and tell you how this nursery provides me with plants for succession planting. I keep my leftover transplants in it and use it to hold our outdoor production of transplants in the modified Styrofoam cups. For example, I start various vegetables from seed directly outdoors in the cups. These transplants are started at various times throughout the season. My choice of crops is not guesswork but deliberate planning for successor crops. When space becomes available, I simply grab several cups and the bulb planter; in just a few minutes I can plant a complete succession crop via the no-dig method.

As a gardener interested in the most for the least, you certainly have numerous choices. I'm not saying you should practice all the methods we just covered. In some cases you must choose one or the other; for example, do you interplant winter squash with early peas or succeed the peas with snap beans? As for myself, I put my major emphasis on intensive planting and vertical gardening. I do use interplanting and successions, but I use them carefully and selectively with certain crops. My aim is to provide enough vegetables for fresh use and some for cellar and freezer storage. It's nice to have several lots of excess vegetables, but make sure your surplus is not for show but for consumption. Use the previous techniques with vegetables your family appreciates.

In the next chapter, you will find helpful hints for individual vegetables. Perhaps the hints will help you to choose among intensive gardening, vertical gardening, interplanting, and succession planting.

Chapter 8
The No-Dig
Vegetable Patch

This chapter will supply you with all the information you will need to grow vegetables and melons. I will list the plants alphabetically, breaking down the information for each plant into the following categories: choices, culture, pests, and harvest. Wherever possible, I will tie the facts to the techniques and information covered in the preceding chapters.

I would like to mention that I intend the figures I give for the days to harvest for each crop to be only rough guides. The range I give results from planting both early and late cultivators at their earliest possible time as seeds. Later plantings, such as those used in succession planting, often mature more quickly because of increasingly warmer weather in which they grow. If you use transplants, remember to count the time required to grow them as part of the time to harvest. Keep the suggested harvest days in mind, but rely more upon visual inspection if the crop is new to you.

Beans

Choices

A large choice of beans confronts the gardener in most general mail-order seed catalogs. I found the most impressive choice of beans in the catalog of the Vermont Bean Seed Company (see Appendix). If you are looking for the extraordinary or heirloom bean, look to this catalog.

174

8-1 This photo shows my no-dig no-weed vegetable garden at the height of the season.

Beans come in three basic types. One type is the snap bean, having edible pods that are usually yellow or green, although purple is also available. The pods are either thin and cylindrical or wide and flat. It is best to eat snap beans while they are young and before they become full sized; otherwise, the pods become inedible. The second type of bean is the lima bean and green shell bean. These beans are best when they have grown to their full size but are not fully mature. The pods of lima and green shell beans are inedible. Gardeners grow the third type of bean, the dry shell bean, for its fully mature, dry beans removed from the pods.

You can find all three kinds of beans in either bush or climbing (pole bean) forms. I happen to prefer climbing beans in my vertical garden, but many of my friends like the bush forms. Pole beans take longer to bear than bush types, but their harvest period is longer. Of course, you can extend the harvest of bush beans by employing succession planting.

Suggesting the best kinds of beans to grow is like picking out a car; essentially it is a matter of personal choice. My own choices of beans to grow after several years of experimenting are the following pole varieties: 'Kentucky Wonder', 'Burpee Golden', and 'Romano'. The first type I mentioned is an old standby, a green, cylindrical bean. The second is a yellow, flat-podded type; and the third is a flat, green bean sometimes called the Italian pole bean. All three types are fine for fresh use or for freezing. If you would like to grow lima beans but have poor luck because of your northern location, try 'Geneva' (Johnny's Selected Seeds). For a change of pace, try growing some of the more unusual dry beans such as 'Garbanzo' (chick-pea) or 'Berken' (mung bean). The former makes a tasty buttered bean or salad addition, while the latter is excellent for preparing bean sprouts.

Culture

Beans form a partnership with nitrogen-fixing bacteria in the soil; to foster this relationship and get a better crop, you should inoculate first-time plantings by dusting the wet seeds with a commercial product sold for the purpose (such as Legume-Aid). You do not have to repeat the inoculation the following year if you plant your beans in the same location.

Snap and shell beans are tender; never plant them into soil below 50°F or they will rot. Lima beans require even warmer soil, about 70°F. I usually wait to plant snap bean seeds and transplants until the soil has warmed up to 55°F as shown by a soil thermometer. Since snap bean seeds are large, direct no-dig sowing is possible with the dibble, furrower, or bulb planter, 1 or 2 inches deep.

If you want a head start or have cold, wet springs, I suggest you grow bean transplants in our Styrofoam cups. In cooler areas, lima bean transplants are a must to allow for proper plant maturation. I usually plant three groups of two seeds each next to the cup rim (12-ounce size) at 12, 4, and 8 o'clock positions. After seed germination, I thin the number of plants down to three plants for pole and bush types. Germination takes roughly seven to ten days at 70°F. Bean seeds do not require any special treatment or light during germination. Start bean seeds three to four weeks prior to the time of transplanting, or sow them in cups outdoors at normal planting time under the outdoor shelter (see Chapter 2, Figure 2-5), if you don't care for early beans but have cold and wet soil.

Cups having three pole bean transplants work out very well in an intensively planted vertical garden. Just place the transplants at 12-inch intervals in a row planted alongside of some form of vertical support. Bush beans, three to a cup, can have an intensive spacing of 6 inches between cups in the row and 12 inches between rows. This spacing gives you a completely filled-in bed or band. For continuous yields, plant bush snap beans at two-week intervals. You can also use bush snap beans as successive plantings after harvesting early crops such as beets, broccoli, early potatoes, lettuce, peas, radishes, or spinach. For succession purposes you can continue bean plantings up to two months prior to your first killing fall frost. You can interplant bush beans with lettuce, onions, peppers, or tomatoes.

Pests

In my opinion the worst bean pest is the Japanese beetle. Bean leaves seem to be their favorite food (Figure 8-2). You can beat Japanese beetles with either the polyester barrier or Reuter's Japanese beetle trap as soon as they appear. You can also knock the beetles into a container of oil or kerosene early in the morning when they are very sluggish. Other bean

8-2 These bean leaves show the damage done by Japanese beetles.

pests include the Mexican bean beetle, bean leaf beetle, bean aphid, leafhopper, tarnished plant bug, spider mites, and whiteflies. You can control all of these pests by using soap spray, rotenone, or pyrethrum.

Rust seems to be the only disease I occasionally see, when the leaves become speckled or covered with a rusty color. You can avoid this disease or others by not picking beans or handling the plants when they are wet. If you have a serious rust problem, choose varieties having rust resistance. Mosaic and anthracnose can also occur, but resistant varieties are available.

Harvest

When picked at the proper time, beans are very tasty. Rough guides to harvest are 40 to 60 days for bush snap beans, 60 to 70 days for pole snap beans, 65 to 75 days for bush lima beans, 80 to 95 days for pole limas, and 70 to 100 days for dry shell beans. If you use bean transplants, you can cut the harvest time by three or four weeks.

Pick snap beans when the beans are about one-quarter to one-third their full size. Their pods are almost full sized at this point, have soft tips, and produce a nice snap when broken. Continue picking the beans to encourage further bean production. For a real treat, prepare snap beans Chinese style, that is, stir-frying quickly. If you plan on freezing snap beans, select a cultivar described as good for freezing and don't overblanch them.

Pick lima beans when the pods are green and full sized with beans nearly full sized. Remove dry shell beans from dry, brown pods. After the pods become dry and brown, cut the entire plant at the soil line. Leave the roots in the soil to build up organic matter. Hang the plants stem end up in a garage or other dry place for further drying. When the pods become brittle, you can remove the beans.

Beets

Choices

The main decision to make concerning beets is whether you want an early or midseason beet for fresh use ('Early Wonder', 'Ruby Queen', 'Red Ball') or a beet for winter storage ('Lutz Green Leaf', 'Long Season'). You can also choose various shapes, such as globular ('Detroit Dark Bed', 'Red Ace') or cylindrical ('Cylindra', 'Formanova'), and you can also choose between two colors, red or golden ('Burpee's Golden Beet'). If you are looking for a baby gourmet variety or a really sweet beet, try 'Little Ball' and 'Sweetheart', respectively.

Beets, while grown as a root crop, also offer the bonus of producing leaf greens. Just remember not to pick all the leaves on a plant prior to harvesting the beets, because you'll get a poor crop of beets if you do. Should you like beet greens, you might want to consider 'Green Top Bunching'. An even better choice if you like beet greens is to grow a beet relative, Swiss chard, which is grown only for its greens. I recommend planting 'Fordhook Giant', 'Rhubarb Chard', or 'Perpetual' Swiss chard.

Culture

Beets are mostly a cool-season crop. The Deep South produces good beets in the late winter and early spring. Swiss chard can take more heat than other greens; it is the best choice of greens for summer harvests.

You can sow beet seeds directly outdoors as soon as you can work your soil. The furrower works best for planting this seed, but you can also use the dibble. For quick germination (ten to fourteen days), soak beet seeds in lukewarm water for 12 to 24 hours. You can mix radish seeds with the beet seeds as a marker and earlier crop. Keep in mind that beet "seeds" are actually fruits that contain several seeds. You must thin to one beet per 3-inch square for intensive gardening, no matter how carefully you space the seeds. Sow beet and Swiss chard seeds ½ to 1 inch deep. Intensive plantings of Swiss chard are one plant per 12-inch square.

To get a head start, you can also sow beets three weeks earlier in our 12-ounce Styrofoam cups. Plant three seeds to a cup at the outer cup edges in equally spaced positions. Thin each spot to leave only the strongest seedling. You can place each transplant triplet such that all bulb-digger holes are equally distant from each other at 6 inches, a spacing that is fine for intensive gardening.

For succession planting, sow beets directly into the garden or in our cups at three-week intervals. Remember, the last crop should mature before the hot weather starts. You can follow beets by planting succession crops such as snap beans, late corn, or late squash. You can also interplant beets with leaf crops such as cabbage, lettuce, or spinach.

Pests

Insects that bother beets include the beet leafhopper, leaf miner, and webworm. Flea beetles can also be troublesome. The polyester barrier can eliminate all of these problems, as can a combined pyrethrum/rotenone spray. Leaf spot and scab may occur in young beets, but good soils and rotations seem to ward off these problems.

Harvest

To produce an excellent beet harvest, you must keep weeds under control. Planting beet transplants through black plastic gives excellent yields.

With the exception of the winter storers, which need roughly 80 days, beets are usually ready to harvest in 50 to 60 days. The best beets are picked in the cooler part of the season and have a 1½-inch diameter, although you can pick beets up to 3 inches in diameter. Swiss chard needs about 70 days to harvest. If you pick *only* the outer leaves when they are up to only 12 inches tall, you'll get tender leaves and have a longer period for harvest.

You can store late beets by packing them in moist sand and placing them in a cool, dark cellar. You can store Swiss chard by freezing it.

Cabbage and Relatives

Choices

I've included a number of related crops here under one heading because they have several similarities. These crops include broccoli, Brussels sprouts, cabbage, cauliflower, Chinese cabbage, collards, kale, kohlrabi, and mustard. We collectively call all of these plants the *cole* crops. A basic similarity among the cole crops is that all are cool-season crops best grown in spring or fall in the North and in spring, fall, and winter in the South.

Gardeners grow broccoli for its edible green flower buds and nearby stems. The main crop comes from the large, terminal cluster of green buds. Later in the growing season, you can harvest the small sprouts at lower positions. Some broccoli varieties produce more and larger lower buds. My favorites for extended harvests are 'Bonanza Hybrid' and 'Green Goliath', but there are at least another dozen cultivars. 'Green Duke' is a good choice for growing in the South; and 'Bravo', 'Green Comet', and 'Packman' are good choices for producing early crops. If you lack garden space, you would be wise to choose a broccoli called 'Green Dwarf'. For harvesting fall broccoli, you can't beat 'Waltham 29'.

Brussels sprouts are grown for their side buds that look like miniature cabbage heads. The best tasting and sweetest sprouts are those you harvest in the fall after a touch of frost. Sprouts mature from the bottom up, so you do get a somewhat extended harvest. I think the best variety is 'Jade Cross E Hybrid', although 'Prince Marvel' also produces an excellent crop. There are about five or six other Brussels sprout choices as well.

Cabbages offer many choices, varying in their head shape and color; their harvest time (early, midseason, late, and winter cabbages are available); and the smoothness or crinkledness of the leaves within the head. I'll make only a few cabbage suggestions, since choices are numerous and good. The earliest producing cabbages are 'Darkri Hybrid', 'Early Jersey Wakefield', 'Golden Acre', and 'Market Victor'. For red or purple cabbage, try 'Mammoth Red Rock', 'Preko', or 'Ruby Red Ball'. If you like crinkled leaves, go for 'Blue Max', 'Early Curly', or 'Savoy Ace'. For winter storage, try 'Lariat', 'Late Danish', or 'Wisconsin All-Season'.

We grow cauliflower for its large, edible head, which is essentially a thick flower cluster. Most cauliflower is white, although a purple form is available. Some kinds of cauliflower require tying of the leaves for blanching the head, while others are self-blanching because of their curved outer leaves. The purple varieties of cauliflower require no blanching and retain their color when used fresh in salads but turn green upon cooking. To grow the purple varieties, try 'Purple Head', 'Royal Purple', or 'Violet Queen'. If you want to grow self-blanching varieties, try 'Albert' or 'Self Blanche'. For standard white varieties, try 'Imperial', 'Snow Crown', 'Snow Queen', and 'Snow King'. If you have hot-weather problems in your area, try 'White Contessa'. An early-maturing variety is 'Garant'.

Chinese cabbage is becoming increasingly popular, with heading and non-heading kinds available. The taste of Chinese cabbage is more like lettuce than cabbage and has a touch of sweetness. The heading choices of Chinese cabbage are more popular and include 'Green Rocket', 'Jade Pagoda', 'Michihli' (an old standard), 'Monument', and 'Nagoda'.

Collards, kale, and mustard all produce leaves that are used as greens. Some of the new hybrids show great promise, including 'Blue Max', 'Heavi-Crop', and 'Hicrop Hybrid' for collards; 'Blue Knight' for kale; and 'Tendergreens II' for mustard. Old standbys or newer nonhybrids for collards include 'Champion', 'Georgia', and 'Vates'; for kale, 'Dwarf Blue

Curled Vates', 'Dwarf Siberian', 'Konserva', and 'Winterbor'; and for mustard, 'Burpee Fordhook Fancy', 'Florida Broad Leaf', 'Green Wave', 'Kyona', 'Southern Giant Curled', and 'Tendergreens'.

Gardeners grow kohlrabi for the swollen bulbous stem portion that grows near ground level. Essentially kohlrabi looks like a small turnip sitting aboveground. Kohlrabi's raw taste is somewhat similar to that of a water chestnut, while its cooked taste seems to mingle the flavors of cabbage and turnip. Some older kohlrabi choices are 'Early Purple Vienna' and 'Early White Vienna'; while some newer versions include 'Blue Danish', 'Grand Duke', 'Karla', 'Purple Delicacy', and 'Purple Danube'. Kohlrabi colors vary from white to purple.

Culture

As a rule all the cole crops, if planted as transplants, will germinate in ten to fourteen days at 70°F. Cauliflower tends to come a little quicker at ten days and kohlrabi later at fourteen days; the other cole crops tend toward the middle of the range. Sow the seeds ½ inch deep. You can easily grow all the cole crops as transplants in our Styrofoam cups with one plant to an 8-ounce or 12-ounce cup.

For intensive plantings of cole crops, use an 18-inch square. If you plant in rows, set the plants 18 inches apart within the rows and have 18 inches between rows. Brussels sprouts work out better with 24-inch spacing. Some specific facts for each cole crop follow.

Broccoli is best set out in the garden as transplants, starting them five to seven weeks ahead of transplanting them. Because broccoli is very hardy, you can place the transplants outside two or three weeks prior to your last spring frost. For a continuous crop, you can use an early and late cultivar, sow transplants at two-week intervals, or select a cultivar noted for continued production of lower buds after the main harvest. Don't forget to start transplants for a fall crop of broccoli, as well. In the Deep South, you can directly sow broccoli seeds in the early fall for a winter crop. Set out fall transplants about two and one-half months before your killing fall frost. Depending upon your garden season, you can follow spring broccoli with beets, carrots, or snap beans, or a fall crop of lettuce, spinach, or radishes. You can also interplant broccoli with lettuce or spinach.

Brussels sprouts taste best when you grow them as a fall crop. You can set transplants out four months before the first killing fall frost. Start the transplants six to eight weeks ahead, or sow seeds directly outdoors at this same time. Brussels sprouts also make a good winter crop in the lower South. Brussels sprouts can follow any early crop that allows enough time for the sprouts to mature, such as radishes, lettuce, peas, or spinach.

Cabbage is hardy, even hardier than broccoli. You can set transplants out three to five weeks before your last spring killing frost. I suggest that you use transplants and put them out early, because heat and cabbage don't mix well. Start cabbage transplants four to six weeks before you wish to plant them in your garden. Fall cabbage transplants can go out about three months prior to the first killing frost. In the Deep South, you can directly seed late cabbage in the early fall for a winter crop. For continuous harvests you can mix early, midseason, late, or winter cultivars of cabbage. You can follow early cabbage with snap beans, squash, or late corn; late cabbage can follow beets, early potatoes, lettuce, peas, radishes, or spinach. You can also interplant cabbage with lettuce, radishes, carrots, beets, or spinach.

Cauliflower is more tender and fussier than the other cole crops. You can put transplants out no sooner than two weeks before the last killing frost in the spring. Start the cauliflower transplants five to seven weeks before you plant them in the garden. Don't delay planting your transplants in the garden much beyond your last spring frost, because cauliflower does very poorly in hot or dry weather. For a fall crop, you can directly sow the seeds in the garden about three months before the fall frost; for a winter crop in the Deep South, directly sow the seeds in the late summer. The interplanting and succession of cauliflower is similar to that of broccoli.

Because heat easily damages Chinese cabbage, your best bet is to grow it as a fall crop in the North and a winter crop in the Deep South. You can either sow seeds directly or as transplants about three months prior to the first killing frost in the fall. You should set out the transplants when they are five to six weeks of age. Chinese cabbage can follow any noncole crop that allows enough free space for the cabbage to grow.

Collards and kale do best in cooler weather but can take more heat than cabbage. As such, both collards and kale are often a substitute for cabbage in the South. Collards and kale are somewhat similar, with collards being the larger of the two. Kale can have either curly or uncurly leaves, but collards only have uncurly leaves. You can sow the seeds directly into the garden as soon as you can work the soil, or you can set out five- to six-week-old transplants two to four weeks before the last killing frost in the spring. For fall crops in the North, sow collards and kale seeds in midsummer; for winter and spring crops in the lower South, sow the seeds in late summer to early fall.

You can plant five- to seven-week-old kohlrabi transplants up to three weeks before the last killing spring frost, or you can directly sow kohlrabi seeds when your garden soil is workable. Sowings at two-week intervals will give a continuous crop. Late summer and fall sowings in the lower South will provide fall and winter harvests.

You can handle mustard transplants and direct spring sowings in the same manner that you handle collards and kale. You can plant seeds at three- or four-week intervals for successive crops. A fall sowing of mustard is possible about eight weeks before the killing frost. Gardeners in lower parts of the South can sow mustard for winter use.

Pests

Cole crops experience similar pests and diseases. Use crop rotations to eliminate pest and disease problems, and be sure that cole crops do not succeed each other in the same place. The cole crop pests that are of most concern include the cabbage aphid, looper, root maggot, worms and harlequin bug. Bacterial pesticides containing *Bacillus thuringiensis*, such as Dipel, will control cabbage loopers and worms. Soap sprays work well for aphids and harlequin bugs. With pyrethrum and rotenone, you can control all of the pests with the exception of the root maggot. To control the root maggot, you must stop the adult fly from laying eggs by using the polyester barrier over the plants. The flies appear about one month after the last killing spring frost in my area. Paper disks placed tightly around the plant stem will also control the root maggot. The disease problems of cole crops include blackleg, black rot, clubroot, and cabbage yellows, all of which you can control by using crop rotation and resistant cultivars.

Harvest

Pick broccoli before the buds start to open and show yellow. Cut the head with a sharp knife, taking a few inches of the main stem. Lower sprouts will develop and give you additional harvests over several weeks.

With Brussels sprouts, cut off the miniature heads close to the stem with a sharp knife. Harvest the lower parts first, when the sprouts are 1 inch to 1¼ inches in diameter. Ripening of Brussels sprouts gradually proceeds from the bottom up to the top of the plant, so your harvest will continue for several weeks. If you want to rush the harvest, remove the upper leaves and terminal leaf cluster to speed ripening.

Pick cabbage when the heads have formed well, are firm, and are glossy green. Heads should weigh 2 pounds or more and be a whitish color inside. Judge the readiness of Chinese cabbage heads by days to maturity and size.

With cauliflower, you have to do some extra work, unless you have a self-blanching variety. Once the upper leaves of the cauliflower curl away and start to expose the head, pull them together and tie them with string. If the weather is warm, the head will be ready to pick in three to five days; in cool weather, up to two weeks. Make sure you pick the head when the curds are white and tight. If the curds are discolored, loose, and look like rice, the head is too old.

Harvest collards, kale, and mustard leaves for salads or greens before they become tough and woody. If you harvest the outer leaves of the plants and don't disturb the growing points, the plants will keep on producing leaves for a longer harvest.

Pick kohlrabi when it is 2 to 2½ inches in diameter, before it becomes tough and stringy. Toughness sets in when kohlrabi is 3 inches in diameter.

Broccoli, Brussels sprouts, cabbage, cauliflower, Chinese cabbage, and collards all mature in 60 to 100 days. Kale and kohlrabi need 55 to 70 days and mustard is ready to pick in 35 to 45 days.

Carrots

Choices

Carrots vary considerably in shape from long and pointed to blunt and cylindrical to short and round. Too many cultivars exist to name them all, but I would like to mention a few. An excellent, all-purpose carrot is 'Burpee's Goldinhart', a blunt, half-long carrot. Shorter carrots, such as 'Short and Sweet' or 'Kundulus', are better to grow if your soil tends to be shallow or heavy. If you like little baby carrots, try 'Little Finger', 'Lady Finger', 'Early French Fame', or 'Amstel'. If you like juicy carrots, then try 'Mokum'. Other good carrots include 'Nantes Half Long' and 'Danvers'; and if you want an early but good-tasting carrot, go for 'Lindoro'.

Culture

Carrots have only one fussy requirement, but it is very critical. The slightest obstruction, such as a stone, can deform the roots of a carrot. Heavy soils also stunt root formation. To grow carrots you need a sandy, deep loam that is free of pebbles. That's one of the reasons California soil produces great carrots. If you don't have sandy, deep loam, use a raised bed, such as the version discussed in Chapter 3, to grow carrots.

You can sow carrot seeds with the furrower as soon as you can work the soil, roughly three weeks before your last killing frost. Cover the seeds with ½ inch of soil. Germination is slow, taking 14 to 21 days. You can put some radishes in the row, because they will germinate quickly and mark the rows. Be sure to rid your garden of weeds as soon as you see them; otherwise, they will have a large head start by the time your carrots come up.

For a really quick carrot crop, start your carrots in our Styrofoam cups, planting seeds at the outer cup edge and thinning to three transplants per cup, equally spaced along the rim. Start the carrot transplants about six to eight weeks before you expect the last killing frost in the spring.

For intensive spacing, thin the seedlings to stand 2 or 3 inches apart in all directions. If you use the transplants in the Styrofoam cups, place the cups equally distant at 3 inches.

You can sow succession crops of carrots at three-week intervals up to 75 days before fall frosts; however, keep in mind that the best growth of carrots occurs at 60° to 70°F. Avoid planting so that carrots finish up during hot weather. Interplantings of carrots with lettuce work well, as do carrots and radishes or onions. You can follow early crops such as peas or radishes with a planting of carrots.

Pests

Carrot rust flies lay eggs that become maggots which tunnel through the carrots. These dark green flies appear about a month after the last spring frost, so you can ward off these pests by covering the carrots early with a polyester blanket. Sage plantings nearby also seem to repel the carrot fly. Later plantings that miss the carrot fly are another possibility for thwarting this pest. Also watch out for leafhoppers, as they can carry a virus called carrot yellows. If you see leafhoppers, put up your polyester barrier to prevent their attack on your carrots. As for diseases, leaf blight can be troublesome, but you can control it by using a three-year crop rotation.

Harvest

You can pick carrots that are from finger size up to 2 inches in diameter. A rough guide to harvesting is that carrots mature in 65 to 75 days from seed. The flavor of the carrot is best closer to maturity when its pale orange color becomes bright orange. If at any time the tops of the carrots expose themselves, cover them with soil to prevent them from turning green. Carrots intended for storage should be a late crop picked near maturity. Storage is best under cool, moist conditions, such as in sand or sawdust in an unheated cellar. You can also leave carrots in the ground and cover them with several inches of hay or straw. You can dig your carrots up to the time the ground freezes.

Corn

Choices

If I could grow only one crop, I would have a difficult time choosing between corn and tomatoes. Your choices in the sweet corn area are tremendous. For colors you can choose white, yellow, or mixed white and yellow. White happens to be my favorite corn, especially the old standby, 'Silver Queen'. Of course the picture becomes even more complicated when you consider the many new varieties that promise more sweetness, greater duration of sweetness, and so forth.

Up until recently, in order to assure sweetness in corn it was necessary to pick the corn and eat it immediately; otherwise, the corn had a very bland taste. The problem resides in a chemical helper in the corn. This chemical helper, which we call an enzyme, has a mission to speed the change of sugar to starch in corn. The enzyme does its job so well that on-the-stalk sweetness is a passing thing. Even worse, when you pick the corn, this enzyme speeds up its action even more, with only refrigeration slowing it down. Few farms cool their corn; this lack plus transportation time explains the dullness of so much grocery store corn. Unless you've had garden-fresh corn, you probably wonder why they call it sweet corn.

Recently, however, breeders have developed new cultivars of corn by experimenting with the genes that control sweetness in corn. Because there is more than one way to alter genes, we have differences in the new hybrids. These sweetness changes have become associated with other changes that you may or may not like. We'll look at these new offerings shortly.

First, let's suggest a few old reliables to plant. The leader in white corn hybrids is 'Silver Queen', but you have to eat it freshly picked to see why experts rate this corn so highly. Although 'Silver Queen' is a late corn, it freezes quite well for storage. Several early white hybrids are also available, but I don't think they beat the 'Silver Queen' in taste. These early hybrids include 'Chalice', 'Spring White', 'White Magic', 'Quicksilver', 'Platinum Lady', and 'White Sunglow'.

Many early, midseason, and late cultivars of yellow corn are available. The early varieties include 'Earlivee', 'Early Sunglow', 'Sundance', 'Blitz', and 'Spring Gold'. The midseason choices include 'Bellringer' and 'Wonderful', while some late choices are 'Jubilee' (almost the yellow equal of 'Silver Queen'), 'Golden Cross Bantam', and 'Iochief'. If you want baby yellows, try 'Golden Midget'. The bicolor corns include 'Butter and Sugar' (an old favorite), 'Honey and Cream', 'Bi-Queen', 'Duet', and 'Calypso'.

Now let's resolve the confusion with the new corn choices. One of the genetic changes that breeders have made, called heterozygous sugary enhancer(s), is essentially a partial modification that affects 25 percent of the kernels, resulting in a 15 percent sugar increase and a slower conversion of starch to sugar (few days on stalk, ten to fourteen days in refrigerator). Other descriptive terms for this altered corn include heterozygous SE, or SE (Sugar Extender), and EH (Everlasting Heritage). The milkiness of this altered corn is similar to that of regular corn and the kernels are soft, not crispy. Examples of SE include yellows like 'Stardust', 'Kandy Korn E.H.', and 'Tendertreat E.H.'; whites like 'Lightnin', 'Platinum Lady', and 'Snow Queen E.H.'; and bicolors like 'Pride and Joy' and 'Peaches and Cream E.H.' These choices also vary from early to late in terms of harvest.

Another genetic alteration is termed homozygous shrunken 2 (sh_2). Other names for this group include Super Sweet, Extra Sweet, and Ultra Sweet. This modification affects all the kernels, resulting in twice as much sugar, which holds for roughly ten days on the stalk and much longer upon refrigeration. The seeds appear shrunken when mature, so the appearance of sh_2 is strange upon sowing. These corns have much lower water-soluble polysaccharides that produce the milky juice in kernels of ripe sweet corn. The low content in sh_2 corn means the kernels have a crispy texture instead of the milky texture of normal corn. The sh_2 types of corn freeze extremely well. Some yellow varieties include 'Summer Sweet 7200', 'Sweet Time', 'Early Extra Sweet', and 'Burpee's Sugar Sweet'. Whites and bicolors include 'Summer Sweet White 8601' and 'Summer Sweet Bicolor 8502', respectively. I like the sh_2 group for its sweet stability and great freezing ability; however, others find it too sweet and prefer the less sweet EH types.

Another less well known, partial modification, heterozygous sugary shrunken, is available and also goes by the names Synergistic and Sweet Genes Hybrid. The sweetness of this corn is comparable to that of the Everlasting Heritage. Examples of heterozygous sugary shrunken are 'Honeycomb' and 'Sugar Loaf'.

The newest modification to corn is homozygous sugary enhancer. The difference between this type and the previously mentioned types is that the breeders have sugar-enhanced all of the genes. The sugar content and sweetness are somewhere in between the Super Sweets and the Everlasting Heritage kinds. Unlike the Super Sweets, the texture of homozygous sugary enhancer corn remains milky and has no crunch. The sugar stability lasts for about four days. I know of only one yellow and a bicolor to date, 'Great-Taste' and 'Double-Taste'. (Incidentally, Twilley Seeds has the best selection of the newer types of sweet corn.)

If you decide to try growing your favorite old corn along with one new type, you have to watch out for cross pollination of breeds. With the heterozygous sugary shrunken and standard sweet corn, there is no cross-pollination problem. With standard sweet corn and heterozygous sugary enhancer or homozygous sugary enhancer types, I suggest isolating the breeds, although isolation is not a definite must. With the homozygous shrunken 2 group, isolation of breeds is essential. By isolation I mean that you should plant the differing corn varieties at least 35 feet apart in a home garden or at separate times so that a few weeks separate the production of pollen on the corn tassels. To make sure you have allowed enough time between plantings, provide for at least fourteen days for planting differences and maturity differences. For example, let's look at 'Kandy Korn E.H.' (89 days to maturity) and 'Jubilee' (85 days to maturity), a conventional older hybrid. In order to get the fourteen-day lag between the tasseling of the two varieties, you would need to plant 'Jubilee' ten days before 'Kandy Korn E.H.' Subtracting the difference in maturity times—four days—from the fourteen-day total gives you the necessary difference in planting time, ten days.

My last suggestion is: Don't try to grow more than one new variety of corn a year with your old corn, because the pollination problems will increase in complexity if you do.

Culture

If you plan to sow seeds directly, do not sow them any sooner than about one week after the last killing spring frost. You can use the furrower, bulb planter, or dibble for seed planting. Corn seed germination and development may be better with later plantings, because corn is a warm-season crop. To obtain the best results, plant corn when the soil temperature is at 65°F (or, as the old adage goes, when oak leaves are the size of squirrel ears). Later planting times are especially important for some corn cultivars such as 'Silver Queen'.

Early plantings of corn can be at a depth of 1 inch, while later plantings are better at a depth of 1½ inches. If you want intensive plantings of corn, put roughly one corn plant to a 12-inch square in intensive beds. Make sure you plant at least four rows of corn side by side for adequate pollination. Corn seeds germinate in about ten days at 65°F.

For the earliest possible corn, I suggest the following technique. Raise corn as transplants in our 12-ounce Styrofoam cups. Start the corn four to five weeks before you plan to put it out in your garden. Remember, the earliest date for planting transplants in the garden is similar to that for planting seeds. Cups of corn germinate in five to seven days at 70°F. Thin the plants to one plant per cup.

At the same time you seed your cups, lay down black plastic in your garden to warm up the soil for your corn transplants. Plant your transplants through the plastic with the bulb planter. If you wish, you can place a polyester cloche over the corn transplants in the black plastic, resulting in the earliest-ever corn.

A second planting method, while not quite as effective as the one I just discussed, is for those who wish to seed directly. You can seed corn directly through black plastic, which has warmed the soil, using either a dibble or bulb planter. Alternately, you can bypass black plastic by preparing 6-inch-deep furrows with the furrower. Next cover your seeds with 1 inch of soil and install a polyester blanket over the furrows to warm the soil and plants. When the corn finally fills in the overhead room and touches the polyester, remove the blanket. Later, pull the furrow sides over on the stalks for improving the corn's anchorage.

If you want to prolong the harvest of corn, you can plant early, midseason, and late cultivars; or if you like only one corn type, sow it at two-week intervals. Corn can follow plantings of beets, lettuce, peas, radishes, and spinach. Interplantings of corn with either winter squash, pumpkins, or pole beans are possible.

Pests

I have experienced few pest problems with my corn, although many pests do trouble corn. Among the insects are the army worm, chinch bug, corn borer, corn earworms, corn flea beetle, and wireworm. Recently I noted that Japanese beetles have a fondness for the leaves, silk, and tassel of corn. The Japanese beetle trap discussed under the section on beans works well for ridding the corn of beetles, or you can knock the beetles into a can of oil or kerosene early in the morning. Pyrethrum and rotenone help in the fight against borers and flea beetles, while Dipel works against earworms. Keeping weeds down near the corn, removing stalks, and rotating crops can help cut down pest problems.

If crows or starlings steal your seeds, cover the newly planted seeds with a polyester blanket. Raccoons may force you to use an electric fence; otherwise, try setting a transistor radio in the garden at night or cheese-cloth bags of human hair to ward off raccoon attacks. (After a few rains, though, the hair loses its effectiveness.)

As far as diseases are concerned, flea beetles and cucumber beetles spread bacterial wilt. If you see these pests, control them with pyre-thrum/rotenone to prevent corn bacterial wilt. Corn blight and corn smut also attack corn plants, but three-year rotations or resistant cultivars can keep these diseases in check.

Harvest

Three factors can help determine the harvesting time for corn. First, you can use the days to maturity as a rough guide (60 to 90 days). Second, you can watch for the corn silk to brown. And third, you can pop a kernel with your fingernail; if a milky fluid appears, the corn is ready for harvesting. A watery or thick mush upon popping the kernel indicates immaturity or over-the-hill corn, respectively. Remember, though, that the newer homo-zygous shrunken 2 corns do not have a milky texture; therefore, you must taste the corn for sweetness instead of looking at the fluid it produces.

If you like to freeze part of your corn harvest, you'll be interested to know that for twelve years now my wife and I have been freezing corn without blanching it, with excellent results. We simply husk the corn, remove the silk, pop the ears into a freezer bag, and freeze them right away. To heat the corn, we drop the frozen ears in a pan of water, bring it to a boil, and boil slowly for four to five minutes. The corn comes out tender and sweet. I've heard from friends that some yellow corn cultivars don't freeze well this way. But I have had good luck with 'Silver Queen' and all the newer cultivars I've tried, Everlasting Harvest and Extra Sweet types.

Cowpeas

Choices

Other names associated with cowpeas include southern peas, black-eyed peas, crowders, and yard-long beans. Not all cowpeas are black-eyed peas, however, because only some have the black spot on the pea. Actually these plants are all beans, but the names stem from the fact that their pods contain beans that look like peas, if you stretch your imagination. You can generally find cowpeas in the South; however, you can grow cowpeas anywhere that corn grows.

The 'Pink Eye Purple Hull', 'Queen Anne', 'Mississippi Silver', 'California Blackeye', 'Big Boy', 'Magnolia Blackeye', and 'Crimson' are all popular cultivars of the cowpea. Although most cowpeas grow on vines, 'Crimson' grows on a bush-type plant.

Culture

Sow cowpeas about ½ to 1 inch deep with the furrower, dibble, or bulb planter at the same time you would normally sow lima beans. Warm soil is a must for cowpea sowing. Also, be sure to use the legume inoculant discussed in the section on beans. Cowpeas can add nitrogen to your soil if you inoculate them. Germination occurs within seven to ten days at 70°F. You can produce cowpea transplants in our Styrofoam cups and grow them intensively under the same condition as beans need. Climbing cowpeas are a natural for vertical gardens.

Pests

Nematodes and aphids seem to be the worst pests that attack cowpeas. By using interplantings of French marigolds with cowpeas, you can control nematodes, because the marigold roots secrete a chemical disliked by nematodes. Studies also indicate that the addition of compost decreases nematode populations. You can use soap sprays to knock out aphid infestations.

Harvest

You can harvest cowpeas like snap beans, shelled green peas, or dried beans. Don't save the seeds, because they quickly lose germination ability. Maturity of cowpeas occurs from 65 to 85 days.

Cucumbers

Choices

When it comes to cucumbers, many more choices exist than you may think. Conventional salad cucumbers are long and narrow, while pickling types are somewhat shorter and wider. Seedless cucumbers, also called European cucumbers, also exist and are milder, much longer, and more slender than conventional cucumbers. Most European cucumbers are greenhouse varieties, but a few cultivars are also available for outdoor planting. You can even find a cucumber that is yellow and looks a bit like a lemon!

Some cucumbers have all female flowers instead of both male and female flowers. These all-female types *(gynoecious)* produce more cucumbers than conventional types do. Gynoecious cucumber packages often include some dyed seeds that you should plant to produce male flowers for pollination. Some gynoecious cucumbers, called parthenocarpic, do not need male pollinators, because they set fruit without pollination.

A few of the many conventional hybrid cucumbers for salads include 'Burpee Hybrid II' (also gynoecious), 'Park's Whopper Hybrid', 'Universal', and 'Marketmore 80'. If you want early conventional cucumbers, try 'Early Triumph' or 'Early Pride'. If cucumbers make you burp, try some of the burpless ones such as 'Sweet Slice', 'Sweet Success', or 'Green Knight'. If you have limited space but you don't want a vertical garden, try the bush forms such as 'Bush Champion', 'Bush Whopper', and 'Spacemaster', or short, vining ones like 'Pot Luck' or 'Streamliner'. For pickling cucumbers try 'Liberty', 'Calypso', 'Lucky Strike', or 'Salvo'. If you like the idea of gynoecious cucumbers with heavy yields, try 'Sweet Success' (also burpless), 'Slice Master', 'Streamliner', 'Gemini', or 'Raider'. If you want a novel white or yellow cucumber, try 'White Wonder' or 'Lemon', respectively. For a taste treat, try some of the European cucumbers such as 'Telegraph Improved'. Japanese cucumbers that are similar to these include 'Suyo Long' (has ridges), 'Chinese Long Green' (smooth), and 'Kyoto' (smooth). Plant these seedless cucumbers away from regular cucumbers to prevent pollination and seed formation. If you are not quite sure what kind of cucumbers you want to plant, try a hybrid that combines the good in both American and European cucumbers such as Park Seed's 'Euro-American Hybrid'.

Culture

Cucumbers are a warm-season crop, so plant them directly outdoors no earlier than one or two weeks after the last killing frost. Moisture is also critical to cucumber growth; cucumbers have a visual way of showing that they are not receiving enough moisture (Figure 8-3). As such, cucumbers and moisture-conserving black plastic mulches make a great partnership. Plant cucumber seeds about ½ inch deep with the furrower or dibble.

To get very early cucumbers, start the seeds indoors four to six weeks before outdoor planting times. At 70°F cucumbers germinate in seven to ten days. I use our Styrofoam cups (12-ounce) and thin to one cucumber plant per cup. Remember, cucumbers are finicky about transplanting, so start them in our specially modified cups. Cucumbers are a natural for vertical gardens. I place seeds or transplants at 12-inch intervals for intensive plantings. Initially you may have to tie the cucumbers to your vertical supports to encourage them to climb.

If you want a longer harvest, grow early and late cucumbers. You can also put in a second sowing four to five weeks after the first, which could also follow an early vertical crop such as peas.

Pests

The most serious problem that affects my cucumbers is the striped cucumber beetle, which transmits bacterial wilt and cucumber mosaic (Figure 8-3). The spotted cucumber beetle is just as serious as the striped one. If you see either of these pests, immediately cover your cucumbers with polyester envelopes. You can also use pyrethrum and rotenone or put in a later second planting to miss the pests. As far as other insects are concerned, you can destroy aphids with soap sprays and the pickle worm with rotenone.

Some diseases that attack cucumbers other than those carried by beetles include downy and powdery mildew, anthracnose, scab, leaf spot, and leaf blight. If these diseases trouble your cucumbers, look for resistant varieties of cucumbers, rotate your crops, and be sure to clean up all debris in the area. These diseases can be carried over in debris from infected plants.

Harvest

Pick cucumbers when they become dark green but are not overly large. As cucumbers get bigger and show yellow or white, seeds have formed and the cucumbers become bitter. European and Japanese types, being seedless, can get much bigger than conventional cucumbers. Days to harvest are 55 to 70, depending upon the cultivar.

A

B

8-3 These photos show two cucumber problems. The cucumber beetle carries cucumber wilt disease, which wipes out plants in no time (A). When cucumbers don't get enough water, they do not develop fully. The cucumber in photo B had enough water when it started growing but not enough later on, as you can see by the smaller end.

Eggplants

Choices

Most eggplants look like a large egg with smooth, shiny, deep purple skin. Cultivars of this type include 'Burpee Hybrid', 'Black Bell', 'Black Magic', and 'Black Nite'. Some more elongated and narrower eggplants, which we refer to as oriental eggplants, include 'Classic', 'Ichiban Hybrid', and 'Imperial'. One eggplant cultivar, the 'Easter Egg', looks like a small egg complete with a color change from white to yellow. Although eggplants are a long, warm-season crop and sometimes fare poorly in more northern areas, breeders have developed cultivars for shorter season areas. These varieties include 'Dusky Hybrid', 'Early Beauty Hybrid', 'Early Black Magic', and 'Epic'. Those of you who enjoy gourmet baby vegetables would like a variety called 'Little Fingers'.

Culture

Gardeners generally start eggplants as transplants because of their long season requirement. Direct seeding is feasible in the lower South, but it is preferable to use transplants. The earliest date for setting out eggplants is about ten days after that for tomatoes or three weeks after the last killing spring frost. Nighttime temperatures should be at least 50°F or even better, 55°F. Daytime temperatures should be over 60°F. Eggplants are a touch more sensitive than tomatoes.

I sow eggplant seeds about ½ inch deep in the 12-ounce modified Styrofoam cups. The seeds germinate in about ten to fifteen days at 70°F or faster on top of the refrigerator. Plants should be thinned to one eggplant for each cup. Start your transplants six to eight weeks before their outdoor planting time. I place my eggplants in an intensive planting pattern using a spacing distance of 18 inches.

Eggplants generally tie up space for most of the garden season. Eggplants can follow an early-season crop like lettuce, peas, or radishes. You can interplant eggplants with established spring lettuce, because the eggplants will fill in the space after you have picked the lettuce.

Black plastic mulch is a natural for eggplants, because they prefer warm, moist soils. Just use the bulb planter to place your transplants through the black plastic. Eggplants are also big feeders; therefore, I suggest that you add organic matter and fertilizer in the no-dig hole for big feeders.

Pests

I have beaten eggplant maggots and the flea beetle, my eggplants' worst pests, by putting up the polyester barrier as soon as they appear. You can also use either pyrethrum or rotenone. Get after these pests right away, because they are carriers of plant diseases. Other pests that affect the eggplants include the Colorado potato beetle, which you can control with pyrethrum or rotenone, and aphids, which you can control with soap spray. As far as diseases go, you can avoid verticillium wilt, fusarium wilt, or blight by using crop rotation. Just make sure you don't follow the eggplants with their relatives, peppers, potatoes, and tomatoes.

Harvest

Eggplants require about 60 to 70 days from transplanting to the first harvest. You can pick eggplants at any time, but you will get the best ones if you pick them before their seeds are hard. With conventional eggplants, pick them when they have a 4-inch diameter and while their skin is shiny. With any eggplant variety, dull color is usually indicative of mature seeds. Pick eggplants by cutting their stems, which are quite tough, with either a sharp knife or a small pruner.

Herbs

I would like to say a few, quick words about herbs. While I don't grow all of them, I do grow a few favorites like parsley, basil, and dill. Many herbs dislike transplanting, so I recommend using our modified Styrofoam cups, which produce great herb transplants from seed that go ever so nicely into the garden with the bulb digger. The ones I've tried grow well with the use of black plastic. Sow the seeds indoors at 70°F about four to six weeks prior to your frost-free date. Use the 12-ounce cups, thinning to one plant per cup. After you harden the transplants, put them into your garden about one week after your frost-free date. Many herb seeds have special requirements for germination, such as refrigeration prior to sowing or light during germination. Other herb seeds have short lives and you can't save them.

I know of about three dozen herbs. Detailed information as such is beyond the scope of this book. If you intend to raise herbs, I suggest you consult other sources of information. Many books exist, but I find two to be most helpful, *The Rodale Herb Book* and *Park's Success with Herbs*. The latter is available from Park Seed Company.

Lettuce
Choices

Head qualities determine lettuce choice. Typical market lettuce has a firm, hard head and is grouped with the crispheads. Some refer to this lettuce as the iceberg type. Crisphead lettuce is the hardest to grow for home gardeners and has the least heat resistance and taste; however, a large number of people still wish to grow it. Of all the crispheads, the only one with which I have luck in terms of good heads is 'Mission'.

A second lettuce group, the butterhead or Boston type, has heads that are loose and soft. The taste of butterhead lettuce is much better than that of the crispheads, and its heat tolerance is slightly better. Some of the butterhead cultivars include 'Bibb', 'Buttercrunch', 'Dark Green Boston', and 'Patty'.

A third group consists of lettuces that have a rosette of loose leaves, essentially no head, and we call them loose-leaf or leaf lettuce. Leaf lettuce has a good taste and moderate heat resistance. Leaf lettuce also has color variations. The red forms include 'Prizehead', 'Red Salad Bowl', 'Red Sails', and 'Ruby'; while typical green leaf lettuces include 'Blackseeded Simpson', 'Crispy Sweet', 'Grand Rapids', 'Green Ice', 'Green Wave', 'Oak Leaf', and 'Slo-Bolt'. 'Slo-Bolt' and 'Green Wave' have a bit more heat resistance than the others should you get early, hot summers. For the lovers of baby or gourmet vegetables, there is 'Tom Thumb'. My favorite of the green forms is 'Green Ice', while my favorite of the red leaf lettuces is 'Red Sails'.

The last group consists of lettuces with tall, slender, upright, loose heads, and we term them cos or romaine lettuce. Romaine cultivars include 'Green Towers', with which I have had great luck, 'Parris Island', and 'Valmaine Cos'.

Incidentally, the best Caesar salad I have ever tasted was a homemade salad with a mixture of the four types of lettuce I just discussed.

Culture

Lettuce is a cool-season crop. Heat causes lettuce to bolt (flower), whereupon the taste becomes bitter. You can plant lettuce seed outdoors as early as you can work the soil. Transplants or seeds can go outdoors one to three weeks before the last killing spring frost. Seeds should be fresh, not saved, because they are short-lived. The germination of lettuce seeds requires light. You can directly seed with the furrower, using ¼-inch-deep scratches. I usually start lettuce transplants four to six weeks ahead of outdoor planting time in 8-ounce cups. Press the seeds lightly into the growing mixture, thinning to one plant to a cup. Twelve-ounce cups can carry two or three lettuce transplants. At 70°F the seeds germinate in seven to ten days. Succession planting at two-week intervals will extend the harvest, but make sure you stop the plantings so that the last lettuce matures at average temperatures no higher than 65°F. You can resume your lettuce plantings in late summer.

Lettuce, especially the heading types, requires considerable moisture to grow. Lack of moisture causes a failure to head. As such, black plastic and lettuce are great partners. I usually place leaf lettuces with the bulb planter at 6-inch intervals for intensive plantings through black plastic, and I give the heading types 12-inch squares in which to grow.

In the spring you can follow lettuce with bush snap beans or beets. In the fall you can follow the snap beans with more lettuce. You can interplant lettuce with summer squash, bush snap beans, cabbage, broccoli, carrots, or onions.

To get a few weeks more time out of lettuce in the warmer weather, shade it by stretching polyester material or cheesecloth across some poles, like a roof. Another approach to extending the growing season of lettuce is to interplant the lettuce with something that shades the lettuce at its maturity, such as squash, pole beans, or tomatoes.

Pests

Aphids, cutworms, and slugs can be troublesome to lettuce plants. Use soap sprays to knock out the aphids, leave part of the Styrofoam cup rim in place to foil cutworms, and hand-collect slugs at dusk with a flashlight. You can also sprinkle wood ashes or limestone around the plants to rid them of slugs, because slugs don't like to cross this dry barrier.

Some diseases that bother lettuce are bottom rot, gray mold rot, downy mildew, lettuce drop, and yellows. Yellows comes from a virus carried by leafhoppers, but you prevent this disease by putting up a polyester barrier if you see leafhoppers. The other diseases are minimal if you use a two-year rotation and make sure you don't follow lettuce with chicory, endive, or dandelions, because they can be hosts for the same diseases.

Tip burn is another lettuce problem, but not a disease, that occurs due to high temperatures with dry soils. You can avoid tip burn by using black plastic over your garden.

Harvest

To get the crispiest lettuce, you will need early morning picking and quick refrigeration. The days to maturity for lettuce from seed are 75 to 90 for crispheads, 65 to 80 for butterheads, 40 to 50 for loose-leafs, and 75 to 80 for cos types. If you take only the outside leaves of leaf lettuce, you can prolong the harvest period.

Melons

Choices

We call them cantaloupes at the market, but they really are muskmelons. The true cantaloupe is grown in Europe. Muskmelons have ribbed and netted skin with orange or salmon flesh. A group of closely related melons are the winter melons: the honeydew, crenshaw, and casaba. These melons have light green, salmon, and white flesh, respectively. Like muskmelons and winter melons, watermelons (although not as closely related as the others) belong to the cucumber family.

Standard choices in muskmelons include 'Burpee's Ambrosia', 'Burpee Hybrid', 'Delicious', 'Gold Star', 'Luscious Hybrid', and 'Saticoy'. If you are short on space, bush varieties of muskmelons such as 'Bush Star', 'Honeybush', or 'Short 'N' Sweet' can help alleviate the problem. Those of you with short growing seasons might appreciate the earlier muskmelons like 'Alaska', 'Earlisweet', 'Early Dawn', 'Early Hybrid', 'Early Northern Queen', or 'Sweet 'N' Early Hybrid'.

The conventional honeydew melon variety is called, as you might expect, 'Honey Dew'. Earlier varieties are also available, including 'Early Dew', 'Honeygrow', 'Limelight Hybrid', and 'Venus Hybrid'. A bush form of honeydew called 'Oliver's Pearl Cluster' is available, too.

Crenshaw melon cultivars include 'Burpee Early Hybrid' or 'Honeyshaw Hybrid', while a good casaba melon choice is 'Golden Beauty'.

Good choices of large watermelons include 'Black Diamond'. 'Charlston Gray', 'Dixie Queen', and 'Sweet Favorite'. Other varieties generally produce smaller melons, somtimes referred to as "icebox melons." Examples include the bush, early, seedless, and yellow watermelons. Bush forms require the same time to grow, but less space, and include 'Burpee Sugar Bush', 'Bushbaby Hybrid', 'Bush Charlston Gray', 'Bush Jubilee', 'Garden Baby Hybrid', and 'Sweetheart'. I've had good luck with the bush types. Early watermelons include 'New Hampshire Midget' and 'Sugar Baby'. Seedless watermelons include 'Burpee Hybrid Seedless' and 'Triple Sweet Seedless'. The seedless melons do require a few pollen donators, such as 'Sugar Baby', in order to set fruit. For a novelty, you might want to try a small, yellow watermelon such as 'Yellow Baby Hybrid' or 'Yellow Doll'.

Culture

Melons need a long period of warm weather to grow and mature. Seeds rot in cool weather or germinate poorly and slowly. At a minimum, the nighttime temperature must be above 55°F for melons to progress. In the North, melons need help. I start my muskmelons or watermelons in 12-ounce modified Styrofoam cups. Melons transplant poorly; therefore, individual transplant containers are essential, and our special ones are the best. Plant muskmelon seeds ½ inch deep and watermelons 1 inch. I start the seeds about four or five weeks before I plan to put them out in my garden. Seeds germinate in seven to ten days at 70°F, but I put them on the top of the refrigerator (75°F), which cuts germination to five to seven days. My aim is to time the transplants so that the nighttime temperature is near 50°F when I put out the transplants, usually about three or four weeks after the last spring frost.

As soon as I start the transplants, I put black plastic mulch down in my garden to warm the soil while the transplants are growing. By using my soil thermometer, I have found that the soil under the black plastic stays several degrees warmer than uncovered soil, and these few degrees make a big growing time difference with melons. I plant the hardened melon transplants with the bulb planter, making a deep hole for big feeders as with eggplants, filling the difference with compost and organic fertilizer, and covering over with a touch of soil. I position four transplants around the milk bottle feeder (see Chapter 4) for later feeding supplements. Then I cover the melons with either a polyester or slitted plastic cloche, which gives the melons an extra shot of heat and gets them off to a quick start. In addition, the polyester cloche wards off the cucumber beetle and the wilt disease transmitted by the beetle. The slitted polyethylene gives a slight edge to the early arrival of melons but is not quite as protective against insects. The black plastic helps the soil retain its moisture, and melons require a lot of moisture during growth. The plastic also prevents rotting of melons, which sometimes happens when they contact soil.

Melons do require a lot of space to grow. The smallest amount of area you can use is 4 square feet for each hill of melons. If you use the 4-foot-wide black plastic as I do, just run the hills dead center at 4-foot intervals, a spacing that works for the bush forms and less aggressive vining types. Large watermelons, however, need more space. Vertical gardening is possible for the smaller melons, if you have a sturdy support system of wood and wire mesh. You must also support the melons with a sling, such as an old nylon stocking or panty hose. In the South, you can use either transplants or direct seeding with the furrower or dibble.

Don't forget to supplement your melons with some organic liquid fertilizer via the milk bottle feeder. You can also add water with the feeder; but once melons have reached full size and have started to ripen, cut back on the water. Drying of the soil during ripening seems to improve the process.

Pests

The insects that attack melons are the same ones you encounter with cucumbers, which I have already discussed. Again, watch out for the cucumber beetle and the wilt disease it carries, keeping the beetle at bay by using the polyester cloche. Troublesome melon diseases include fusarium wilt, downy mildew, powdery mildew, and anthracnose (with watermelons only). Using a three year rotation or resistant cultivars eliminates these disease problems.

Harvest

Harvest melons with care, because an unripe melon, once picked, will sweeten poorly. The days to maturity offer one clue as to when to judge the melons as being ripe. Standard muskmelons require 75 to 90 days to harvest; earlier varieties of muskmelons require 75 days. Conventional honeydews require 110 days to harvest, while earlier cultivars are ready in about 90 days. The standard crenshaw melon requires 110 days to harvest, and earlier varieties need about 90 days. The casaba melon needs 120 days to reach ripeness. The standard large watermelon needs 85 to 95 days to harvest, but earlier varieties will ripen in 70 to 75 days. Keep in mind that when we discuss the number of days melons need to mature, we are speaking of warm days when the temperature is at least 70°F. I have a growing season of roughly 190 days, but only half of the season is actually suitable to growing melons.

In addition to the number of days to maturity, there are several other clues to aid you in determining the ripeness of your melons. First let's look at muskmelons. Ripe muskmelons have a fragrant musklike aroma. The end opposite the stem will give a little with slight pressure. At the stem end, you should see cracks around the stem along with a slight shriveling of the stem. The acid test is that the stem should separate from the melon with slight pressure; if it doesn't, wait a few more days.

With the winter melons, the ripeness signal is a color change of the skin. Honeydews develop a yellowish cast in either their ivory white or light green skin, depending upon the cultivar. The skin of a casaba becomes golden yellow and that of a crenshaw, yellow-tan. All three of these melons, under slight pressure, show a yielding of the end opposite the stem when ripe.

The watermelon is perhaps the hardest to judge for ripeness. Some people can tell by tapping the melon. Unripe melons have a sharp sound, like "pink-pank," while ripe ones give out with a dull "punk." The bottom, where the melon is in contact with the soil or mulch, develops a whitish to yellow color. Usually the three tendrils nearest the stem end are dead and dry. With care you should be able to pick your own delicious melons.

Onions and Relatives

Choices

Choices abound in the onion group. You can have yellow, red, or white domestic onions. Sweeter versions also exist, which we refer to as foreign or Spanish and Bermuda onions. These latter onions require a longer growing season than do the domestic onions. If you pick onions when they are immature, that is, pencil-thin to marble-size onions, we refer to them as scallions. Somewhat similar to scallions, Japanese bunching onions have more pronounced leaves and a bulb that is thinner and softer but more thickened at the neck than that of scallions. Unlike scallions, Japanese bunching onions do not develop into large onions if you let them grow longer. There are also mini-onions, sometimes referred to as pearl onions. Pearl onions are popular creamed or in a mixed pea and onion dish. There is even an onion variety that forms bulblets on top (the tree or Egyptian onion).

Chives, garlic, leeks, and shallots are also members of the onion family. We grow chives for their small leaves with a delicate onion flavor. One form of chive grown infrequently has a garliclike flavor. We grow garlic for its flavorful bulb, which splits into cloves. Leeks have a slight, soft, flattened bulb with a sheath of leaves. The flavor of leeks is milder and sweeter than that of onions. Shallots have a multiple bulb that we use when young. Shallots have a delicate flavor and find use in gourmet cooking, as do leeks.

Most of the yellow domestic onions are the cultivar 'Ebenezer' or closely related types. Some other popular yellow onions include 'Early Yellow Globe' and 'Yellow Stuttgart' (Dutch). If you want sweetness in a raw yellow onion, try 'Sweet Sandwich'. 'Crystal Wax' and 'White Ebenezer' are popular white onions. Some reds include 'Benny's Red', 'Red Hamburger', 'Red Wethersfield', and 'Southport Red Globe'. These red and white onions are a touch milder than yellow onions. The "foreign" onions are milder and sweeter yet and include 'Bermuda', 'Sweet Bermuda', 'Sweet Spanish', and 'Walla Walla'.

You can pull any one of these onions young as scallions. Cultivars that essentially remain scallions throughout their development are the Japanese bunching or spring onions, such as 'Ishikuro', 'Kujo Green Multistalk', and 'White Lisbon'. A good pearl onion is 'Quicksilver', while the tree onion usually sold as Egyptian tree onion is probably 'Perennial Tree'.

There are few other names for garlic. Usually it is classified as either the early white, or Mexican, type or the late pink, or Italian, type. There are no other names for chives either, with the exception of the garlic version called garlic chives. A number of leeks are available, such as 'American Flag', 'Broad London', 'Electra', 'Inverno', 'King Richard', 'Leader', or 'Titan'. Suppliers sell shallots as 'Dutch Yellow' or 'Giant Red'. We also call the yellow forms multiplier onions and the red forms French shallots. Gourmets prefer the French shallots.

Culture

You can grow domestic or regular onions (yellow, red, or white) from seeds, sets, or plants. Sets are convenient, plants produce more quickly, and seeds are cheaper but take longer to mature than sets or plants. You can produce your own transplants easily with seeds or get results with direct seeding. One plus with seeds is that you have a much larger choice of cultivars. You can plant all forms outside two to four weeks before the last killing spring frost, using the furrower for seeds, sets, and plants, or the dibble for sets or plants.

An important point to know is that onion bulb formation depends on day length; therefore, you can't use all cultivars in all places. For example, the Spanish and Bermuda types might not form bulbs in the North, unless you planted them early and as good-sized transplants. To be sure you use proper cultivars for your area, buy your onions locally or check with your local extension service. If you order sets by mail, order them from a reputable dealer to ensure that you get the right onions.

When planting onions, be sure you use fresh seeds; onion seed ages rather quickly. Start your seeds eight to ten weeks ahead of your putting-

8-4 *These onions need to have soil mounded around their bases to cover the exposed bulbs.*

out date. I use the 12-ounce Styrofoam cups for my transplants and cover the seeds with ½ inch of growing medium. Seeds come up in ten to fourteen days at 70°F. You can thin the plants to about three equally spaced transplants per cup. When you plant the transplants in your garden, put in the whole group with the bulb planter or each transplant separately with a dibble. If you don't want this bother, just buy and plant sets, covering the sets with 1 inch of soil. Set transplants to the depth at which they were growing. You can also plant seeds directly outdoors in a ½-inch furrower scratch. Use a 3-inch spacing between every plant for intensive plantings of onions. You can follow onions with snap beans or interplant them with lettuce.

You must raise leeks as transplants because they take a long time to mature. Use the same standards for cups, seed depth, and germination time as you used for onions. Place each leek transplant in a dibble hole so that only 2 inches of leaf protrudes. If you do this, you won't have to mound soil at the plant base to blanch the lower part of the leek later. In the lower South, you can seed leeks directly, but do so as soon as the soil is workable. Leeks are a touch hardier than onions.

You can easily raise chives as transplants, but be sure to use fresh seeds. Lightly press the seeds into the growing medium. Use a 12-ounce cup, and thin to four transplants per cup. Seeds germinate at the same rate as onions. Put the transplants into the garden with the bulb planter, placing four holes close together and putting in four groups. This pattern will fill in nicely and give you a good clump. These plants are perennials; therefore, planting chives is a once-and-done job. Just divide the clump every two or three years.

Gardeners usually plant shallots as a clove from the multiple bulb, and you can use either the dibble or bulb planter. Set the cloves deeply enough so that the soil barely covers them. You can also plant garlic cloves with the bulb planter, covering the cloves with about 1 inch of soil.

Pests

Two insects are real pests to onions and their relatives: onion maggots and thrips. If these pests arrive on the scene, put up your polyester barrier. You can also use rotenone against thrips. Diseases that affect the onion family include onion smut, downy mildew, bacterial soft spot, basal rot, pink root rot, neck rot, yellow dwarf, and yellows, with the last two being viral diseases. I never have these disease problems, most likely because I rotate my onions on a three-year schedule. Remember also to keep the space free of chives, garlic, leeks, and shallots during this time, because the same diseases can attack these onion relatives.

Harvest

Domestic onions require 110 to 130 days from seed to harvest, while foreign onions need 125 to 185 days. In the North, you must use transplants for the foreign cultivars because of their need for a long growing season. Shallots usually need 90 to 110 days to mature, garlic needs 150 to 180 days, and leeks need 180 days. You can pick immature onions as scallions and immature shallots as green onions. Onions, shallots, and garlic are mature when their tops fall over and dry. At this point, you can lift the bulbs, air-dry them on a rack inside a garage and store them in a cool, dry place. You can pick chives at any point, but take only part of the leaves or a fraction of the total leaves if you take the whole leaf, so the plant can keep on growing. You can rinse, chop, and freeze chives in a plastic bag for later use. Pick leeks when they are 1 to 1½ inches in diameter, and pick bunching onions any time during the season.

Peas

Choices

As my first crop to go into the soil, peas mark the start of a new garden season. You have some choice with peas. The standard garden pea comes either smooth or wrinkled, with the wrinkled ones having the sweeter (and better) taste. Next we have the old edible-podded peas, snow peas, sugar peas, or oriental peas. More recently another edible-podded pea appeared, snap peas. The difference between this new cultivar and the older ones is that the edible pod lasts much longer and is sweeter, and you consume the pod with larger peas than with the snow peas.

Standard garden peas include 'Alderman', 'Green Arrow', 'Lincoln', and 'Patriot'. For early peas, try 'Alaska', 'Burpee's Blue Bantam', 'Knight', 'Laxton's Progress', 'Little Marvel', 'Maestro', and 'Sparkle'. If heat comes on too quickly and ruins your peas or you want to stretch the pea season, try 'Wando', which has good heat resistance. Should disease get you down, I suggest 'Almota', the most disease-resistant pea presently available. If you're into freezing peas, try 'Freezonian', 'Fridget', or 'Frosty'. You say you love pea soup? Then go for 'Century'.

Snow pea cultivars include 'Dwarf Grey Sugar', 'Mammoth Melting Sugar' (a late variety), 'Oregon Sugar Pod II', 'Snowbird', and 'Snowflake'. The first new snap pea, 'Sugar Snap' is tall, requires support, and harvests later than newer introductions; but I think that taste-wise, it's the best. 'Sugar Rae' is short but not early. Short and early choices include 'Sugar Anne', 'Early Snap', 'Sweet Snap', 'Sugar Bon', and 'Sugar Daddy'. Although 'Sugar Daddy' is a stringless pea, its taste is not up to that of 'Sugar Snap'. Besides good taste, 'Sugar Snap' shows a touch more heat tolerance and frost resistance than do garden peas.

Culture

Peas are an early, cool-season crop that produce best as a spring or fall crop in the North and a fall, winter, or spring crop in the South. Peas are also a legume crop like beans and pull free nitrogen fertilizer from the air if you inoculate the seeds with the required bacteria (see Beans).

You can seed peas directly into your garden as soon as you can work the soil. In most cases this time period works out to be anywhere from one to five weeks before your last killing frost in the spring. You can use the furrower, dibble, or bulb planter to plant pea seeds, covering the seeds with 1 to 2 inches of soil.

I suggest the following intensive planting system. First provide some support for the peas, whether it be brush, growth panels, nylon net, or a pea fence (see Chapter 7). Next plant a double row, one on each side of the support and 9 inches away from the support, which gives you roughly 18 inches between the rows. Seeds germinate in seven to fourteen days, depending on soil temperature.

If you lose a lot of seeds to rot prior to germination or just want the earliest peas possible, try the following planting system. Soak pea seeds overnight at room temperature; then plant several seeds 1 inch deep in each 12-ounce modified Styrofoam cup. The seeds should come up in seven days or less. Perform the steps just mentioned four to six weeks before normal outdoor seeding time. At the same time, lay down a strip of black plastic where your peas will go in the garden; then put up your vertical supports. The black plastic will warm the soil just enough to get your transplants off to a good start. Thin each cup to three nicely spaced transplants. Put the transplants through the plastic with the bulb planter, using the double row concept and leaving 3 inches between each cup hole in the row. About one month later, cut and remove the plastic to prevent overwarming of the pea roots. This entire process will give you the earliest-ever peas.

For a more continual pea harvest, you can plant early and late cultivars or sow the same peas at ten-day intervals. Make sure your last sowing occurs before daytime temperatures frequently start to reach 60°F. You can follow peas with another climbing crop, such as pole beans or cucumbers, or with crops such as corn, beets, carrots, bush snap beans, late cabbage, or squash.

Pests

The pea aphid and pea weevil are sometimes troublesome to pea plants. You can control the aphid with either soap sprays, pyrethrum, or rotenone. Rotations and garden sanitation ward off weevil problems. Disease problems of peas include root rot, powdery mildew, bacterial blight, and wilt; but crop rotation appears to control these diseases.

Harvest

Peas mature in 58 to 75 days, depending upon the cultivar. For the best pea quality, carefully pick them in the morning. Damaged vines yield less for later pickings. With garden peas, look for well-developed green peas, making sure that you pick them before the peas start to harden; otherwise, they become starchy and lose their sweetness. You can also pick dried peas for pea soup. You should refrigerate peas upon picking and use them quickly if you wish the peas to be sweet.

Pick snow peas when their pods are flat and the peas are just forming. If you miss this stage, treat snow peas in the same manner as garden peas. Pick snap peas with green pods and nicely developed but not hard peas. The sweetness of snap peas is much more stable than with the other kinds of peas. Most snap peas have a string, which you remove prior to raw or cooked consumption. Freezing of snap peas is possible, but the results are not as good as with garden peas.

Peppers
Choices

We can divide peppers into three basic groups: sweet bell, frying, and hot. Sweet bell peppers are mild and go from green to red or yellow when ripe. You can use sweet bell peppers raw in salads, or you can stuff or fry them. Frying peppers tend to be longer, narrower, and more tapered than bell peppers; they are also a bit more pungent than sweet bell peppers. Hot peppers vary from zesty hot to steamy knockouts. Although usually long and tapered, hot peppers also come in round or sausage shapes.

Standard bell peppers of the green to red type include 'Annabelle', 'Bell Boy', 'Burpee Tasty Hybrid', 'Lady Bell', 'Ma Belle', 'Park's Whopper Hybrid', 'Ringer', and 'Sweet Bell'. Early varieties of this type are 'Ace' and 'Gypsy Hybrid'. If you want huge peppers, try 'Big Bertha'. Yellow bell versions include 'Golden Bell' and 'Golden Summer'. 'Sweet Banana' is similar to the two yellow bell versions, except its shape is longer and tapered.

Good frying peppers, which usually are yellowish green when young and red upon maturity, include 'Cubanelle', 'Karlo', and 'Key Largo'. If you like 'Cubanelle' but wish it were earlier, try 'Hy Fry'.

Some hot peppers that become red in color when they're ripe are 'Anaheim M', 'Cayenne Long Slim', 'Early Jalapeno', or 'Jalapeno M'. A yellow hot pepper is 'Hungarian Yellow Wax'. Some of the really hot peppers are 'El Cid' and 'Thai Hot'. 'Red Cherry' is good for pickling. If you want large and hot peppers, try 'Hot Portugal'. Should you have an interest in trying hot peppers but want to start easy, I suggest 'Zippy Hybrid'.

Culture

Peppers require warmth and time for results. Yields are often fickle for several reasons. Blossoms fail to set fruit below 55°F or if the humidity is low. Low soil moisture or prolonged high temperatures also reduce fruiting. The first fruits, unless picked off, reduce subsequent yields.

It's preferable to start peppers as transplants six to eight weeks ahead of setting-out time. Peppers can go out about one week to ten days after the last killing spring frost. I place seeds ½ inch deep in the modified Styrofoam cups. At 70°F seeds come up in roughly two weeks; however, placing transplants on the top of a refrigerator (75°F) can cut this time to ten days. Thin the pepper plants to one plant per 12-ounce cup.

For the earliest and biggest yields of peppers, put down black plastic about three weeks before you put out the transplants. The plastic warms up the soil, giving your peppers a quick sendoff. Later, the plastic helps retain soil moisture, which encourages fruiting. Plant the peppers at an intensive,

12-inch spacing with the bulb planter. You can add organic matter to the hole if you wish; but don't add any more fertilizer other than the organic rapid starter solution, because adding too much nitrogen to the soil causes peppers to leaf excessively with few fruits.

After your peppers are in the ground, cover them with a polyester cloche; you can quite easily apply the polyester cloche and leave it on the plant if pepper maggots or flea beetles appear. The cloche warms up the air, giving you earlier fruit set. Remember, fruit set ceases below 55°F. When the first one or two pepper flowers just start to fruit, pinch them off, and you will improve later total yields.

Pests

Several insects attack peppers: the aphid, cutworm, flea beetle, leaf miner, pepper maggot, pepper weevil, and stalk borer. If you have cutworms, leave the upper half of the Styrofoam cup around the transplant, allowing it to protrude about 1 inch above the ground. The worst pepper pest I have had is the pepper maggot, which I ward off with the polyester barrier. Later peppers miss the pepper maggot, because it appears in early to midsummer. Pyrethrum, rotenone, or polyester barriers can control the flea beetle, and soap sprays work on aphids. If you have trouble with other pests, try the polyester barrier. Incidentally, the pepper weevil can breed on black nightshade, so keep the adjacent garden areas free of this weed.

Diseases of the pepper plant include bacterial spot, blight, anthracnose, tobacco mosaic virus, cucumber mosaic virus, and curly top virus. Aphids and leafhoppers spread the diseases, so keep after these pests if they appear. Smokers can also transfer tobacco mosaic virus; therefore, if you smoke, wash your hands well before touching peppers. Rotations help to keep disease problems down as well, but make sure you keep the areas free of pepper relatives: eggplants, potatoes, and tomatoes.

Harvest

Peppers start producing in 55 to 75 days from transplants, depending upon the cultivar. You can pick peppers green or when they turn yellow or red. Cut the fruit and leave a piece of attached stem, because you can very easily damage pepper plants and cause yields to go down if you pull the peppers off the stem. In addition, just before frost you may find that you have a huge crop of green peppers in various stages of development, as I usually do. I pick them all when frost threatens. After washing them, I core the pepper and cut it into strips, placing the strips (without blanching first) into freezer bags to freeze them. As recipes call for peppers, as in pizza or submarines, I take what I need from the bag. While softer than freshly cut peppers, frozen peppers taste great after a little cooking. My wife and I enjoy the pepper strips all winter long, especially uncooked in salads.

Potatoes

Choices

Potatoes come with either brown or red skins. We grow some potatoes specifically for baking and others for boiling. We grow early potatoes for fresh, short-term use and late potatoes for storage.

The most popular early potato, 'White Cobbler', has good baking qualities but poor storage qualities. 'Red Pontiac', a red-skinned potato, is an early-to-midseason, all-purpose potato that stores reasonably well. 'Kennebec' boils well and 'Russet Burbank' is a good baker. Both of these cultivars are late, brown-skinned, and have good storage qualities.

Culture

Potatoes are a cool-season crop with moderate frost tolerance. The potatoes or tubers form best when days are on the short side and temperatures are around 60° to 65°F. As such, some cultivars do not grow well in the South; therefore, Southerners should choose cultivars appropriate to their area.

We don't plant potatoes from seed but rather from seed potatoes, because potatoes do not grow uniformly true from seed. That is, young plants grown from seed will not produce plants (or potatoes) exactly like the parents. Although there is a potato called 'Explorer' that comes true from seed, I was quite unhappy with its size and yield when I grew it. The best seed potatoes are little tubers that weigh between 1 and 2 ounces and have at least one eye, such as 'Spud Buds' from Park Seed. You can also buy cut pieces of potato that have dried and contain one eye as seed potatoes or make your own, but be sure you get medium-sized, certified seed potatoes to avoid disease problems. Cut each potato into four to six pieces, making sure each piece has at least one eye. Let the pieces dry in a cool place (50° to 60°F) until the cut surfaces heal over.

You will easily grow the best potatoes you have ever had if you lay black plastic mulch down two weeks before your last killing frost in the spring. Using your bulb planter, place 4-inch-deep holes at spacings of 12 inches in all directions. After the organic rapid starter solution soaks into the soil, put a piece of seed potato in each hole and cover it. You will get sprouts in two to three weeks. You need not worry about weeds or mounding with soil; just remove the plastic at harvesttime and dig.

You can plant late potatoes a few weeks or more after you have planted early potatoes and in the same manner. Plant late potatoes so that they will mature around the time you expect the killing fall frost for best results.

Pests

Trouble can come to your potatoes in the form of aphids, flea beetles, Colorado potato beetles, and leafhoppers. Soap sprays can control aphids and leafhoppers, while pyrethrum or rotenone will control all four pests. The polyester barrier is quite effective also.

Diseases that affect potatoes are scab, early blight, late blight, verticillium wilt, black leg, mosaic, and leaf roll. The last two are viral diseases that aphids carry, so aphid control is important. If scab disfigures your spuds, adjust your soil pH to about 5; the microorganism that causes scab fares poorly at a soil pH of 5. Rotations and sanitation in the garden help to prevent diseases, and some degree of resistance is available with some cultures.

Harvest

Harvest new potatoes when the potato top flowers. New potatoes boil and cream well, but you must use them quickly. Harvest mature potatoes when the tops wither or about two weeks after the tops have frost-blackened. Carefully dig the potatoes with a spading fork. Don't wash them, but allow them to air dry for a day or two in a cool place, such as a garage. Store the potatoes in a cool, dark place. Potatoes mature in 90 to 120 days, depending upon the cultivar. A final note: Discard any potatoes showing green, because this discoloration means there is a toxin present.

Radishes

Choices

Pungent radishes come in either globular, elongated globular, or long, narrow shapes; and they can be red, white, red and white (bicolor), or black in color. Based upon days to maturity, heat resistance, and planting time, radishes can be grouped as early (spring) radishes, midseason (summer) radishes, and late (fall or winter) radishes.

Examples of red spring radishes are 'Champion', 'Cherry Belle', 'French Breakfast', 'Inca', 'Marabelle', Red King', and 'Ribella'. 'Sparkler' is a bicolor spring radish; 'Pax', 'White Giant', and 'White Icicle' are white varieties. An interesting novelty is 'Easter Egg', a mixture of differently colored (red, white, pink, and purple) radishes. 'Easter Egg' might be just the thing to start children off as gardeners. Midseason radishes include 'April Cross', 'All Seasons White', and 'Summer Cross Hybrid'; while late radishes are 'Black Spanish Long', 'China Rose', 'Mino Early No. 1', 'Miyashige', 'Round Black Spanish', 'Tama Hybrid', 'Tokinashi', and 'White Chinese'.

Culture

You can sow radishes as soon as you can work your soil but not earlier than a month before your last killing frost in the spring. Use the furrower to plant them, and cover the seeds with ½ inch of soil. While radish transplants are possible in the Styrofoam cups, I see no advantage to using this approach. Seeds germinate rapidly, usually in four to six days. You can sow spring radishes at seven- to ten-day intervals for successive harvests, stopping at midspring and resuming in the fall because spring radishes do poorly in warm weather. Thin the radishes to roughly 2 or 3 inches in all directions.

To stretch the radish season, use successive plantings of midseason radishes, which tolerate more heat than the early ones. Start planting midseason radishes about a month after you have planted the spring radishes, and discontinue plantings in the late spring. For fall and storage radishes, sow late radishes in the late summer to early fall, leaving about 5 to 6 inches between the fall radishes.

You can also interplant spring radishes as seeds with beets or carrots. The radish seeds germinate quickly and mark the rows long before the slow beets or carrots appear. After you harvest the radishes, the beets or carrots fill in the space. You can interplant radishes with early crops such as lettuce or spinach, as well. Bush snap beans make good fillers between spring and fall radishes.

Pests

The only radish pests of note are flea beetles and root maggots. Use pyrethrum or rotenone to control the beetles. The root maggot is the same one that attacks cabbages, so don't utilize the same space for both crops. You can stop the root maggot with the polyester barrier. Some people even use the radish as a trap crop to keep root maggots away from cabbage.

Harvest

Spring radishes mature in 20 to 30 days, and you can pull them when they are the size of a large marble or bigger. Don't let them go much beyond maturity, as warm weather causes splitting, pithiness, and extreme pungency. Summer radishes are ready in 35 to 45 days, and late radishes need 50 to 70 days. Store late radishes in moist sand in a cool cellar.

Spinach

Choices

We differentiate between the different kinds of spinach based on whether its leaves are smooth or crinkled (savoyed). We also describe some spinach as being bolt-resistant. Bolting refers to the formation of flower stalks and seeds by the spinach, an event that warm weather brings. Spinach is not worth harvesting after it bolts because the flavor turns bitter. Bolt-resistant spinach can take a bit more heat than ordinary cultivars, adding a week or two of extra harvest time.

Spinach varieties include 'America', 'Avon Hybrid', 'Bloomsdale Long Standing', 'Fabris', 'Indian Summer', 'Iron Duke Hybrid', 'King of Denmark', 'Melody Hybrid', 'Skookum', 'Tyee', and 'Winter Bloomsdale'. The differences among these varieties involve bolt resistance, disease resistance, and degree of uprightness, a characteristic involving the leaf angle. The more upright forms of spinach experience less soil splash from rain, and thus require less washing prior to cooking. There is also a spinach substitute available, New Zealand spinach, which when cooked tastes like spinach. Its advantage over spinach is that it grows in the warmer months.

Culture

You can plant spinach seed as soon as you can work the soil, usually one to five weeks before your last killing spring frost. Use the furrower to plant the seeds, and cover them with ½ inch of soil. Seedlings appear in eight to ten days. Transplants are possible with Styrofoam cups but offer no advantage except a few weeks extra on harvest time. Thin the seedlings to stand 3 inches apart in all directions for intensive plantings. For a continuous harvest, continue sowings at seven- to ten-day intervals until about six weeks before daytime temperatures will exceed 75°F. You can resume plantings in late summer, stopping about five weeks before your killing fall frost. You can follow early plantings of spinach with corn, snap beans, squash, or tomatoes; and you can interplant spinach with onions or carrots.

Fill the summer void with a sowing of New Zealand spinach about two weeks after the last spring frost. You can make successive plantings at two-week intervals, but stop about ten weeks prior to the killing fall frost. Regular spinach can take a few light frosts, but New Zealand spinach can't. Soak the seeds for one to two hours in water, starting out at 120°F, to improve germination. Using the furrower, sow seeds about 1 inch deep. The seeds will germinate in twelve to twenty days. Thin the plants to stand about 4 inches apart in all directions for intensive plantings.

Pests

Aphids and leaf miners are sometimes troublesome to spinach. Soap spray rids your spinach of aphids; but the only remedy for leaf miners is to put up the polyester barrier to prevent the adults from laying eggs. If you already have leaf miners, put your polyester barrier up about two weeks before the last killing spring frost, and keep it in place for six to eight weeks, roughly when egg laying takes place. Also, make sure you keep the garden free of lamb's-quarters, because this weed hosts the leaf miner.

Harvest

Harvest spinach and New Zealand spinach by picking individual leaves. Don't take more than a fraction of the plant's leaves and you will be able to stretch the harvest. If you have successive spinach plantings, you can harvest the entire plant. Spinach is ready to harvest in 40 to 50 days, New Zealand spinach in 70 days.

Squash
Choices

Pumpkins and squash are relatives; therefore, their culture is similar. I will discuss them together and will include pumpkins, winter squash, and summer squash.

Winter squash and pumpkins usually grow on large, sprawling vines, although a few bush cultivars are available. Pumpkins are usually round with yellow to orange skin and flesh. Their size ranges from small to immense. Winter squash are similar to pumpkins and have a hard rind and a yellow to orange flesh. The skin color of winter squash, however, can vary from tan to orange to blue-green. Winter squash shapes also vary considerably, from half-dumbbells through acorns to ovals. Both pumpkins and winter squash mature in the fall and possess a hard rind when ready for use.

Summer squash grow on bushy plants. We use immature summer squash in the summer and don't store them for winter as we do pumpkins and winter squash. The skin of summer squash is fragile and yellow, green, or whitish green in color, while the flesh is usually a white to cream color. Summer squash are generally cylindrical, clublike, or flattened and acornlike in shape.

Many cultivars of squash exist; therefore, it's difficult to choose favorites. New introductions also occur frequently, making the decision even harder. As such, we can't cover all cultivars in this book. Bill and I have favorites, which we realize may not be yours. We try new kinds of squash every year, always comparing them to our "old reliables." Our following thoughts on squash we have known may help you make your decision on what varieties to grow.

First, let's start with the easy group, pumpkins. For those giant prize-winners, try one of these: 'Atlantic Giant', 'Big Max', 'Big Moon', 'Big Tom',

'Connecticut Field', 'Hungarian Mammoth', and 'Kentucky Large Field'. If you wish to grow pumpkins for pies, why not start with 'New England Pie', 'Small Sugar Pie', or 'Triple Treat'? You can actually carve just about any pumpkin for Halloween, but you might want to try 'Jack-O'-Lantern'. If garden space is a problem, try the bush-like (short vines) pumpkin, 'Bushkin'.

We have two favorites in the winter squash category. 'Waltham Butternut' and 'Buttercup' (Burgess strain preferred). Our reasons for choosing 'Waltham Butternut' over other winter squash cultivars are its resistance to squash vine borer, high vitamin A content (highest of any), good taste, and excellent storage quality. While 'Buttercup' doesn't quite measure up to 'Waltham Butternut' in that it has more susceptibility to the borer, lower vitamin A content, and equal storage quality, it surpasses 'Waltham Butternut' in taste. As a matter of fact, the taste of 'Buttercup' rates as the best of all, as the majority of squash lovers will attest. Both cultivars bake extremely well. Another buttercup cultivar is 'Sweet Mama'.

Some gardeners like 'Golden Delicious', a butternut that has the highest vitamin C content of the winter squash but a taste somewhat below that of 'Waltham Butternut'. In the South, the preferred butternut cultivar is often 'Alagold'. Although not a butternut variety, 'Banana' is favored in the West; its flavor is quite good, and the yield is especially prolific. Still other gardeners like the various hubbard squash, such as 'Blue Hubbard', which have good flavors, moderate vitamin A content, and rather large size. Acorn-type squash don't keep all that well, and their taste and vitamin content don't compare very well to butternut kinds; but their baking qualities and smaller size appeal to some gardeners. If interested in acorn squash, try 'Table Ace' (green) or 'Jersey Golden Acorn' (yellow). Finally, the oriental winter squash are notable for novelty and good performance in warmer, more humid climates. Examples of the oriental winter squash are 'Red Kuri' and 'Green Hokkaido.' The most novel winter squash to try is 'Vegetable Spaghetti', if you like spaghetti that tastes like squash.

The one drawback to growing winter squash is its vining habit, which means it needs more room than the bush summer squashes. Although there are a number of bush cultivars of winter squash, I must say they are a disappointment thus far. First, the taste is never as good as their vining counterpart. I have also noticed decreased resistance to the squash vine borer with the bush forms of butternut. However, I'll try any new bush cultivars, always hoping that breeders will solve these problems.

Our favorite yellow squashes are the yellow straightneck ('Early Prolific Straightneck') and crookneck ('Yellow Crookneck') types. Improved versions of the crookneck in terms of earliness and appearance (fewer or no warts) are 'Pic-N-Pic', 'Dixie', 'Cracker Hybrid', 'Tara', and 'Sundance'.

'Goldbar Hybrid' and 'Smoothie' are similar improvements upon the straightneck. The straightneck picks a little more easily than the crookneck does, but the taste of the crookneck has a slight edge over the straightneck.

Many, especially in the South, favor the scallop or patty pan, and more recent Peter Pan cultivars of squash. These squash look a bit like a flattened acorn and are whitish to light green or yellow in color. Examples of the scallop cultivars include 'Benning's Green Tint', 'Peter Pan Hybrid', 'Scallop Yellow Bush', and 'Sunburst'.

My favorite green summer or zucchini squash is 'Richgreen Hybrid Zucchini', although other good varieties include 'Buccaneer', 'Burpee Hybrid Zucchini', 'Cocozelle', 'Green Magic', and 'Grey Zucchini'. Yellow forms of zucchini are also available, such as 'Gold Rush'.

Culture

Plant squash or pumpkin seeds 1 inch deep. It doesn't pay to put the seeds out until two to three weeks after the last killing spring frost, because squash and pumpkins are warm-season plants. Seeds germinate in seven to ten days at 70°F. You can use the furrower, dibble, or bulb planter for outdoor sowing of seeds.

The question of whether or not to grow squash and pumpkin transplants depends upon the cultivar you wish to grow. For instance, you need not grow winter squash as transplants because you will be storing them; therefore, early maturity poses no advantage. In fact, winter squash need cold temperatures to sweeten.

On the other hand, you should grow summer squash as transplants if you want to have them early for food. Also, early plants often resist some insect pests much better than young squash. Start the squash in the 12-ounce modified Styrofoam cups about four weeks before you wish to set them in the garden. You can set them out two weeks after the last spring frost. If you use a polyester or slitted polyethylene cloche, you can put the squash transplants in the garden a week or two earlier. The cloche combined with black plastic will give you a three-week edge on early squash.

Make sure you put down black plastic at the same time you start your transplants. In this way, you will warm the soil to prepare it for the transplants, especially if you put a cloche over the plastic. Intensive plantings of summer squash consist of placing single plants down the middle of 4-foot-wide sheets at 3-foot intervals. For winter squash I place groups of four plants around a milk bottle feeder (see Chapter 4), repeating the groups at 4-foot intervals. Put the plants in the soil with the bulb planter, making sure that you put some organic matter and fertilizer in each hole, as suggested for big feeders in Chapter 4. You can also plant squash in mini-hills (see Chapter 3). You can interplant pumpkins or winter squash with corn, or use them to follow early crops such as lettuce, peas, or radishes.

Pests

Squash borers and squash bugs are especially troublesome to the squash family. The cucumber pests — aphids, cucumber beetles, and pickle worms — also attack squash (see methods of control under Cucumbers). In addition, whiteflies and cutworms can be a bother to squash. Use the yellow sticky cards to eliminate whiteflies and the Styrofoam cup collars for cutworms. Control squash bugs and aphids with soap sprays or rotenone.

Only the polyester barrier can really control the squash borer. The barrier must go up when the reddish-looking adult lays eggs. The squash borer danger period starts roughly two months after the last frost and persists for four weeks. Early plantings with black plastic and cloches can realize considerable yields before the pests kill the plant. If you don't use polyester, plant your squash early and make a second planting in midsummer after the pest has gone.

Diseases that bother cucumbers can also attack squash, with the most troublesome being downy and powdery mildew. Rotations and early plantings avoid most of these diseases; but watch out for the cucumber beetles, which can infect squash with the same wilt disease that kills cucumbers. The polyester barrier or pyrethrum and rotenone will control the cucumber beetle.

Harvest

Pick summer yellow or zucchini squash when they are 5 to 8 inches long; pick patty pan or scallop types when they are 3 inches in diameter. Your fingernail should easily pierce the skin of yellow, zucchini, or patty pan squash if they are ripe. Make sure you keep picking the squash to assure continued later yields. Pick winter squash when it's fully mature; the rind should be hard and resist denting by fingernails. You can leave winter squash on the vine until the first light frost, which often improves its taste.

Tomatoes
Choices

Tomatoes come in essentially two shapes: round and oblong. Round tomatoes vary from small, cherry-size ones to 1-pound or 2-pound bruisers. Their colors vary from red through pink and orange to yellow. Oblong tomatoes are plum tomatoes and pear tomatoes. Most are red, except for the yellow pear form. The plum tomatoes have a higher solids-to-liquid ratio, and we mainly grow them for making tomato sauce. With their lower liquid content, they simmer to a thick sauce in less time.

When speaking of tomatoes, another choice that confronts gardeners is the descriptive words *determinate* and *indeterminate*. The word *determinate* refers to the fact that flowering and fruiting of the plant terminate the growth of the stem that bears the fruit. As such, determinate tomato plants tend to be short and stocky, generally about 2 to 3 feet tall. Determinate tomato plants do not require staking, but you can easily adapt them to cage culture. *Indeterminate* refers to a continuous branching of the tomato plant, unstopped by fruit formation; in other words, you find two or more fruit clusters to a branch. Indeterminate tomato plants get much larger in height than do determinate plants and can bear large tomatoes. Determinate tomatoes tend to be small to medium in fruit size, while indeterminate tomatoes can be almost any size, and the plants' growth is checked only by frost.

The choices in tomatoes are extensive, so I will mention only some of the varieties. For the earliest tomatoes, you should start with early cultivars. For early but moderate sized tomatoes, I suggest 'Burpee's Big Early', 'Burpee's Early Pick', 'Champion', 'Earlibright', or 'Early Girl'. If you like small, early, cherry-type tomatoes for salads, go for 'Burpee's Pixie Hybrid', 'Small Fry Hybrid', or 'Tiny Tim'. These three tomato cultivars are determinate types.

Midseason, cherry size tomatoes include 'Gardener's Delight', 'Patio' (determinate), 'Red Cherry', and 'Sweet 100'. Large, indeterminate, midseason tomatoes include 'Better Boy', 'Jackpot', and 'Red Express'; while determinate varieties are 'Celebrity', 'Freedom', and 'Independence'.

Late cultivars tend to be the largest tomatoes. These tomatoes are the ones that fill the entire hamburger bun and taste so good. Some of my favorites are 'Beefmaster VFN' (resistant to verticillium and fusarium wilts plus nematodes), 'Better Bush' (determinate), 'Burpee's Big Boy', 'Burpee's Big Girl Hybrid VF', 'Burpee's Supersteak Hybrid VFN', 'Park's Whopper VFNT', and 'Ramapo'.

Lesser used tomatoes are the sauce and paste types such as 'Bellstar' (large plum), 'Roma VF', and 'Royal Chico'. A small pear-shaped salad tomato you might want to try is 'Yellow Pear'. 'Sundrop' and 'Burpee's Jubilee' are large, orange tomatoes, while 'Ponderosa' and 'Pink Girl' are pink. For yellow versions, try 'Golden Boy', 'Lemon Boy', or 'Taxi'. If you have multiple disease problems, try 'Floramerica', which has tolerance against 15 diseases. Finally, for a real storage cellar tomato, try 'Long Keeper'.

Culture

Tomatoes are a long warm-season crop best grown from transplants. I suggest using the 12-ounce modified Styrofoam cups to grow your transplants, planting seed about six to eight weeks before your outdoor planting time. Plant three seeds in each cup, covering them with ½ inch of soil. At 70°F seeds germinate in eight to ten days; if you keep them on top of a refrigerator at 75°F, the seeds will germinate in five to seven days. Thin to the strongest plant for each cup. Use the bulb planter to put the transplants in the soil, making sure you dig the hole deeper than the plant to accommodate some fertilizer and organic matter. For normal plantings, put the transplants out in the garden about two weeks after the last killing spring frost.

If you want the earliest possible tomatoes, pick an early cultivar, be it large or small. Plan on putting your transplants out in the garden either on the date of your last killing frost or a few days later. Start your transplants about six to eight weeks before that date. About four weeks before your hardened transplants will go out in the garden, put black plastic over the garden soil, covering it with either a polyester or slitted plastic cloche. The combined unit will raise the soil temperature considerably, so your tomatoes will go into warm soil. Also, tomatoes fail to set fruit below 55°F, so this extra soil warmth is especially important.

When you put your tomatoes out in the garden, undo one side of the cloche. Make a hole in the ground 2 to 3 inches deeper than the soil ball from the cup. Place a few tablespoons of combined organic fertilizer, compost, and soil into the hole; then add your rapid starter solution. After the solution drains into the soil, insert your transplant root ball, adding soil as needed. Finally, replace the side of the cloche. When you see blossoms on your tomato plants, either shake the plants for pollination or leave the cover off for an hour at noon. When temperatures consistently start getting above 75°F, remove the cloche cover. Sit back and enjoy those early tomatoes!

Intensive plantings at 18-inch intervals are possible for determinate and staked, indeterminate tomatoes. If you stake your tomatoes, insert the stakes with your transplants to avoid root disturbance. Place large, unstaked tomatoes at 4-foot intervals. The use of black plastic is essential with unstaked tomatoes to eliminate the number of rotted tomatoes resulting from soil contact.

Some pruning is usually necessary with staked tomatoes. I suggest that you use a 6-foot-tall stake, tying the main stem to the stake and allowing the first sucker to become a second stem, which you tie to the stake. Trim off any other suckers. At weekly intervals, check the plant growth and continue to add ties.

You can, if you prefer, grow tomatoes in special wire cages instead of using stakes. You can buy ready-made square or circular cages. They often have wire prongs that let you anchor them into the soil without stakes. You can also make your own cages, and a special wire is available for the purpose, with openings large enough to let you insert your hand to pick tomatoes. I make my own circular cages, 18 inches in diameter, and anchor them by tying each one to a short stake.

For a succession of tomatoes, plant either early and late choices or early, midseason, and late cultivars. You can interplant tomatoes with various established cole crops such as broccoli, cabbage, or cauliflower.

A few words about the long storage tomatoes are in order. Start 'Long Keeper' tomatoes as transplants one month to six weeks after you start regular tomatoes, because you will plant it and pick it later than regular tomatoes. You can store 'Long Keepers' in the cellar. Mine have lasted until the end of January! The taste, while not as good as fresh summer tomatoes, is definitely superior to store-bought tomatoes.

Pests

Tomato pests include aphids, cutworms, flea beetles, tomato hornworms, and whiteflies. The corn earworm will also eat tomatoes; when it does, we call the worm the tomato fruit worm. You can rid your plants of aphids with soap sprays and of whiteflies with yellow sticky cards or soap sprays. Flea beetles, young tomato hornworms, and whiteflies also give in to pyrethrum and rotenone. You can also plant dill nearby as a trap crop for the hornworm, which you hand-pick and drop in kerosene. Use the Styrofoam cup collar to ward off cutworms.

Some troublesome tomato plant diseases are anthracnose, bacterial wilt, curly top virus, early blight, fusarium wilt, leaf spot, mosaic, tobacco mosaic virus, and verticillium wilt. Use of a three-year rotation will keep diseases in check. Make sure you control aphids and leafhoppers with soap sprays or pyrethrum/rotenone, because they can be carriers of viral diseases.

Two nondisease disorders are sunscald and blossom end rot. If you don't cut away foliage, sun scald will be minimal. Blossom end rot comes from a combination of acid soil, low calcium, and inadequate water. A soil test with the addition of limestone, and mulching with black plastic will solve the blossom end rot problem.

Harvest

Early tomatoes need 54 to 62 days to harvest from transplants, midseason tomatoes need about 70 days from transplants, and late cultivars require 78 or more days from transplants. Pick tomatoes when they are close to or fully ripe. For best taste, refrain from refrigerating them after picking. Pick 'Long Keeper' tomatoes just before frost, while most of them are still green. After picking them, lay the tomatoes out on cellar shelves in a single layer. Use any orange tomatoes first; although they have an orange skin, their interior is red. As the green 'Long Keepers' turn orange, you can either use them or let them sit for weeks. Periodically check the tomatoes, and discard any that have rotted. My supply of winter storage tomatoes usually lasts into late January.

Turnips

Choices

Rutabagas and turnips are part of the cabbage group; but unlike the crops treated under cabbage, we grow rutabagas and turnips for their roots. As such, I prefer to treat them separately. These two root crops do differ from one another. Rutabagas are larger, hardier, require a longer growing season, and have more neck at the leaf crown than do turnips. Rutabagas have a more pungent taste as opposed to the sweeter, milder taste of turnips. While the rutabaga greens are edible, they are quite strong in flavor and are smooth and waxy. The more preferable turnip greens are rough and hairy. Most turnips have white flesh and most rutabagas have a yellow interior, but exceptions do exist. Rutabagas go by other names such as Canadian, Swedish, yellow, or winter turnips. The latter name comes from their storage qualities and the former ethnic names from their association with cold, northern areas and nationalities.

Rutabaga choices include 'American Purple Top', 'American Yellow', 'Champion Purple Top', 'Laurentian', 'Pike', and 'Purple-Top Yellow'. Many choices of turnips exist, such as 'Early Purple-Top Milan', 'Gilfeather', 'Just Right', 'Ohno Scarlet', 'Petite White', 'Presto', 'Purple Top White Glove', 'Royal Glove II', 'Shiro Hybrid', 'Shogoin', 'Showtop', and 'Tokyo Cross'. For a real quick turnip, try 'Yorii Spring'; and for greens only (no root harvest at all), try 'All Top'.

Culture

Turnips are the preferred crop in the South and rutabagas in the North, although either area can grow both. It is best to grow rutabagas as a fall crop, because of their cool-season requirement and longer growing season. Treat turnips as either a spring or fall crop.

Plant both rutabagas and turnips about ¼ to ½ inch deep with the furrower, using either transplants or direct sowing. You can obtain earlier turnips with transplants; but it is impractical to try to obtain earlier rutabagas with transplants because you should harvest them near frost to get the best taste. However, rutabaga transplants started at normal seeding time offer improved germination over direct seeding in the summer.

You can start turnip transplants four to six weeks ahead of their garden planting time and rutabaga transplants at the outdoor seeding time. For rutabagas, sow the seeds three to three and one-half months before the expected fall frost. You can plant spring crop turnips, either as transplants or as direct seedings, three to five weeks before the last killing spring frost. Fall turnip crops go in two to three months before the fall frost. I use 12-ounce Styrofoam cups for each transplant. Seeds germinate in seven to ten days at 70°F.

Intensive plantings of rutabagas and turnips need 8- and 4-inch spacing, respectively. As a fall crop, both can follow peas or snap beans, early corn, or early potatoes. You can also interplant spring turnips with lettuce or spinach.

Pests

The pests and diseases that attack turnips and rutabagas are the same as those that attack cabbage. The most serious pest is the root maggot, but the polyester barrier can keep it in check. You must use crop rotations, remembering to keep the space free of any plants listed under Cabbage.

Harvest

Rutabagas need 90 to 110 days for maturity, with the best harvest time being just before or after a light fall frost. You can store rutabagas in moist sand in a cellar for three or four months. Turnips mature in 60 to 80 days; but you should harvest them when they are 2 to 3 inches in diameter, because mature turnips become tough and woody. Turnips fare poorly in storage. You can harvest greens at any time, but they are best at a young age in terms of taste and tenderness.

Chapter 9
The No-Dig Flower Garden

I do enjoy my vegetable garden and hope to have one every year for as long as I can. And I'm sure that no-dig and no-weed methods will certainly make more years of gardening pleasure possible; however, to paraphrase a famous quotation, Man cannot live by bread, or vegetables, alone. Each year I look forward to another side of gardening which offers its harvest in beauty and pleasure. Vegetables may be the "bread" of gardening life, but flowers are the beauty.

Each year I plant those stalwarts of the flower garden, annuals. Their continuous parade of color satisfies my need for attractive displays in my front and rear yards. Annuals also keep our table vase full of color. If you think about annuals, I'm sure you'll find many more uses to add to the list. Let's take a closer look at annuals.

We consider any plant that produces stems and leaves with flowers and seeds and then dies in one growing season an annual; however, this definition can change with location. For example, the tomato is an annual in much of the United States. In the southernmost parts of Florida, though, tomatoes can continue much beyond one growing season; therefore, tomatoes become perennials in that area. Some annuals, however, are true annuals, no matter where you grow them. Annuals can be flowers or vegetables, but we will only concern ourselves with annual flowers in this chapter.

221

When considering annuals, most people think of about one dozen popular flowering plants: ageratum, alyssum, begonias, celosia, coleus, geraniums, impatiens, marigolds, petunias, salvia, verbena, and zinnias. But did you know that there are actually over 150 annuals? Most of us get into the top-dozen rut simply because gardening centers push these plants during their spring bedding plant sales and all our neighbors have these plants. The point I'm trying to make is: Dare to be different! Make a point of trying at least one new annual each year. You'll never run out of choices among the various seed catalogs.

Why do so many gardeners plant annuals? I think a very basic answer to this question is that annuals are easy to grow. Just about anyone can have good luck with growing annuals like marigolds or zinnias; and by using the no-dig approach, no one can say they have an excuse for not growing annuals in terms of work. Annuals also supply the greatest reward for the least amount of money. An inexpensive package of annual seeds can easily produce two dozen or more quickly growing plants and in no time reward you with colorful flowers. If you think of just about any color or shade you'd like to see in your yard, some annual will fill the bill. There are even many annuals with two colors in their flowers, such as with some petunias and zinnias. Often, flowers such as marigolds and zinnias will last all season.

But color is not the only characteristic that gives variety to flowers. Some annuals, like alyssum, are low to the ground; while others, like snapdragons, zoom upward. Flowers can be tiny verbena or big sunflowers. Some flowers are simple in form, as with single petunias, while others are complex, like salvia. Yet other flowers, like impatiens, grow and bloom in shade; while zinnias fill your hot, dry corners with color.

What can you do with annuals? Certainly, annuals are flowers of many uses. Anywhere you want a touch of color, plant annuals. Put an island of flowers in your lawn or along a border, such as your property line, driveway, or walkway. If you have limited space, plant them in a window box. How about planting flowers in a container for touches of color that you can move in a flash? You can use the colorful blossoms of annuals to hide the yellowing foliage of early spring bulbs. Need a touch of color while your perennials are getting larger, or to compensate when they are not in flower? Just add annuals and water. Need something to jazz up the space around a tree trunk or in a shaded corner? Then plant some shade-tolerant annuals.

Do annuals work with the no-dig methods? Certainly! Figure 9-1 is a time sequence showing my no-dig raised flower bed on my front lawn. This

A

B

9-1 This sequence of photographs shows a no-dig no-weed flower garden from the time of transplanting through the growing season. The flower garden is located on my front lawn.

C

9-2 *The no-dig planting method allows you to make holes wherever you want to pop in a few annual flowers for extra color, without disturbing other plants. This photo shows annual begonias planted in my perennial bed near the chrysanthemums.*

garden, along with a flower island in my backyard, resulted from transplants I produced in our modified Styrofoam cups and planted with the bulb planter. You can use the bulb planter to put transplants anywhere that you want a touch of color (Figure 9-2). If you want rows of annuals raised directly from seeds for cutting purposes, use the furrower. If you just want to plant a few seeds here and there, use the dibble.

It is very easy to raise annuals as transplants for planting with the bulb planter; essentially you grow annual transplants in the same manner as you grow vegetable transplants (see Chapter 2). You can raise annuals directly in the modified Styrofoam cups or start them first in flats. You can leave them in flats after thinning or transplant them into the cups.

Descriptions of some of my favorite annuals, along with cultural information and suggested uses, follow. You should be able to find annuals to fit all your needs. Please note that I omitted the depth at which to plant seeds, because the seed packages supply this information. As a rule of thumb, you can cover any seed to two to three times its thickness, except for seeds that need light for germination, which you just lightly press into the soil. I will indicate any special requirements, like light for growing the seeds.

Ageratum

Otherwise known as floss flower, ageratum is popular for its blue flowers, a color that's somewhat uncommon in annuals. Other ageratum colors are available but to my eye they are not as attractive as the blue. The flower heads are dainty little fluff balls under 1 inch in diameter. Flowers appear throughout the summer and fall until frost. Dwarf compact plants have a height of 5 to 6 inches, which makes them great for edging borders or for placement in rock gardens. There are also taller forms available, which are suitable for use as cut flowers.

Ageratum seeds require light to germinate and you can sow them outdoors after all frost danger has passed. For earlier bloom, start ageratum transplants eight to ten weeks ahead of the time you will place them out in the garden. The seeds germinate in five to eight days. Pick any dead flowers to promote continuous blooming. In the fall, you can pot up some of your plants for indoor color. Cultural needs include full sun to light shade and plenty of water, with 6- to 8-inch plant spacing.

Alyssum

Another name for alyssum is sweet alyssum, because of its fragrant blossoms. In very warm areas, this plant becomes a perennial. Its flowers are numerous and tiny, giving the impression of mounds of flowers. Alyssum colors include white, violet, and rose. Most cultivars tend to be 3 or 4 inches tall, although a few kinds can reach 9 inches in height. Alyssum blooms quickly from seed (45 to 70 days) and is ideal for edging purposes or for rock gardens. Mix alyssum with low-growing spring bulbs for color and for screening of yellowing foliage after the bulbs have finished blooming.

You can directly sow alyssum seeds when your last killing spring frost passes. For very early bloom, start alyssum transplants six weeks earlier. The seeds germinate in eight to fifteen days. Space alyssum plants at 5 to 8 inches when you plant them. If the plants become shaggy, quickly shear them and follow with water and fertilizer to bring back heavy flowering. It is best to plant alyssum in full sun.

Amaranthus

Some gardeners call this flower amaranth for short. Two of its cultivars are better known as love-lies-bleeding and Joseph's coat. Noted for its brightly colored foliage, amaranthus comes mostly in hues of scarlet, with some gold or bronze shades. It grows to a height of 3 feet and finds use as scattered color accents or massed groups in flower beds.

You can plant amaranthus seeds outdoors after all frost danger is past or you can start transplants six weeks ahead of the time you would plant amaranthus outside. Amaranthus seeds need about ten days to germinate. Space the plants at 12 to 18 inches, and use them in your hot, dry areas where the soil is only ordinary to poor.

Arctotis

This daisylike flower, often called African daisy, displays hues of white, orange, apricot, yellow, pink, red, and terra cotta. The stem grows 10 to 18 inches tall, but I prefer the dwarf forms at 10 inches. Arctotis flowers are good for cutting and for displaying in flower beds. Blooms appear during the summer and fall.

I suggest growing transplants about six to eight weeks ahead of out-door planting time. Plant the transplants in your garden when frost is no longer a possibility, spacing them at 12-inch intervals. The seeds germi-nate in about 25 days. Arctotis plants need full sun and can tolerate heat and dryness. Use them freely for cut flowers to promote further blooming.

Asters

We sometimes call these flowers annual or China asters. Aster flowers are full bodied and available in many shades of blue, crimson, lavender, peach, pink, purple, rose, white, and wine. Plant heights vary from dwarfs of 6 inches to giants of 3 feet. The lower aster forms are good to use for edging and massing in flower beds, while the taller ones are excellent for long-lasting cut flowers and color groups in the flower bed. Asters also make good container plantings. The one drawback to asters is that after you have cut the first midsummer blossoms, few additional flowers will appear; therefore, I suggest you make succession sowings for continuous cut flowers.

Aster wilt can be a serious problem to your asters, so make sure you get varieties that offer wilt resistance. The best approach to producing asters is to grow transplants about six to eight weeks ahead of outdoor planting time, putting the transplants out in your garden after all frost danger has passed. Aster seeds germinate in eight to fourteen days. Space tall varieties at 12 to 15 inches and dwarfs at 6 inches. Asters need full sun to grow; and be sure you rotate asters each year to prevent the serious aster yellows disease.

Balsam

This relative of the impatiens has small, roselike blossoms available in cerise, mauve, pink, purple, red and white. The usual height for balsam is 30 inches, but 10-inch dwarf forms are also available. While unsuitable as a cut flower, this plant is beautiful for color masses in the flower bed. Use the dwarf varieties for edging and containers. Flowering starts in early sum-mer and continues until frost.

You can plant balsam seeds directly in your garden after all frost danger has passed. For earlier blooming, start balsam transplants six to eight weeks ahead of outdoor planting time. Balsam seeds germinate in eight to fourteen days. Space the larger forms at 12-inch intervals and the dwarf forms at 6- to 8-inch intervals. Balsam plants grow best with full morning sun, followed by afternoon shade, and they need plenty of water.

Begonias

These plants, sometimes called wax begonias, are popular garden annuals. Their leaves vary from waxy green to bronze in color; and their small, simple flowers come in pink, red, rose, and white and are prolific and continuous from summer until fall. Double roselike flowers and variegated foliage are also available. Begonia heights vary from 6 to 12 inches. Begonias are great for edging, color masses in flower beds, color accents, window boxes, and container plantings.

Begonia seeds are very tiny and require light for germination, a slow process requiring two weeks to occur. The initial growth of begonias is also slow; therefore, it is best to start begonias as transplants ten to twelve weeks ahead of outdoor planting time. Put the plants outside after all frost danger has passed. When planting begonias, space them 8 to 12 inches apart from each other in light shade. They make great companions for impatiens. You can lift begonias out of the soil in the fall and use them as house plants. Also, begonia cuttings root easily in sand, soil, and water.

Blue Lace Flowers

These flowers look like soft, lavender-blue versions of Queen Anne's lace, or wild carrot, a perception that is not surprising when you consider that these annuals also belong to the carrot family. Blue lace flowers grow to heights of 30 inches and have long-lasting virtue as cut flowers.

You can sow blue lace flowers outdoors at the same time you sow carrots, or you can start transplants six to eight weeks ahead of outdoor planting time. I suggest that you use individual containers for your blue lace flower transplants, because transplanting these flowers is no easy task. Blue lace flower seeds need darkness and are slow to germinate, usually requiring two weeks or more. Space the plants 10 inches apart from each other. Full sun and cool weather allow best growth, while hot weather usually terminates the flowering period.

Brachycome

Also known as the swan river daisy, this 9-inch plant bears daisylike, fragrant flowers in shades of blue, rose, violet, and white. The summer-flowering plants are useful for edging, bed color masses, rock gardens, and cut flowers for small bouquets. The bloom period of the brachycome is relatively long.

You can directly sow brachycome seeds outside after all frost danger has passed, or start them four to six weeks ahead of outdoor planting time as transplants. Since the plant requires a long season, transplants are better to use than direct seeding. Germination usually occurs in two weeks. When planting, space the plants 6 inches apart. Cutting the plant encourages more flowers to appear. The brachycome plant tolerates dryness.

Browallia

Most gardeners grow browallia for its heavenly blue flowers—an unusual color among annuals. Cultivars are also available with lavender and white flowers. The browallia flower is small and simple with five petals. The plant grows to a height of 10 to 15 inches and is best used for color masses in flower beds, window boxes, and containers. Flowers appear during the summer.

I suggest that you grow browallia transplants, starting them indoors eight to ten weeks ahead of outdoor planting time. Browallia seeds require light and germinate in about two weeks. You should not place these plants outside until all frost danger has passed. Space browallia plants at 8 to 10 inches, assuring they will have good sun with some afternoon shading. The browallia also makes a good potted greenhouse plant.

Calendula

Some call these annuals pot marigolds. The name comes from the use of their petals to flavor soups and add color as a substitute for saffron. Calendula flowers are chrysanthemumlike and come in colors of apricot, cream, gold, orange, or white. You can expect flowers from early summer until frost. The plants grow from 1 to 2 feet tall. Calendulas are good cut flowers, if you pick them when they are near to or in bud. For color, plant them in masses in your flower border.

Calendulas are cool-season plants; therefore, you can sow calendula seeds outdoors after the danger of heavy spring frost has passed. For maximum bloom, start calendula transplants six to eight weeks ahead of outdoor planting time. The seeds require darkness and germinate in ten to fourteen days. You can space plants at 8- to 12-inch intervals in full sun, being sure to provide a good water supply. Pick the dead flowers to assure further blooming.

California Poppies

California poppy blossoms are silky, single or double petaled, and have a saucerlike shape. They can be bronze, gold, orange, rose, scarlet, yellow, or white in color. The plants grow 1 to 2 feet tall and have interesting, lacy, silver-gray foliage. Blooms appear most of the summer. California poppies make beautiful color masses or accents in flower beds. For cut flower use, pick them while they are in bud.

Poppies transplant poorly but bloom quickly from seed. Although poppy transplants are feasible in individual containers, they offer little advantage over direct seeding. Sow seeds as soon as you can work the soil; germination will occur in ten to twelve days. Thin the plants to an 8-inch spacing and provide them with full sun and dry, sandy soil. Remove dead poppy flowers to encourage continued blooming.

Candytuft

Also known as annual candytuft, edging candytuft, or globe candytuft, this flower appears in masses of lilac, pink, purple, rose, or white in late spring or early summer. The plant reaches a height of 12 to 15 inches; and you can use candytuft for rock gardens, edging, in flower borders, or as a cut flower. It has a pleasant fragrance and looks especially nice among the foliage of the smaller spring bulbs.

You can either sow the seeds outside as soon as you can work the soil or start transplants six to eight weeks ahead of outdoor planting time. Seed germination occurs in ten to fifteen days. Candytuft requires cool weather, full sun, and 6- to 8-inch spacing. Pick dead flowers to encourage the growth of new flowers.

Cape Daisies

We also call these flowers African daisies, but don't confuse them with arctotis, because their genus is *Dimorphotheca*. Yet another name for them is Cape marigolds. The flowers are daisylike with dark centers and come in buff, cream, orange, salmon, and yellow. Good uses for Cape daisies include edging, massing, and cut flowers. Keep in mind that, like all daisies, the flowers close at night. Flowers bloom throughout the summer and fall.

Although you can plant seeds outdoors after frost danger has passed, you would be wise to grow transplants, starting them about five weeks ahead of outdoor planting time. Seeds germinate in ten to fifteen days. Make sure you have fresh seed, because it doesn't last very long. Space the plants at 8- to 10-inch intervals in full sun. Cape daisies can tolerate hot, dry areas.

Carnations

You can get perennial carnations to bloom in one season. Since they are tender perennials, you should treat carnations as summer-flowering annuals in the North. Carnations possess a well-known spicy fragrance and delicately fringed petals. The ones we grow at home are similar to the florist's carnations but smaller. Carnations grow 12 to 18 inches tall and come in colors of pink, purple, red, scarlet, white, and yellow. Carnations are great for cutting purposes and for adding color plus fragrance to the flower border.

To get flowers in one year, start transplants eight to ten weeks in advance of outdoor planting. Carnation seeds germinate in five to ten days. Put plants out when frost dangers have passed, using 10-inch spacing and planting them in a sunny location.

Celosia

Another name for celosia is cockscomb, and two forms are available. One form is plumed or feathery, while the other is velvety, crested, and more like a rooster's comb in appearance. Celosia heights vary from 1 to 3 feet. The crested form is usually red or gold; the plumed form comes in red, orange, apricot, yellow, rose, pink, or bronze. This plant makes a colorful display in flower groups in borders or islands. It is good as a cut flower and quite valuable for dried flower arrangements. Celosia flowers appear throughout the summer.

You can directly sow celosia seeds after frosts have passed, or you can start transplants four to six weeks ahead of outdoor planting. The seeds germinate in ten to fifteen days. Plant smaller cultivars at 12-inch spacings and larger forms at 18- to 24-inch spacings. Celosia requires full sun and a good water supply.

Cleome

Some people call this flower the spider flower, because of the appearance of its seed pods. The delicate, orchidlike flowers come in lavender, pink, rose, and white and appear throughout the summer. The plant is somewhat large at 3 to 6 feet in height. You can use cleome for backgrounds or unusual accents. For cut flowers, pick cleome in the bud stage.

Do your outdoor sowing after all danger of frost has passed, or start transplants four to six weeks earlier. Space the plants 2 feet apart in a sunny location. The cleome plant can tolerate heat, drought, and even some shade.

Cobaea

Another name for cobaea is cup and saucer vine. Although this plant is perennial, its rampant growth makes it a good candidate for annual use. Cobaea flowers are either blue or white "cups" resting on a green "saucer," and the vine can grow as much as 20 feet in one season. You can best use cobaea for temporary screening or a rapid cover for a trellis or wall. Its flowers last throughout the summer.

Sow cobaea seeds outdoors when all frost danger has passed, or start transplants six weeks in advance of outdoor planting. Put the seeds into the medium vertically, as they germinate poorly with the broad side down. Seed germination takes place in fifteen to twenty days. Plant cobaea at 2-foot intervals in full sun, although some shade is acceptable. The cobaea needs moderate amounts of water.

Coleus

We treat this tender perennial, noted for its colorful foliage, as an annual. The variegated leaves come in many color combinations, such as pink, white, and green or red and light green. Coleus leaf shapes also vary somewhat, with edges from notched to frilled. Plant heights usually vary from 1 to 2 feet, although some plants can be smaller or larger. You can use coleus for colored accents or masses in the garden, and in window boxes or other containers.

I suggest you use coleus transplants, starting them about eight weeks ahead of outdoor planting time. Coleus seeds need light and germinate in ten to fifteen days. Bottom warmth can be quite helpful, too. Do not put transplants outside until all danger of frost has passed. Depending on their height, space the transplants at 10 to 18 inches. You will get the best color from the coleus if you plant it in a sunny area, but it can tolerate shade. Pinch back the plant, if you want it to get bushy. Also pinch off the unattractive lavender flower spikes that grow on the plant. You can remove the coleus from the soil in the fall for an indoor potted plant, or you can root coleus cuttings in sand or water.

Coreopsis

Other names for coreopsis include calliopsis and annual or golden coreopsis. This daisylike plant has single, semidouble, or double flowers in brown, crimson, orange, or yellow. Dark centers and banding occur in some varieties. Both low and high forms, reaching heights of 12 and 36 inches, are available. You can use coreopsis as color masses, edging (the low form), or for cut flowers. The flowers appear all summer long.

You can sow the seeds outdoors when frosts no longer threaten or start transplants six to eight weeks ahead of outdoor planting. Coreopsis seeds germinate in five to ten days. Place coreopsis plants at 8- to 12-inch spacings in full sun. The plants can tolerate heat and dryness.

Cornflowers

Other popular names for cornflowers are bachelor's buttons, blue bottles, and ragged robins. Although most people are familiar with the blue variety, there are also pink, purple, red, rose, white, and wine varieties available. The ruffled and tufted flowers bloom on plants that vary in height from 12 to 36 inches. The taller forms are best for backgrounds to lower plants, because the lower leaves of cornflowers often look ratty. The dwarf forms are nice for edging. Cornflowers are good for cutting, and yes, for sticking in a buttonhole.

You can directly sow cornflower seeds as soon as you are able to work your soil, as these are hardy annuals. You can also start transplants four to five weeks early. Cornflower seeds require darkness and germinate in one to two weeks. Thin dwarf varieties to 6 inches and tall varieties to 12 inches. Keep the flowers picked to encourage continuous blooming, which at best doesn't last long. To lengthen blooming time, you will need to make succession plantings. Plant cornflowers either in full sun or light shade.

Cosmos

These daisylike single and semidouble blossoms come in lovely warm shades of crimson, lavender, pink, purple, rose, and white. The plant heights vary from 30 to 48 inches. Flowers appear from midsummer to frost and are good for cutting; however, the best use for cosmos is in border backgrounds, especially against fences or walls. Taller cosmos varieties may need staking.

After all danger of frost has passed, you can sow seeds outdoors; however, I suggest that you start transplants six to eight weeks ahead of outdoor planting time for earlier flowering. Seeds come up in five to ten days. Plant cosmos at 18-inch intervals, and continue picking the flowers to promote further flowering. Cosmos require a sunny location and can tolerate poor soil.

Dahlias

You can grow bedding or dwarf dahlias from seed as annuals. Flowers can be single, semidouble, or double in shades of apricot, lavender, pink, purple, red, white, or yellow. Bicolors, such as red and white combinations, also occur. Flower shapes, as with the large perennial dahlias, also vary and include anemone, cactus, pompom, and quill forms. Dahlias can grow from 12 to 36 inches in height. You can use them for color masses all summer in the border or as cut flowers, if you pick them before they fully open and dip the cut stem ends briefly in boiling water.

It is best to start dwarf dahlias as transplants four to six weeks ahead of outdoor planting. Their seeds germinate in five to ten days. You can plant your dahlia transplants outside in full sun after all danger of frost has passed, spacing them 18 inches apart. You can dig the tubers in the fall after the tops have blackened from frost. It is best to store tubers with some dry peat moss in a plastic bag in a cellar; however, because bedding dahlias grow so easily from seed, I don't bother saving the tubers.

Dianthus

Other names for dianthus are China pink or annual pink. Dianthus flowers are fragrant and available in lilac, pink, rose, white, and bicolor varieties; and they have either single or double frilled petals. Dianthus heights vary from 6 to 18 inches, and the flowers bloom in the early summer. Pinks are good for color masses, edging, and for cut flowers.

After the danger of frost has passed, sow seeds directly into your garden; or start transplants six to eight weeks ahead for earlier and longer flowering. Germination occurs in five to ten days. Set the plants 6 to 9 inches apart and, after flowering, give the plants a light shearing to initiate more blossoms.

Four O'Clocks

In warmer areas, these flowers from grandmother's early garden days become perennials and, of course, open in mid to late afternoon, or all day when the sky is cloudy. The trumpetlike flowers come in lavender, pink, red, salmon, white, and yellow. Appearing late in the season on 18- to 36-inch plants, these fragrant flowers are good for border color late in the summer.

Plant the seeds outdoors when all frost danger has passed, or start transplants four to six weeks earlier for faster blooming. Plant spacings of 12 to 18 inches are acceptable. Four o'clocks require full sun and can tolerate heat and poor soils.

Gaillardia

Also called blanket flower, this asterlike flower comes in shades of gold, orange, red, and yellow on 18- to 24-inch-tall plants. The gaillardia lasts all summer and makes a good cut flower. You can best use gaillardias in colorful masses for the border or bed. A dwarf form for edging purposes is also available, as are bicolors in the larger cultivars.

After frost danger has passed, you can sow the seeds directly in your garden. You can also start transplants four to six weeks ahead for earlier flowers. Germination requires fifteen to twenty days. Be sure to use 1-foot spacing when planting gaillardias and keep picking the flowers to promote further blooming.

Gazania

Other names for the gazania include treasure flower and African daisy. It comes in colors of cream, gold, orange, pink, and yellow, although dark centers and bicolors also occur. Gazania heights vary from 8 to 12 inches, and the flowers appear all summer, closing at night like other daisies. The best use for the gazania is for colorful masses in borders or beds.

Sow gazania seeds outdoors when the danger of frost has passed. To get earlier blooms, start transplants five to seven weeks ahead of outdoor planting time. Germination takes eight to fourteen days to occur and requires darkness. Space the gazania plants 6 to 10 inches from each other in full sun. The plant performs just fine in hot, dry conditions. You can lift this plant from the garden in the fall and use it indoors as a potted plant.

Geraniums

Bedding geraniums, which we know well for their colorful flower clusters of pink, red, salmon, and white, grow to heights varying from 15 to 24 inches. Besides providing color in the flower bed, these plants also look beautiful in containers and window boxes. The flowers bloom all summer long, and you can cut geranium flower heads and float them on shallow water for an unusual flower arrangement.

Although you can buy plants, you can more economically grow your own. Make sure you get seeds of hybrid series specially developed for raising from seed, such as the Sprinter hybrids. Start the seeds ten to twelve weeks before the last heavy spring frost, as geraniums grow slowly. Geranium seeds need bottom heat (top of refrigerator) and germinate in twenty days. Plant your transplants in the garden after the frost danger has passed, placing the plants 12 to 16 inches apart. Pick off spent flower clusters to allow continuous blooming. Geraniums need full sun and moderate dryness to grow.

Globe Amaranth

The globe amaranth has cloverlike flower heads in lavender, orange, pink, reddish purple, rose, and white and grows on plants 18 to 24 inches tall. Blooming occurs from midsummer to late fall. The globe amaranth dries well for arrangements when fully developed, makes a good cut flower, and provides interesting massed plantings in borders.

You can directly sow seeds after frost dangers have passed, but you will get quicker results by using transplants. Start transplants six to eight weeks ahead of outdoor planting. The seeds germinate slowly in fifteen to twenty days. Soaking the seeds overnight in lukewarm water helps to quicken germination. Space globe amaranths at 10 to 15 inches from each other and plant them in full sun. The globe amaranth can tolerate heat and dryness.

Gloriosa Daisies

Improved versions of the black-eyed Susan, these plants have single, semidouble, and double dark-centered daisies in shades of gold, mahogany, and yellow. These hybrids bloom easily from seed the first year, so you can treat these plants as annuals even though they are perennials. Gloriosa daisies grow 24 to 36 inches tall, and you can use them as colorful masses and cut flowers.

Start gloriosa daisy seeds six weeks ahead of outdoor planting, if you wish to use them as annuals. Seeds germinate in five to ten days. Space the plants at 12 to 24 inches in your garden after the frost has passed. The plants grow best in full sun and will tolerate heat, drought, and poor soil. Being perennials, gloriosa daisies will reappear in gardens located in USDA Zone 5 (where wintertime low temperatures average −20° to −10°F) and warmer.

Gypsophila

Another name for gypsophila is annual baby's breath, although a perennial species also exists. The dainty masses of flowers come in pink, red, and white, and the plant grows 12 to 24 inches tall. Blooming starts in early summer and doesn't last very long. To lengthen the time of flowering, you must use succession plantings. This plant adds an attractive touch to borders.

Baby's breath is hardy, and you can sow it as soon as you can work the soil. You can also start transplants six to eight weeks ahead of outdoor planting. Gypsophila seeds need ten to fifteen days to germinate. Plant spacings of 8 to 12 inches are adequate, and full sun provides the best results with baby's breath.

Heliotrope

This plant has small clusters of violet flowers and a delightful fragrance and grows to 12 to 20 inches in height. The vanilla-scented flowers appear throughout the summer. The heliotrope plant makes an attractive addition to the border or window box.

Heliotrope is perennial in Southern Florida, Texas, and California, but for most of us it is an annual. The best approach to growing it is to start transplants ten to twelve weeks early. Seeds need three to four weeks for germination. After all frost danger has passed, put the transplants outside at spacings of 12 inches between plants. Full sun affords the best results. You can pot heliotrope in the fall or take cuttings for a winter potted plant.

Hollyhocks

Make sure you get the annual, not perennial, form of hollyhock. This 3- to 5-foot tall plant produces many single, semidouble, or double flowers along its spike throughout the summer. Flower colors include cerise, pink, rose, scarlet, white, and yellow. Tall hollyhocks may require staking, but they make a nice background in borders or against fences.

The best method for attaining sure blooms is to start transplants eight to ten weeks ahead of outdoor planting. Hollyhock seeds need light and germinate in ten to fourteen days. Put the transplants outside once the frost has passed, spacing small forms at 18 inches apart and larger ones at 24 inches. The hollyhock needs full sun.

Impatiens

Other names for impatiens include busy Lizzie, patient Lucy, and patience plant. These succulent plants have simple flowers in shades of fuchsia, orange, pink, salmon, scarlet, and white. Their heights vary from dwarfs at 6 inches to large forms at 30 inches. Impatiens bloom throughout the summer and add color to edgings, borders, and containers.

You can directly sow seeds after all danger of frost has passed, but it is preferable to use transplants. Start seeds ten to twelve weeks ahead of outdoor planting time and be sure to provide the seeds with light. The seeds will germinate in fifteen to twenty days. When transferring the transplants to the garden, space small varieties of impatiens at 12 inches and larger ones at 18 inches. These plants do well in shaded areas and make good companion plants to begonias. If you grow impatiens in the sun, you must keep them evenly moist.

Kochia

Other names for kochia are burning bush and summer cypress. This bushy plant looks like a small evergreen and possesses foliage that turns a reddish color in the fall. It grows 24 to 36 inches tall, and you can use it as a temporary hedge, background, or an unusual accent.

You can directly sow kochia seeds after all frost has gone, or you can start transplants four to six weeks ahead of outdoor planting. The seeds need light to germinate, a ten- to fifteen-day process. Space kochias 18 to 24 inches apart and provide full sunlight and adequate moisture. You can give kochias a light shearing to improve the plant's shape.

Larkspur

Other names for larkspur are annual or rocket larkspur. This delphinium look-alike is noted for its blue flower spikes up to 4 feet tall. Shades of pink, purple, red, and white are also available. The larkspur blooming period is from late spring to early summer. You can use larkspur for cut flowers and border backdrops, such as in front of fences. Make sure foreground plants conceal the often unattractive lower foliage of larkspur.

Sow the seeds of this hardy annual as soon as the soil is workable. Better yet, start transplants six to eight weeks early. Seeds require darkness and germinate in eight to fifteen days. Get fresh seed, as larkspur seed does not stay fresh for long. A spacing of 12 inches between plants is acceptable. You may have to stake the plants, and you definitely must keep picking the flowers to encourage continued blooming. Larkspur need full sun but not heat, because they are cool-season plants.

Lobelia

This low, compact or trailing plant grows 4 to 6 inches high and is covered with dainty, simple flowers throughout much of the summer. Flower colors include blue, rose, violet, and white. You can use lobelia for edging borders and rock gardens, and the trailing forms are nice in containers and window boxes.

Lobelia grows slowly, so I recommend using transplants started ten to twelve weeks ahead of outdoor planting, putting them outside after all frost danger has gone. Seed germination takes fifteen to twenty days. Space the lobelia plants at 6-inch intervals; and if blooming slows, give them a light shearing. Lobelia does well in full sun to light shade. You can root cuttings for use as potted plants at the end of the season.

Lupine

Annual lupines are lower growing and not as showy as perennial lupines, but they are nevertheless worth growing. Pealike flowers in blue, orange, pink, purple, red, white, or yellow appear on 18-inch-tall spikes. Lupines provide color in beds, borders, and backgrounds. They bloom in late spring and early summer.

You can directly sow seeds as soon as the soil is workable, but it is wiser to start transplants in individual containers, which provide room for the taproot to grow. Soak the seeds overnight to quicken germination, which takes fifteen to twenty days. Start the plants six to eight weeks ahead of outdoor planting. When transplanting, space the lupines 12 to 18 inches apart, depending on their height. Tall forms may need staking. Full sun to light shade is best for plant growth. If your summers get hot early, you may need to use an organic mulch to keep roots cool, because lupines are cool-season plants. Regularly remove any dead flowers.

Marigolds

Marigolds are clearly the favorite American annual, having come close to being named the national flower through congressional action. Marigold colors include several variations of mahogany red, orange, and yellow. A white marigold is also available. The plant heights vary from 6-inch dwarfs to 36-inch giants. Most of the flowers are of the double form, but a few singles and semidoubles are available. Marigolds, depending upon the choice of cultivar, are useful in beds, borders, and containers, or for edging and cutting purposes. The flowers bloom throughout the summer until frost.

You can directly sow marigold seeds after frost; however, you will find that transplants are really easy to grow and they bloom much earlier than directly sown seeds. Start transplants four to six weeks ahead of outdoor planting and allow five to seven days for germination to occur. Space marigolds at 6- to 18-inch intervals, depending on their height; and be sure they receive full sun. Except for mule (triploid) forms, which will not stop blooming when flowers mature, remove dead flowers to assure continual bloom.

Morning Glories

These vines with their funnellike flowers grow from 3 to 20 feet, depending upon the cultivar. While the blue variety is popular, morning glories also come in crimson, lavender, pink, violet, and white. The flowers wilt in full, hot sun but bloom beautifully in the morning (hence, morning glory) and on cloudy days. Use morning glories on a trellis, lattice, or net.

Soak morning glory seeds in warm water for 24 hours, because their hard coat will prolong germination. After soaking, the seeds germinate in five to seven days. You can directly sow the seeds after all danger of frost has passed or start transplants four to six weeks ahead of outdoor planting. Use 12-inch spacing when planting outside, and be sure the plants receive full sun and moderate watering. Morning glories tolerate dry soil.

Nasturtiums

These old-time flowers vary from the 12-inch bushy kind to an 8-foot climber needing support. The colors include orange, rose, red, and yellow; and the flowers can be single or double, with some being fragrant. The blooms appear throughout the summer. The bush forms are useful in beds and borders, while the climber is good as a background screen or in hanging baskets. Some people use peppery-flavored nasturtium leaves in salads.

The seeds need darkness to germinate in seven to twelve days, and you can sow them in your garden after the danger of frost has passed. You can also grow nasturtiums from transplants in individual containers started four to six weeks ahead of outdoor planting. Space plants 8 to 12 inches apart in the garden, and be sure they receive full sun to light shade. Don't overfertilize nasturtiums or you'll end up with lots of leaves and few flowers.

Nicotiana

Another name for nicotiana is flowering tobacco. Nicotiana has star-like trumpet flowers that are especially fragrant in the evening. The flowers can be lavender, pink, red, or white in color. The flowers continue to bloom throughout the summer until frost, and they make colorful accents for borders.

Direct sowing of seeds is possible after all danger of frost has passed; however, transplants are better, especially to achieve earlier flowers. Start transplants six to eight weeks ahead of outdoor planting time, and be sure to provide light for seed germination, which takes ten to twenty days. Space the plants at 10-inch intervals in your garden. If flowering stops, cut off the spent flower stalks to allow for additional blooms.

Nierembergia

This plant, also called cup flower, is a perennial from the lower part of USDA Zone 7 and south that you can treat as an annual if you live further north. The cuplike, small, violet-blue flowers bloom on 6- to 12-inch plants; another type of nierembergia grows 24 to 36 inches tall and has white flowers. Nierembergia flowers appear in late summer. The low forms are good for edging, rock gardens, and borders, while the larger ones are good for borders.

For use as an annual, start nierembergia as transplants ten to twelve weeks early. The seeds need fifteen to twenty days to germinate. Put the plants outside after all frost dangers have gone, spacing them at 6- to 12-inch intervals. Light shade to full sun is acceptable for growing nierembergia.

Nigella

Love-in-a-mist is another name for this plant whose flowers can be pink, purple, red, or white and resemble cornflowers (bachelor's buttons). The plant grows 12 to 24 inches tall, and you can use it for colorful massing in a bed or border. You can also use it as a cut flower or dry its unusual seed pods for use in dried arrangements. Nigella flowers appear from midsummer through the fall.

Nigella is a hardy annual whose seeds you can sow as early in spring as you can work the soil. The seeds germinate in ten to fifteen days. You can also use transplants, starting them four to six weeks ahead of outdoor planting and using individual containers, because the nigella doesn't transplant well. Place the plants at 8-inch intervals and in full sun.

Ornamental Grasses

For an unusual accent, why not try a clump of ornamental grasses? Many are tall, upright, graceful plumes; some are dainty; and others nod gracefully in the breeze. Many ornamental grasses are available, including cloud grass, hair grass, green foxtail millet, quaking grass, and ruby grass. Their heights very considerably, with some cultivars approaching 4 to 5 feet. You can use ornamental grasses in dried arrangements.

Lightly press the seeds into the ground as soon as frost dangers have passed, or start transplants four to six weeks ahead of outdoor planting time. Plant ornamental grasses in scattered clumps for best effect, and be sure they receive full sun.

Petunias

These attractive annuals are another American favorite, with their simple funnel, exquisite double, or ruffled flowers. Their fragrance is slight, but their colors include just about every hue, with a number of bicolors also available. Petunia heights vary from 10 to 18 inches. Petunias bloom throughout the summer and make colorful additions to beds, borders, window boxes, hanging baskets, and other containers.

Petunia seeds are extremely fine. It is best to sow them indoors and grow transplants, starting about ten weeks ahead of outdoor planting and providing light and some bottom warmth (top of refrigerator) for germination. At 70°F, petunia seeds germinate in twelve to fourteen days; while at 75°F, they germinate in ten. Place plants outside after all danger of frost has passed, spacing the smaller petunias at 8 inches and larger ones at 12 inches. After the first flush of bloom, cut back the tips and spent flowers to allow for more blooms. Allowing petunias to go to seed stops blossoms, so continue to pick spent blooms throughout the season. Full sun and moderate moisture provide the best growing conditions for petunias.

Phacelia

We also call this plant the California bluebell, because it comes from California and has lovely, blue, bell-like flowers. It reaches a height of 9 inches and blooms throughout the summer. Use the phacelia as a colorful mass in the rock garden or as edging for borders and beds.

After frost, you can sow phacelia seeds directly in the garden. If you choose to grow transplants, start them six weeks before outdoor planting time and use individual containers for these somewhat fussy plants. Germination occurs sporadically in 12 to 25 days. Space phacelias at 6-inch intervals, and pinch their tips when young to encourage fullness. Full sun and warm to hot summers are best for growing this plant.

Phlox

Make sure you get the annual forms of phlox, which have colorful clusters of simple flowers in lavender, pink, red, and white. Phlox heights vary from 7-inch dwarfs to 15 inches, and flowering occurs throughout the summer. Use the dwarf forms in edgings and rock gardens, and use the tall ones for massing in beds or borders or for cut flowers. The flower clusters may show sporadic wilting of individual flowers; therefore, pick the wilted ones off of the cluster for best appearance.

You can sow the seeds outdoors as soon as the soil is workable, because phlox are hardy annuals. You can also start the seeds as transplants in individual containers six to eight weeks earlier, putting them outside when frost dangers have passed. Save some of the weaker transplants, as they often develop the best colors. Phlox seeds require darkness, cool conditions (55° to 65°F), and ten to fifteen days for germination. Use a spacing of 10 to 12 inches for phlox, be sure the plants will receive full sun, and remove faded flowers to encourage further blooming.

Polygonum

Other names for this annual are fleeceflower and knotweed. You can treat this attractive perennial as an annual in the North. The dense heads of pink flowers bloom on plants only 3 or 4 inches tall. You can use polygonum for edging and in rock gardens. The flowers appear during the summer.

To grow polygonum as an annual and get flowers in one season, you must start transplants six to eight weeks ahead of planting outdoors. Germination occurs slowly, in 20 to 25 days. Put the transplants outside only after the danger of frost has gone. Polygonum spreads vigorously; therefore, place transplants at 18-inch intervals. Polygonum can spread quickly and become invasive in areas where the winter temperature does not fall below 0°F (USDA Zones 7 and up). The plants can tolerate full sun to light shade.

Portulaca

Another name for this sunny plant is moss rose. The ruffled, cup-shaped flowers can be single or double. Colors are numerous and include warm shades of cream, gold, pink, red, rose, salmon, white, or yellow. The portulaca plant is only 4 to 6 inches high but forms a spreading mound up to 2 feet across. The flowers close in cloudy weather and at night. Portulaca works nicely as edging or in a rock garden. The flowers appear from midsummer on.

You can sow the seeds directly in your garden after all danger of frost is past or start transplants about six weeks ahead of outdoor planting. Portulaca seed germinates in about ten to fifteen days and requires light. Space the plants at 12- to 24-inch intervals in full sun. Portulaca can tolerate heat and dryness quite well.

Salpiglossis

Salpiglossis, or painted tongue, has velvety flowers resembling deep petunias, with splashes of contrasting color on their petals. The colors include blue, purple, red, rose, and yellow, and the plant grows about 30 inches tall. Salpiglossis flowers appear from midsummer to frost. They make colorful backgrounds in beds or borders and work well as cut flowers.

Seeds can be sown outside when frost dangers have passed, but for early flowers, start transplants eight weeks earlier. The seeds require darkness and are so fine that you must press them into the growing mixture and cover them with cardboard or newspaper. Germination requires fifteen to twenty days. Place plants in the garden at 8- to 12-inch intervals in full sun. They also may require staking. Salpiglossis does not grow well where summers are hot.

Salvia

This attractive plant, also called sage, has spikes of flowers that appear from early summer through frost. Salvia colors include the well-known red, as well as lavender, pink, purple, rose, and white. Another closely related species of salvia has blue flowers. Both forms of salvia are perennials in the warmer zones, but we can grow them as annuals throughout much of the United States. Ten-inch dwarf cultivars and 3-foot giants are available. Salvia makes a bright addition to the border or bed, and you can dry the blue form.

Because salvia takes a long time to reach flowering, it is best to start it as a transplant. Start red salvia six to eight weeks ahead of outdoor planting, and be sure to provide light. Salvia seeds have short lives, so be sure you use fresh ones. Start blue salvia twelve weeks early. Germination for both forms takes twelve to fifteen days. Plants can go outside after the danger of frost has passed. Give the blue forms a spacing of 12 inches and the red forms 15 inches. Be sure your salvia gets full sun and plenty of water.

Scabiosa

Other names for this annual are pincushion flower and sweet scabious. The pincushionlike flowers are fragrant and available in blue, pink, purple, red, rose, or white. Plant heights vary from 18 to 36 inches. The flowers are attractive in borders and beds and are good for cutting. They bloom throughout the summer.

You can sow scabiosa seeds directly after the danger of frost has gone; however, for earlier flowering, start transplants four to six weeks ahead of outdoor planting time. Seed germination takes ten to fifteen days. Space the plants 6 to 12 inches apart, depending upon their final expected height, and in full sun. Remove spent flowers to encourage the blooming of more flowers. Scabiosa does not grow well in extreme heat.

Shell Flowers

Another name for shell flowers is Bells of Ireland. The flowers are apple green and bell-like, appearing all along the tall stem. The flowers bloom late in the summer on plants 24 to 36 inches tall. The actual flower is tiny, white, and fragrant and grows in the base of the green shells or bells. You can use these flowers freshly cut, but they are best known for use in dried flower arrangements.

Sow shell flower seeds outside as soon as you can work the soil, because they are hardy annuals; or start transplants about eight weeks earlier in individual containers, a necessity due to the shell flower's taproots. Seeds need light and coolness (55°F) for germination, which is slow at 25 to 35 days. Space the plants at 12-inch intervals in full sun or light shade and provide moderate watering. For drying purposes, cut the flowers when they are at their peak.

Shirley Poppies

These annual poppies have single or double flowers in brilliant shades of apricot, crimson, pink, red, salmon, or white. The silky flowers appear on 30- to 36-inch plants throughout the summer. You can create wonderful color masses in the bed or border with Shirley poppies. You might want to sow separate groups in succession so that the main display does not occur all at once.

Shirley poppies are quite hardy, so you should sow them as soon as you can work the soil. You can also prepare transplants about six weeks earlier, but use individual containers, because poppies transplant poorly. Space the plants 9 to 12 inches apart in full sun. Pick off spent flowers, as seed formation ends blossoming. Shirley poppies do not grow well in extreme heat.

Snapdragons

These colorful annuals are a tradition in many flower gardens. The flowers are thought to resemble the jaws of a dragon, and generations of children have learned how to open the jaws by pressing the bottom of the flower. Snapdragons come in every color except blue, and double flowers are also available. Snapdragons can range from 7 to 36 inches in height. The flowers appear from summer through frost. Use the smaller forms for edging and larger forms for backgrounds. You can also use snapdragons for colorful massing in beds or borders and as cut flowers.

While you can sow seeds in place, it would be wise to use transplants because snapdragons are actually perennials that we use as annuals. Start your transplants six to eight weeks ahead of outdoor planting. Germination requires ten to fourteen days and light. Plants can go outside after all danger of frost has passed at spacings of 6 inches for small forms and up to 12 inches for the larger ones. Some tip pinching will encourage young plants to branch and produce more flowers. Snapdragons require full sun.

Snow-on-the-Mountain

This annual, usually sold as euphorbia, has white-edged green foliage and flower bracts. One hardly notices the actual flower. The plant grows from 24 to 30 inches tall and contains a milky juice that can irritate eyes and skin. The best use for the plant is for accents or to separate more colorful flower groups. Because the lower parts of euphorbia tend to become bare, you might want to use some low annuals in front of it for concealment.

You can sow the seeds directly in your garden after the danger of frost has passed or start transplants six to eight weeks earlier. Germination is in six to eight weeks. Provide 12-inch spacing of plants. This plant can take full sun to light shade, heat, and drought. If you use it in a cut flower arrangement, seal the cut stem end by dipping it in boiling water. Wash off any milky sap that gets on your hands.

Statice

We sometimes call statice by another name, sea lavender. Its delicate, airy flower clusters come in blue, lavender, purple, rose, and yellow and appear in late summer on 30-inch plants. Statice dries well and is very popular for use in dried arrangements. Other uses include bed, border, and rock garden displays, and cut flowers.

You can start statice directly outside when frosts have passed, but transplants are better to use because statice blooms late. Start transplants eight to ten weeks early. Germination requires fifteen to twenty days. Space the plants at 18-inch intervals, and be sure they have full sun and good drainage. Keep statice drier than your other plants.

Stock

Gardeners in most of the United States treat stock as an annual even though it is actually a perennial. The flowers are fragrant during the summer and fall and appear as blue, pink, purple, red, rose, white, or yellow rosettes. The single or double flowers bloom on plants 12 to 30 inches tall. Stocks make good cut flowers and colorful masses in the bed or border.

Because summer heat can prevent flowering, it is best to start stock as transplants six to eight weeks ahead of putting them outside. The seeds require light and germinate in seven to ten days. After frost dangers have gone, put the plants in the soil at 12-inch intervals. Stock requires sun and plenty of moisture and does poorly in extreme heat.

Strawflowers

These annuals have full paperlike or strawlike flowers in orange, pink, purple, red, salmon, white, and yellow and reach heights of 12 to 30 inches. Strawflower blossoms appear from midsummer through frost and are excellent for dried arrangements, cut flowers, and bed or border use.

You can directly sow the seeds after frosts have passed, or as transplants four to six weeks before outdoor planting time. Germination requires light and occurs in seven to ten days. You can space the plants at 9- to 12-inch intervals in your garden. Full sun and heat make for great strawflowers. Be sure you pick strawflowers just before or at their peak for drying, for the flowers open further as they dry.

Sunflowers

Although we know these annuals best for their large, daisylike flowers, which form big, central, seed heads, there are also some cultivars of dwarf size, 15 to 36 inches; some with double flowers; and some with brown, bronze, gold, or even red flowers. The most familiar form reaches up to 12 feet in height with flowers over 1 foot in diameter. We use sunflowers for screening, bird food, and fun for children, who love to watch the little seed slowly grow into a gigantic plant that's taller than they are.

Sunflowers grow so rapidly that transplants are unnecessary. Sow the seeds after all danger of frost has passed. Germination is in ten to fourteen days. Depending upon the cultivar, space the plants from 24 to 48 inches apart. You may need to do some staking. Sunflowers need full sun but can succeed even in poor soil.

Swan River Everlasting

Suppliers often sell this annual as acroclinium. The flowers are semi-double or double, and the daisylike plant is about 15 inches tall. The flowers come in pink, rose, and white and appear from midsummer to early fall. This annual makes a colorful bed or border planting and is suitable for cutting and dried arrangements.

Sow the seeds directly in the garden after frosts have passed, or start transplants six to eight weeks ahead of outdoor planting time. Germination takes about fourteen to twenty days. Use individual transplant containers, because this plant can be difficult to transplant. Space the plants at 6- to 9-inch intervals in full sun. Swan river everlasting can tolerate dryness. If you wish to dry the flower, pick them before they fully open.

Sweet Peas

Sweet peas have fragrant, pealike flowers in colors of blue, pink, purple, red, rose, and white. The plants vary in size from 9-inch bushy dwarfs to 7-foot vines. Blooming occurs from late spring through early summer. You can use the dwarf forms in beds or containers and the vining types for screening or background purposes.

Sow the seeds outdoors as soon as you can work the soil, or start transplants four to six weeks ahead of outdoor planting time. Soak the seeds in water for 24 hours or put a nick in the seed coat with a file to improve germination. Germination can take ten to fourteen days. Space the plants 6 to 9 inches apart and provide support for the climbing forms. Full sun and cool weather afford the best growth. If your summers heat up early, use some of the more heat-resistant varieties. An organic mulch can keep the roots cool and improve warm-weather performance.

Thunbergia

Other names for this annual include black-eyed Susan vine or clock vine. The simple, five-petaled flowers with their dark centers faintly suggest an image of black-eyed Susans; however, there is no resemblance to the daisy. The vine reaches a height of 5 feet and produces orange, yellow, and white flowers in the summer. Incidentally, not all thunbergia have the dark center. The vine is useful for screening purposes or for cascades in a window or porch box.

You can sow the seeds outdoors after frosts have passed, or start transplants six to eight weeks ahead of outdoor planting time. Germination takes ten to fifteen days. Space the plants at 6- to 12-inch intervals in full sun to light shade. Thunbergia does poorly in extreme heat.

Tithonia

Mexican sunflower is another name for this colorful annual. The daisylike flowers have a brilliant orange-red color and appear in midsummer through fall. The plant varies from 3 to 6 feet in height. This annual makes a good background planting and cut flower.

You can sow the seeds outside after all danger of frost has passed, or start transplants six to eight weeks earlier. Light helps germination, which takes five to ten days. Space the plants 2 feet apart in full sun. Tithonia can tolerate heat and dryness.

Torenia

Another name for torenia is wishbone flower, due to the wishbone appearance of the stamens inside the flower. The flowers look like miniature gloxinias with violet-blue lips and a yellow throat. The plant grows from 8 to 14 inches tall and produces flowers during the summer through frost. The torenia is useful for edging, containers, and as a substitute for pansies in the South.

It is best to start transplants ten to twelve weeks ahead of outdoor planting time. Germination requires fifteen to twenty days. Space the plants 6 to 8 inches apart in full sun in cool climates only and in light to partial shade in warm climates. Dryness results in poor plant performance.

Verbena

We treat verbena as an annual, even though it is actually a perennial. The sprawling and trailing plant generally reaches 15 inches, although it sometimes spreads as much as 24 inches. Clusters of tiny flowers having contrasting centers (usually white) cover the plant and come in blue, maroon, pink, purple, rose, scarlet, and white. The plant is a good edging for borders, looks nice in rock gardens or window boxes, and is reasonable as a cut flower. Blooming occurs through the summer and early fall.

For best results, start verbena transplants twelve to fourteen weeks before outdoor planting time. The seeds need darkness for germination, which takes 20 to 25 days. Plant the transplants outside in full sun after the danger of frost has passed, using a spacing of 12 inches between each plant. Shear off spent flowers to afford continuous blooming. Verbena will tolerate heat.

Vinca

Periwinkle is another name for this perennial, which we often grow as an annual. The trailing plant varies from 6 to 18 inches tall and has simple pink, rose, or white flowers that appear in the summer. Some forms have a darker, or contrasting, center eye. The plant is useful for groundcovers, edging, bedding, and containers.

Start the seeds as transplants eight to ten weeks ahead of outdoor planting to assure blossoms, since vinca is a perennial. Germination takes ten to fifteen days. Space vinca transplants 6 to 12 inches apart in a sunny to lightly shaded location. Vinca can tolerate heat and dryness.

Xeranthemum

Another name for this annual is immortelle. The papery flowers are single or double and daisylike in colors of pink, purple, red, rose, and white. The plants grow 24 to 36 inches tall, with flowers appearing in late summer and early fall. Xeranthemum is colorful in the border and makes a good cut or dried flower.

You can sow the seeds once the frost danger is over, or you can start transplants in individual containers six to eight weeks earlier. These flowers are somewhat fussy as transplants, hence the need for individual containers. The seeds germinate in ten to fifteen days. Plant xeranthemums 8 to 10 inches apart in full sun. If you dry the flowers, cut them when they are not quite fully open.

Zinnias

In my book, zinnias rate as highly as marigolds do in terms of substantial returns for little work. Zinnias are available in all colors, with the exception of blue. You can also buy bicolor forms. Zinnia heights vary from 10 to 30 inches. The flowers are single through double and come in many forms, such as daisylike, chrysanthemum, cactus, pompom, and ruffled. Zinnias are great cut flowers and excellent additions to the bed or border. You can also use them as plantings for containers and edges. The flowers appear from summer to frost and contrast nicely with marigolds.

You can sow zinnias after the danger of frost has gone, or you can prepare transplants four to six weeks ahead of outdoor planting in individual containers. Germination takes five to seven days. Space the small cultivars at 6-inch intervals and large ones at 12-inch intervals. Zinnias thrive in full sun and can take the heat or dryness. Avoid crowding them and overhead watering if powdery mildew is a problem in your area.

Appendix

As a fellow organic gardener and reader, I find it annoying when I read about some new gardening product but can't locate it. I have put this appendix together with this thought in mind. Every tool, accessory, supply, or seed choice mentioned in the book is available from the suppliers listed here.

Unhappily, some things change. Products are discontinued, companies go out of business, or catalogs once free suddenly cost money. Therefore I have provided telephone numbers for the suppliers, except when the number was not listed in the catalog. Should you wish to get a catalog in a hurry, ask if it is still free, or check on product availability or cost over the phone, you can. Otherwise a note to the listed address should get you a catalog.

Incidentally, if a firm is not listed, it is no reflection on its merits or product availability. By all means go with your favorite supplier. These companies are just ones that I happen to know supply what I have mentioned in the book. Another suggestion is to check with your local garden supply source. Your dealer may have the item you need right there.

The supplies are listed in categories. After the item you will find a number or numbers. These numbers can be used to identify the supplier from the list found later.

The Supplies

Accessories

Kneepads: 1, 2, 3, 4, 5, 20
Kneeling mat: 2, 5, 9, 14, 20
Row seeders: 3, 6, 9, 20
Soil sampler probe: 1, 6, 10
Soil test kit: 1, 3, 4, 6, 7 ,8, 10, 14, 18
Soil thermometer: 1, 3
Straightline or row marker: 3, 5, 20

Aids for the Elderly or Handicapped Gardener

 Book, *Gardening for the Handicapped and Elderly*, by Mary Chaplin:
  20
 Kneeling stool/bench: 5, 6, 14, 21
 Three-wheeled scoot (stable rolling seat for sitting and moving between
  rows while planting, weeding, and picking): 2, 5, 6

Cloches

 Hot caps: 3, 6, 7, 18
 Polyester (Reemay): 6, 8
 Shade cover (for extending cool season crops into summer): 6
 Slitted polyethylene: 6, 8

Mulches

 Black plastic: 1, 3, 7, 8, 19
 Paper (peat) mulch: 6

Organic Fertilizers

 Complete powders (Fertrell or similar mixtures containing various
  amounts of nitrogen, phosphorus, and potassium): 9, 10, 18, 19
 Fish emulsion: 6, 10
 Meals (blood, leather, etc.): 10
 Rock dusts: 10
 Seaweed (kelp) extract: 3, 6, 10, 19
 Seaweed meal: 6, 10, 19
 Seaweed extract combined with fish emulsion (Sea Mix): 6, 8, 9, 10
 Worm castings: 6, 10

Pest Controls

 Dipel: 6, 8, 9, 10
 Electric fence: 6
 Japanese beetle trap: 3, 9, 10
 Milky spore disease: 6, 9, 10
 Polyester (Reemay): 6, 8
 Pyrethrum: 8, 10
 Pyrethrum/rotenone combination: 8, 10
 Rotenone: 3, 6, 8, 10
 Safer's soap spray: 3, 6, 8, 9, 10, 12
 Sticky yellow cards: 9, 10, 19, 20
 Tanglefoot, Tangletrap: 1, 6, 10

Seeds

 Flowers, herbs, and vegetables: 3, 7, 8, 11, 12, 13, 15, 16, 17, 18, 19
 Legume inoculant: 3, 8, 10, 18, 19

Tools

 Action or oscillating hoe: 1, 5, 9, 14
 Bulb planter (long handle): 1, 2, 6, 21
 Burpee Seeder: 3
 Combination tools: 3, 14, 20
 Dibble: 2, 3, 4, 5, 14, 20
 Easi-Weeder: 6
 Furrower: 9, 20
 Furrowlike hoes: 1, 2, 3, 14, 20
 Plant-Rite Seeder: 20
 Precision Row Seeder: 6

Transplant Supplies

 Cold frame: 3, 5, 6, 7, 9, 12
 Growing mixtures (Jiffy Mix, Peat Lite Mix, etc.): 3, 7, 8, 12, 18, 19
 Paper pots: 6
 Peat pots: 1, 3, 7, 12, 18, 19, 20
 Perlite: local supplier
 Propagation mat (for bottom heat): 1, 6, 8
 Self-watering propagation unit: 6, 7
 Solar vent (nonelectrical cold frame window opener and closer): 7, 8, 12, 18, 20
 Sphagnum moss: 7
 Trays: 7, 8, 12, 19
 Various plastic propagation containers: 3, 8, 12, 19
 Vermiculite: 7

Vertical Gardening Supplies

 Netting: 3, 7, 9, 12, 18, 19
 Pea fence: 3, 9

Watering Systems and Accessories

 Adaptors (for hooking two or four separate watering systems to one faucet): 2, 3, 6, 8, 20
 Backflush valves: local hardware or plumbing supplier
 Computerized water timers and moisture meter detectors: 2, 4, 5, 6, 14
 Drip irrigation set-ups: 3, 9, 10, 14
 Fogging nozzles: 1, 2, 8
 Hose extenders: 1, 2, 8
 Mechanical water timers: 3, 6, 8, 20
 Pressure regulators: 3

The Suppliers

1. A. M. Leonard, Inc.
   P.O. Box 816
   Piqua, OH 45356-0816
   (513) 773-2694
   Horticultural tools and supplies.
2. Brookstone
   127 Vose Farm Road
   Peterborough, NH 03460
   (603) 924-7181
   Hard-to-find tools, many garden tools and accessories.
3. Burpee
   W. Atlee Burpee Company
   300 Park Avenue
   Warminster, PA 18974
   (215) 674-4900 Ext. 222
   Wide seed selection, garden tools and accessories.
4. Clapper's
   1121 Washington Street
   West Newton, MA 02165
   (617) 244-7909
   Garden tools and accessories.
5. Gardener's Eden
   P.O. Box 7307
   San Francisco, CA 94120-7307
   (415) 428-9292
   Garden tools and accessories.
6. Gardener's Supply Company
   133 Elm Street
   Winooski, VT 05404
   (802) 655-9006
   Garden tools, supplies, and accessories.
7. Harris Seeds
   Joseph Harris Co., Inc.
   Moreton Farm
   3670 Buffalo Road
   Rochester, NY 14624
   Seeds and supplies.
8. Johnny's Selected Seeds
   Albion, ME 04910
   (207) 437-9294
   Seeds, supplies, and accessories.

9. Judd Ringer's Natural Lawn & Garden Care
   6860 Flying Cloud Drive
   Eden Prairie, MN 55344
   (612) 941-4180
   Garden tools, supplies, and accessories ($2 for catalog).
10. Necessary Trading Company
    328 Main Street
    New Castle, VA 24127
    (703) 864-5103
    Garden supplies and accessories ($2 for catalog).
11. Nichol's Garden Nursery
    1190 North Pacific Highway
    Albany, OR 97321
    (503) 928-9280
    Herbs and unusual seeds.
12. Park Seed Company
    Greenwood, SC 29647
    General seeds, supplies, and accessories.
13. Shepherd's Garden Seeds
    7389 West Zayante Road
    Felton, CA 95018
    (408) 335-5400
    Seeds of European vegetables, herbs, and salad plants.
14. Smith & Hawken
    25 Corte Madera
    Mill Valley, CA 94941
    (415) 383-4050
    Garden tools and accessories.
15. The Cook's Garden
    Box 65
    Londonderry, VT 05148
    (802) 824-3400
    Seeds for salad lovers.
16. The Urban Farmer
    P.O. Box 444
    Convent Station, NJ 07961
    International seed selection ($1 for catalog).
17. Thompson & Morgan Inc.
    P.O. Box 1308
    Jackson, NJ 08527
    (201) 363-2225
    Wide selection of international and unusual seeds.

18. Twilley Seed Company
    P.O. Box 65
    Trevose, PA 19047
    (215) 639-8800
    Seeds, supplies, and accessories ($1.25 for catalog).
19. Vermont Bean Seed Company
    Garden Lane
    Bomoseen, VT 05732-0308
    (802) 265-4212
    General seeds, especially beans and heirloom seeds.
20. Walter F. Nicke
    Box 667G
    Hudson, NY 12534
    (518) 828-3415
    Wide selection of garden tools and accessories.
21. White Flower Farm
    Litchfield, CT 06759-0050
    (203) 567-0801
    Unusual plants and supplies ($5 for catalog).

Index

Page numbers in italic type indicate photographs or illustrations.

A Accessories, 16-18, *17*, 130-32, 251
Acroclinium. *See* Swan River
  everlasting
Aeration, of soil, 7-8, 24
African daisy. *See* Arctotis; Cape
  daisy; Gazania
Ageratum, 224-25
Alyssum, 225
Amaranth, globe, 234-35
Amaranthus, 225
A. M. Leonard, Inc., 15, 254
Annual(s)
    definition of, 221
    for flower gardens, 221-49, *223,*
    224
        ageratum, 224-25
        alyssum, 225
        amaranthus, 225
        arctotis, 225-26
        aster, 226
        balsam, 226-27
        begonia, 46, *224,* 227
        blue lace flowers, 227
        brachycome, 227-28
        browallia, 228
        calendula, 228
        California poppy, 228-29
        candytuft, 229
        Cape daisy, 229
        carnation, 229-30
        celosia, 230
        chrysanthemum, *222,*
          224
        cleome, 230
        cobaea, 230-31
        coleus, 20, 46, 231
        coreopsis, 231
        cornflowers, 232
        cosmos, 232
        dahlia, 46, 47, 232-33
        dianthus, 233
        four o'clocks, 233
        gaillardia, 233-34
        gazania, 234
        geranium, 20, 234

        globe amaranth, 234-35
        gloriosa daisy, 235
        gypsophila, 235
        heliotrope, 235-36
        hollyhock, 236
        impatiens, 20, 46, 236
        kochia, 236-37
        larkspur, 237
        lobelia, 237
        lupine, 237-38
        marigold, 19, 45, *222,* 238
        morning glory, 238-39
        nasturtium, 239
        nicotiana, 239
        nierembergia, 239-40
        nigella, 240
        ornamental grass, 240
        petunia, 20, 46, 240-41
        phacelia, 241
        phlox, 241-42
        polygonum, 242
        portulaca, 242
        salpiglossis, 242-43
        salvia, 243
        scabiosa, 243
        shell flower, 244
        Shirley poppy, 244
        snapdragon, 244-45
        snow-on-the-mountain, 245
        statice, 245
        stock, 245-46
        strawflower, 246
        sunflower, 246
        Swan River daisy. *See*
          Brachycome
        Swan River everlasting,
          246-47
        sweet pea, 247
        thunbergia, 247
        tithonia, 247-48
        torenia, 248
        verbena, 248
        vinca, 248-49
        xeranthemum, 249
        zinnia, *222,* 249

Annual(s) (*continued*)
    transplants, 46, 224
Annual pink. *See* Dianthus
Anthracnose, control of, 177, 192,
    207, 218
Aphid
    beans and, 177
    cabbage and, 183
    control of, 143-44, 145, 146,
        190, 192, 194, 207, 209, 211,
        215, 218
    cowpeas and, 190
    cucumbers and, 192
    eggplant and, 194
    lettuce and, 196
    peas and, 205
    peppers and, 207
    potatoes and, 209
    spinach and, 211
    squash and, 215
    tomatoes and, 218
    transplants and, 148
    viral disease and, 140, 149
Arctotis, 225-26
Army worm, 189
Aster, 226
Aster wilt, 226
B Baby's breath. *See* Gypsophila
Bachelor's button. *See* Cornflower
Bacillus thuringiensis, 183
Bacterial blight, 205
Bacterial spot, 203, 207
Bacterial wilt, 189, 192, *193*, 199,
    218
Balsam, 226-27
Band planting, 76, 164
Basal rot, 203
Bean(s), 174-77, *177*
Bean aphid, 177
Bean leaf beetle, 177
Bees, pollination and, 140, 141
Beet(s), 178-79
Beet leafhopper, 179
Beetles
    bean leaf, 177
    Colorado potato, 145, 194, 209
    corn flea, 189
    cucumber, 145, 149, 189, 199,
        215
        spotted, 192
        striped, 192, *193*
    flea, 134, 139, 141, 145-46, 148,
        179, 189, 194, 209, 210, 218
    Japanese, 146, 176, *177*, 189

    Mexican bean, 145, 146, 177
Begonia, 46, 224, 227
Birds, control of, 135, 137, 189
Black-eyed peas. *See* Cowpeas
Black-eyed Susan. *See* Gloriosa daisy
Black-eyed Susan vine. *See*
    Thunbergia
Black leg, 183, 209
Black rot, 183
Blanket flower. *See* Gaillardia
Blight
    carrots and, 185
    corn and, 189
    cucumbers and, 192
    early, 209, 218
    eggplant and, 194
    late, 209
    leaf, 185, 192
    peppers and, 207
    potatoes and, 209
Blossom end rot, 218-19
Blue bottle. *See* Cornflower
Blue lace flowers, 227
Bottom rot, 197
Brachycome, 227-28
Broadcasting
    of fertilizers, 78, 95
    of seeds, 38
Broccoli, *171*. *See also* Cabbage
    family
Browallia, 228
Brussels sprouts. *See* Cabbage family
Bulb planter, 9-10, *10*, 11, *98*
    for planting seeds, 69-70, *70*
    for planting transplants, 62-63,
        63, 68, *68*, 224
Burning bush. *See* Kochia
Busy Lizzie. *See* Impatiens
C Cabbage aphid, 183
Cabbage family, 179-84
Cabbage looper, 145, 183
Cabbage worm, 145, 183
Cabbage yellows, 183
Calendula, 228
California bluebell. *See* Phacelia
California poppy, 228-29
Calliopsis. *See* Coreopsis
Candytuft, 229
Cantaloupe. *See* Melons
Cape daisy, 229
Carnation, 229-30
Carrot(s), 184-85
Carrot rust fly, 145, 185
Carrot yellows, 185

Cauliflower. *See* Cabbage family
Celosia, *45*, 230
China aster. *See* Aster
China pink. *See* Dianthus
Chinch bug, 189
Chinese cabbage. *See* Cabbage family
Chives. *See* Onion family
Chrysanthemum, 222, 224
Cleome, 230
Cloches, 155-62
    application and removal of,
      140-42
    black plastic mulch and, 118,
      149, 155-57
    crops suitable for, 159-60
    for early gardening, 155-60, *158*,
      160
    for late gardening, 161-62, *162*,
      163
    polyester, 157-59, *160*
      for insect control, 133-42,
        139, *140*, 149, 192, 194,
        197, 199, 203, 209, 215
      installation of, 134-37, *135*,
        136, *137*, 158-59
      reuse of, 161
    "poor man's," 162, *162*, *163*
    slitted plastic, *158*, 159, 161
    sources of, 252
Clock vine. *See* Thunbergia
Clubroot, 183
Cobaea, 230-31
Cockscomb. *See* Celosia
Cold frame, 48
Cole crops. *See* Cabbage family
Coleus, 20, 46, 231
Collards. *See* Cabbage family
Colorado potato beetle, control of,
    145, 194, 209
Compost, 86-92, 97, 98, 111
Compost piles, 86-88, *89*
Containers, for transplants, 21-27,
    23, *26*, *27*
    covers for, 39-40, *39*
Coreopsis, 231
Corn, 185-90
Corn blight, 189
Corn borer, 189
Corn earworm, 189, 218
Corn flea beetle, 189
Cornflower, 232
Corn smut, 189
Cosmos, 232
Cowpeas, 190-91

Crop rotation, for disease control,
    150
Crowders. *See* Cowpeas
Cucumber(s), 139-40, 191-93, *193*
Cucumber beetle, control of, 145
    149, 189, 192, *193*, 199, 215
Cucumber mosaic virus, 192, 207
Cucumber wilt, 140, 149, 189, 192,
    193, 199, 215
Cup and saucer vine. *See* Cobaea
Cup flower. *See* Nierembergia
Curly top virus, 207, 218
Cutworm, control of, 147, *147*, 148,
    196-97, 207, 215, 218
D Dahlia, 46, 47, 232-33
Daisy
    African. *See* Arctotis; Cape
      daisy; Gazania
    Cape, 229
    gloriosa, 235
    Swan River. *See* Brachycome
Damping-off, 34, 83, 107, 108
Deer, control of, 151, 152-53
Dianthus, 233
Dibble, 11-12, *12*, 68-70, *69*, *70*
Digging, no-dig method vs, 3-8
Disease(s). *See also names of
    individual diseases*
    control methods
      crop rotation, 150
      organic, 149-50
      polyester cloches, 137-40,
        139
      for seedlings, 34-35
      solarization, 119, 150
    plant resistance to, 150
Downy mildew, control of, 192, 197,
    203
Drainage, 7-8
E Earwig, 145
Eggplant(s), 141, 148, 193-94
Eggplant maggot, 141, 194
Euphorbia. *See* Snow-on-the-
    mountain
F Fences, 151-54
    pea, 168-69
Fertilizers, 77-105. *See also names of
    individual fertilizers*
    application of, 78-79, 94-96
      broadcasting, 78, 95
      foliar feeding, 80-81,
        100-101, *100*
      milk-bottle dispenser for,
        102, 104, *104*

Fertilizers *(continued)*
mulching and, 102, *103*, 118
organic oasis mixture, 68, *68*, 92-93, 105
rapid starter solution, *63*, 64, 73, 92
for seedlings, 43-45, 72, 73, *73*, 74, 93
for soil improvement, 93-99, *98*, *99*
for soil maintenance, 99-105, *100*, *103*, *104*
solid, 84-92
sources of, 252
supplemental treatments with, 102-4, *103*, *104*
water-soluble organic, 77-84
Fish emulsion, 43-44, 84
foliar feeding with, 44, 79-80, 100-101, *100*, 146
Flats, 11, 27, 35, 37, 65-66, *66*
Flea beetle, control of, 134, *139*, 141, 145-46, 179, 189, 194, 209, 210, 218
Fleeceflower. *See* Polygonum
Floss flower. *See* Ageratum
Flowering tobacco. *See* Nicotiana
Foliar feeding, 80-81, 100-101, *100*
Four o'clocks, 233
Frost protection, 83-84, 101, 118
Fungus gnat, 145
Furrower, 13-14, *13*, 70, 71-74, 72
Fusarium wilt, 150, 194, 218
G Gaillardia, 233-34
Gardening techniques, 162-73
intensive planting, 163-65, *165*
interplanting, 169-71, *169*
succession planting, 171-73, *171*
vertical gardening, 166-69, *166*
Garlic. *See* Onion family
Gazania, 234
Geranium, 20, 234
Germination, 20, 40-41, 82
Globe amaranth, 234-35
Gloriosa daisy, 235
Grass, ornamental, 240
Gray mold rot, 197
Gypsophila, 235
H Handicapped gardeners, aids for, 17, 252
Hardening off, 48, 49
Hardpan soil, 56, 57, 61
Harlequin bug, 183
Heliotrope, 235-36

Herbs, 195
Hiller. *See* Furrower
Hoe, 12-13, 14, *See also* Furrower
for seed planting, 12-14, *13*
for weeding, 15, *71*, 121, *121*
Hollyhock, 236
I Immortelle. *See* Xeranthemum
Impatiens, 20, 46, 236
Insect(s), 138. *See also names of individual insects*
Insect control, 133-49
with cloches, 133-42, *139*, *140*, 149, 192, 194, 197, 199, 203, 209, 215
foliar feeding and, 101
with sprays, 144-46
with Styrofoam cups, 147-48, *147*
Insect traps, 142-44, 145, 176, 189
Intensive planting, 163-65, *165*
Interplanting, 169-71
Iron deficiency, in plants, 83
J Japanese beetle, control of, 146, 176, *177*, 189
Judd Ringer's Natural Lawn & Garden Care, 13, 255
K Kale. *See* Cabbage family
Kneeling aids, 16, *17*, 72
Knotweed. *See* Polygonum
Kochia, 236-37
Kohlrabi. *See* Cabbage family
L Larkspur, 237
Leaf blight, 185, 192
Leafhopper
control of, 140, 145, 146, 149, 177, 179, 185, 197, 209, 218
viral disease and, 140, 149
Leaf miner, control of, 179, 207, 211-12
Leaf roll, 209
Leaf scab, 179
Leaf spot, 179, 192, 218
Leeks. *See* Onion family
Lettuce, *169*, 195-97
Lettuce drop, 197
Lettuce rot, 150
Light requirements, for germination, 40, 41
Lima beans. *See* Bean(s)
Lobelia, 237
Lupine, 237-38
Love-in-a-mist. *See* Nigella
M Maggots
eggplant, 141, 194
onion, 203

pepper, 207
root, 137, 139, 140, 150, 183, 210, 220
Marigolds, 19, 222, 238
as nematode repellent, 190
pot. *See* Calendula
transplanting, 45
Mealybug, 145, 146
Melons, 149, 197-200
Melonworm, 146
Mexican bean beetle, 145, 146, 177
Mexican sunflower. *See* Tithonia
Mildew
downy, 192, 197, 203
powdery, 192, 205
Mini-hills, 75, 76, 137
Morning glory, 238-39
Mosaic
bean, 177
cucumber, 192, 207
potato, 209
tomato, 218
Moss rose. *See* Portulaca
Mulches, 106-20
advantages of, 106-7
application of, 94
black plastic, *103*, 134, *135*
application of, 112-18, *114, 115, 116, 117*
cloches and, 118, 149, 155-57
length of use of, 118-20
seed planting and, 74, *74*
soil temperature and, 108, 109
disadvantages of, 107-10
fertilizers and, 102, *103*, 118
organic, 74, 110-12
paper, 112, 113, *116*
plastic, 123-24
sources of, 252
for weed control, 54-55, 106-20
Muskmelons. *See* Melons
Mustard. *See* Cabbage family
N Nasturtium, 239
Neck rot, 203
Nematodes, control of, 150, 190
New Zealand spinach. *See* Spinach
Nicotiana, 239
Nierembergia, 239-40
Nigella, 240
Nitrogen
in compost, 89, 90, 91
deficiency of, 44
excess of, 44

Nutrient(s), 94-96. *See also names of individual nutrients*
O Onion family, 200-203, *202*
Onion maggot, 203
Onion smut, 203
Opossums, control of, 151, 152
Organic matter
for disease control, 149-50
leaching of, 8, 78
soil content of, 96-99, *98, 99*
soil maintenance and, 104-5
Organic oases, 68, *68*, 92-93, 105
Ornamental grass, 240
P Painted tongue. *See* Salpiglossis
Patience plant. *See* Impatiens
Patient Lucy. *See* Impatiens
Pea(s), 203-5
Pea aphid, 205
Pea fence, 168-69
Peanut rot, 150
Peat pots, 27
Pea weevil, 205
Pelleted seeds, 38
Pepper(s), 141, 145, 206-7
Pepper maggot, 207
Pepper weevil, 207
Periwinkle. *See* Vinca
Pest control, 252. *See also* Insect control; *names of individual pests*
Petunias, 20, 46, 240-41
Phacelia, 241
Phlox, 241-42
Phosphorus
deficiency of, 44-45, 96
soil availability of, 81
Pickle worm, 146, 192, 215
Pincushion flower. *See* Scabiosa
Pink root rot, 203
Pinks. *See* Dianthus
Planting, 51-76
garden preparation for, 53-61
patterns of, 75-76
soil tests and, 51-53
tools for, 12-14, *13*, 71-74, *72*
of transplants, 62-69, *63, 64, 65, 66, 67, 68, 69*
Pollination, 140-41, *142*
Polygonum, 242
Poppy
California, 228-29
Shirley, 244
Portulaca, 242
Potato, 208-9
Potato mosaic, 209

Potato scab, 150
Pot marigold. *See* Calendula
Powdery mildew, 192, 205
Pumpkin. *See* Squash
Pyrethrum, for insect control, 145, 177, 179, 189, 192, 194, 205, 209, 215, 218

R Rabbits, control of, 151-52
Raccoons, control of, 151, 152, 189
Radishes, 209-10
Ragged robin. *See* Cornflower
Raised beds
    planting, 75-76
    for small gardens, 57
    for stony soil, 58-61, 58, 59
Rapid starter solution, 63, 64, 73, 92
Rhizoctonia, 150
Ridge plough. *See* Furrower
Rocky soil, 58-61
Root maggot, 137, 139, 140, 150, 183, 210, 220
Root rot, 205
    pink, 203
Rot
    basal, 203
    black, 183
    blossom end, 218-19
    bottom, 197
    gray mold, 197
    lettuce, 150
    neck, 203
    peanut, 150
    root, 203, 205
Rotenone, for insect control, 145-46, 177, 179, 183, 189, 192, 194, 203, 207, 209, 210, 218
Row marker, 16-17
Row planting, 75-76, 163-64, 165
Row seeder, 17-18
Rust, bean, 177
Rutabagas. *See* Turnips

S Sage. *See* Salvia
Salpiglossis, 242-43
Salvia, 243
Scab, 192, 209
Scabiosa, 243
Scale, 145
Sclerotium, 150
Sea lavender. *See* Statice
Seaweed extract, 43, 44, 46, 82-84, 146, 149
    for foliar feeding, 79-81, 100-101, 100
Seaweed meal, 85

Seed(s)
    ordering, 33
    planting, 37-39, 37, 69-70, 70
        tools for, 12-14, 13, 71-74, 72
    polyester cloches for, 135-37
    sources of, 252
    watering, 41
Seedlings
    care of, 41-46
    damping-off, 34, 83, 107, 108
    disease prevention for, 34-35
    fertilizing, 43-45
    starter solution for, 63, 64, 73, 92-93
    thinning out, 45-46, 45
    transplanting, 45-46, 45, 47
    watering, 42-43, 43
Seedling helper, 72, 73, 73, 74
Seed sower, 73
Seed tapes, 38-39
Shallots. *See* Onion family
Shell beans. *See* Bean(s)
Shell flowers, 244
Shirley poppy, 244
Skunks, control of, 151
Slugs, 148, 196, 197
Smith & Hawken, 13, 15, 255
Snap beans. *See* Bean(s)
Snapdragon, 46, 244-45
Snow-on-the-mountain, 245
Soap spray, 145
Soil amendments, 84-92
Soil compaction, 8, 56-57
Soil helper mixture, 93
Soil improvement techniques, 93-99
    fertilizing, 82-83, 94-96
    organic matter content and, 96-99, 98, 99
Soil maintenance, 99-105, 100, 103, 104
Soil pH, 93-94
Soil sampling, 52-53
Soil substitute, 60-61
Soil temperature
    effects of cloche on, 157
    effects of mulch on, 107, 108-9
Soil testing, 51-53, 93-94
Solarization, 119, 123-24, 150
Southern peas. *See* Cowpeas
Sphagnum moss, 28-29
Spider mite, control of, 83, 101, 145, 146, 177
Spinach, 210-12

Spotted cucumber beetle, 192
Sprays, for insect control, 144-46
Sprinklers, 125-26, 127-28, 129
Squash, 138-39, 141-42, *169*, 212-15
Squash bug, 146, 215
Squash vine borer, 148, 215
    polyester barrier for, 138-39,
      141-42
Squirrels, control of, 135, 137, 151,
    152
Stalk borer, 207
Starter solution, *63*, 64, 73, 92-93
Statice, 245
Stock, 245-46
Stony soil, 58-61
Strawflowers, 246
Striped cucumber beetle, 192, *193*
Styrofoam cups
    for insect control, 147-48, *147*
    as transplant containers, 24-27,
      26, 27, 34, 35
Styrofoam "peanuts," as growing
    media, 29-30, *31*
Succession planting, 171-73
Summer cypress. *See* Kochia
Sunflowers, 246
    Mexican. *See* Tithonia
Sunscald, 218
Swan River daisy. *See* Brachycome
Swan River everlasting, 246-47
Sweet alyssum. *See* Alyssum
Sweet peas, 247
Sweet scabious. *See* Scabiosa
Swiss chard. *See* Beet(s)
T Tarnished plant bug, 177
T-bar, *35, 37*
Temperature, seed germination and,
    40-41
Thrips, control of, 146, 203
Thunbergia, 247
Tillage, 3-4
Tip burn, 197
Tithonia, 247-48
Tobacco mosaic virus, 207, 218
Tomato, 215-19, 221
    pests and, 148, 218-19
    pollination of, 141
    transplants, 20, 27
Tomato hornworm, 146, 218
Tools, 9-15
    for plastic mulch application,
      112-13
    for seed planting, 12-14, *13*
    sources of, 253

    for transplanting, 9-12, *10, 12*
    for weeding, 15, 71, 121, *121*
Torenia, 248
Transplants, 19-50. *See also*
  Seedlings
    advantages of, 19-21
    of annuals, 224
    containers for, 21-27, *23, 26, 27,*
      34, 35, 36-37, *36*, 147-48, *147*
    covers for, 39-40, *39*
    growing areas for, 31-33, *32*
    growing media for, 27-31
    growing techniques for, 33-50,
      35, 36, 37, 38, 39, 41, 43, 45,
      47, 49
    insect resistance and, 148
    planting, 62-69, *63, 64, 65, 66,*
      67, 68, 69
    root systems of, 22-24, *23, 27*
    soil organic matter levels and,
      104-5
    sources of, 253
    tools for, 9-12, *10, 12*
    watering, 67-68
Transplant nursery, 49-50, *49*, 173
Treasure flower. *See* Gazania
Turnips, 219-20
V Verbena, 248
Vermont Bean Seed Company, 174,
  256
Vertical gardening, 166-69, *166*
    supply sources for, 253
Verticillium wilt, 150, 194, 209, 218
Vinca, 248-49
Viral disease. *See also names of*
  individual diseases
    aphids and, 140, 149
    leafhoppers and, 140, 149
    prevention of, 140
W Walter F. Nicke, 11, 12, 256
Watering
    of seedlings, *41*, 42-43, *43*
    of transplants, *23, 23*, 67-68
Watering systems, 124-32
    accessories for, 130-32, 253
    drippers, 127-28, *128*, 129
    hoses, 128-30, *129*
    sprinklers, 125-26, 127-28, 129
    supply sources for, 253
    tubing, 128-30
Watermelons. *See* Melons
Webworm, 179
Weed control 6-7, 121-22, *121*
    cultivation depth and, 122-23

Weed control *(continued)*
 with mulch, 54-55, *106-20*
 without mulch, 120-24
 by solarization, 123-24
 tools for, 15, *71,* 121, *121*
 weeding schedule and, 122
Weed seeds, 6-7, 121
Weevil, pepper, 207
Whitefly, control of, 143, 144, 145, *145,* 146, 177, 215, 218
Wilt
 aster, 226
 fusarium, 150, 194, 218
 pea, 205
 verticillium, 150, 194, 209, 218
Wireworm, 189
Wishbone flower. *See* Torenia

Woodchucks, control of, 151-52
Worm castings, as fertilizer, 86, 105
X Xeranthemum, 249
Y Yard-long beans. *See* Cowpeas
Yellow dwarf, 203
Yellows, 183, 185, 197, 203
Yield
 intensive planting and, 163-65, *165*
 interplanting and, 169-71
 succession planting and, 171-73, *171*
 vertical gardening and, 166-69, *166*
Z Zinnia, 222, 249